THE CHILDREN'S ILLUSTRATED BIBLE

THE NEW TESTAMENT

THE CHILDREN'S ILLUSTRATED BIBLE

THE NEW TESTAMENT

Retold by VICTORIA PARKER
Consultant: JANET DYSON

southwater

CONTENTS

THE STORY OF THE NEW TESTAMENT......6-9
A CHILD IS BORN......10

THE MAN OF MIRACLES......68

DEATH AND RESURRECTION......126

SPREADING THE WORD......184

The Story of the New Testament

The 27 books of the Bible that make up the New Testament tell of the life and death of Jesus Christ, and how His followers later spread His teachings.

THE ANGEL GABRIEL
Mary was given the good news by the Angel Gabriel that she was to have a very special son.

Setting the Scene

Jesus lived in Palestine and Judea when these areas were under occupation by the Romans. It was an extremely tense time. The majority of people were Jews, but many groups of non-Jews (Gentiles) lived there too, and there was a lot of dislike and mistrust between the communities. Some groups of angry locals, such as the Zealots, tried to fight the Romans. They never stood a chance of success. The Romans were always on the lookout for new ringleaders who might stir up trouble and were quick to suppress any rebels. Everyone deeply resented having to pay their hard-earned wages in taxes to the Roman invaders. All important legal decisions were also in Roman hands, although the Jewish elders still had some authority over everyday life, such as how people should behave and what customs they should follow. Everything had to be approved by the Roman provincial or district governor, and sometimes by the Roman emperor himself!

BAPTISM
Water from a font such as this is used to baptize people when they join the Christian Church.

Links Between Old and New

The Jews were always waiting for the savior or "Messiah" promised by the ancient prophets in their holy scriptures. It is this ancient promise that links the New Testament of the Bible with the Old Testament. The Jews lived in hope of the glorious future that had been prophesied, when the Messiah would establish the most mighty of all kingdoms for the people of Israel. The books of the New Testament were written by people who

WISE MEN AND JESUS
After Jesus was born, He was visited by wise men from far away in the East. They found Him by following signs that they had read in the stars.

believed that Jesus of Nazareth was the Messiah. They wrote in Greek, the most common language in the Roman Empire. The Hebrew (the language of the Jewish people) "Messiah" translates into Greek as "Christ." The oldest complete copy of the New Testament that still exists today is a papyrus version which dates from 400 AD. However, there exists a manuscript fragment of John's writing that dates back to the early part of the 200s AD.

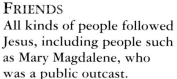

FRIENDS
All kinds of people followed Jesus, including people such as Mary Magdalene, who was a public outcast.

CHILD PRODIGY
Jesus was obviously special, even as a boy, when He was able to talk learnedly with Jewish elders.

The first four books of the New Testament are called the Gospels, a word that means "good news." Each Gospel follows Jesus's life, death and resurrection, so the four accounts cover many of the same events. However, each Gospel was written by a different person, and focused on different aspects of Jesus's story, and so every account is quite unique.

Different Authors

The disciple Matthew was a tax collector who also went by the name of Levi. (You can read about him in the story *Matthew is Called*.) Matthew's Gospel shows how Jesus reached out to those who were scorned by society. He aimed his Gospel at a Jewish audience, and concentrated on showing how Jesus fulfilled the prophecies of the Old Testament and was the Messiah.

Mark's Gospel focuses on Jesus's actions more than His words, and was probably written for a no-nonsense Roman audience. It is the shortest Gospel, but it contains several

INTERPRETATIONS
Five chapters of John's Gospel were about what Jesus said at the Last Supper before He died.

events not included in the other three books.

Luke was a doctor who wrote his Gospel for Gentiles. Luke did not claim to be an eyewitness to the events of Jesus's life, but he knew many people who had been very close to Jesus, such as His mother, Mary.

John was one of Jesus's closest friends. He outlived most of the other 11 disciples and wrote his Gospel after years of reflection on all that had happened. His account is therefore very different in tone from the others.

RESURRECTION
Each of the Gospels tells of Jesus's resurrection slightly differently, but all agree on the basic story.

It relates only a few events and concentrates on unraveling the meaning of Jesus's life.

Spreading the Word

The rest of the New Testament is made up of *The Acts of the Apostles* and 22 *Epistles*.

Acts was written by Luke. It tells what happened to the disciples once Jesus had left them, and how they traveled around the Mediterranean, spreading Jesus's teachings and establishing churches of His followers. This

HOLY GRAIL
The chalice used in Christian Church services symbolizes the Holy Grail, the cup from which Jesus drank wine at the Last Supper.

Matthew

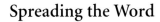

Mark

Luke

John

A NEW BEGINNING
The New Testament story does not end with Jesus's death on the cross. It covers events in the years following, when the apostles spread Jesus's teachings.

THE GOSPEL AUTHORS
Matthew, Mark and John were friends and followers of Jesus during His lifetime, while Luke wrote his Gospel about 50 years after Jesus's death.

SPECIAL POWERS
When Jesus was gone, the Holy Spirit filled the 12 disciples with courage and wisdom.

was a difficult and dangerous activity. *Acts* focuses mostly on the activities of Paul and Peter, the disciples that Luke knew best (Luke was, in fact, one of Paul's helpers).

The *Epistles* are sometimes called *Letters*. The disciples wrote them to the people they had met on their travels, who needed guidance and encouragement in their following of Jesus. The only letter without a clear author is *Hebrews*, which refers heavily to the writings of the Old Testament. Most of the letters are from Paul, who led the teaching of Jesus's word to non-Jewish communities. He wrote several of them while he was in jail, facing the death sentence for being a Christian "trouble-maker."

THE GIFT OF HEALING
The disciples carried out many miracles in the name of Jesus Christ and were able to heal the sick.

DANGEROUS JOB
The first followers of Christ were often at risk of being imprisoned by both the Jewish and Roman authorities.

THE BEGINNING OF CHRISTIANITY
The stories in this book draw together all the essential facts from the different accounts of Jesus's life in the Gospels, and retells all of the most important stories. It covers Jesus's early life *(A Child is Born)*, His ministry (*The Man of Miracles*) and His death, resurrection and ascension into Heaven (*Death and Resurrection*). You can marvel at the many extraordinary miracles that Jesus performed in stories such as *The First Miracle, Jesus the Healer, Feeding the Five Thousand* and *Jesus Walks on Water*. His task was not easy, and some of the difficulties He faced are recounted in stories such as *Trouble Begins to Brew* and *Judas Plots Betrayal*. Jesus's teachings about the Christian way of life come to light in *The Sermon on the Mount, Jesus and the Children* and *The Last Supper,* and in the parables that He made up to help people understand Him better, such as *The Good Samaritan, The Story of the Prodigal Son* and *The Pharisee and the Tax Collector.*

Spreading the Word follows the travels, trials and adventures of Luke, Paul and other early Christians as they laid the foundations of Christianity. Finally, the story *The Revelation to John* tells of a vision of heaven, and of good triumphing over evil.

A CHILD IS BORN

*Jesus's birth and early childhood, the gathering of the disciples
and the first miracles that heralded the start of His ministry*

A Child is Born

ABOUT 2,000 years ago an event happened that was to change the world for ever. Jesus Christ was born. From His birth the modern calendar is dated (although the actual year of Jesus's birth was probably 7B.C. or 4B.C., not the year 0, because a medieval monk made a mistake in his calculations!). Every time we look at a calendar and write down the number of the year, we are reminded of the birth of Christ and the existence of the Christian Church since then.

Jesus in the temple
When Jesus was separated from Mary and Joseph in Jerusalem, He went to His Father's house, God's temple in Jerusalem, where He amazed the religious elders with His knowledge.

The story of Jesus's birth and His early years is also very familiar. Even today, when people are less religious than they used to be, many public Christmas displays will include a Christmas manger with the baby Jesus, Mary, Joseph, the shepherds, and the wise men, some angels, and a few animals nosing around.

The birth and beginning of Jesus's ministry, or teaching, is one of the most important parts of the Bible story, with a clear link to modern times. Yet most of Jesus's early years are completely obscure. Only a few events are recorded in the Gospels. There are so few details that, later, people added to the stories to make them more interesting or exciting, or to make a point. Many of these stories, though, have no basis in history.

Even the familiar Christmas story owes more to tradition than to the facts that we are given in the Gospels. The only evidence that Jesus was born in a stable is the statement that Mary laid him in a manger, which was the normal crib for a newborn child in an ordinary Israelite home. A baby was safer there than on the floor, where everyone else slept!

The Christmas story also features the amazing sights of the chorus of angels singing to the shepherds, and a new star appearing in the sky. These events have led

many people to question the truth of these stories. However, the Gospel writers include these details to make an important point. The baby Jesus was not an ordinary child. He was the Son of God, who came into the world as a human to share human life. His aim was to bring humans and God back together in a relationship of trust and service.

The miracles of Jesus's birth continue as Jesus begins His ministry. The paralyzed man is healed outwardly and has his sins forgiven. The madman is made mentally and spiritually healthy again; the centurion's servant is healed, even though many people at the time thought that God did not care for Gentiles (people who were not Jewish). In each case the story enlarges on Jesus's mission: to bring God's forgiveness and to break through the barriers of human pride.

The miracles finish with the great act of stilling the storm. With the voice of the Creator's authority, Jesus bids the waves to be still. "Who is this?" cry the amazed disciples in fear and trembling. The message of the Gospel writers is clear: "We believe He is the Son of God." They leave their readers to decide if they are right.

Dead Sea and the wilderness
Before Jesus could begin His ministry in Galilee, He was tempted by the Devil in the wilderness around the Dead Sea. When it was proved He could resist temptation, He began His ministry.

⁕ A Child is Born ⁕

This section covers the birth and early life of Jesus, His baptism by John the Baptist, His temptation by the devil, and the early part of His ministry in Galilee
JUDEA BEFORE JESUS
Luke, Ch. 1.
THE BIRTH OF JESUS
Matthew, Ch. 2; Luke Ch. 2.
JESUS'S EARLY LIFE
Matthew, Ch. 2; Luke Ch. 2.
JESUS BEGINS HIS MINISTRY
Matthew, Ch. 3 & 4; Luke Ch. 4.
THE FIRST MIRACLE
John, Ch. 1 & 2.
JESUS'S MINISTRY IN GALILEE
Matthew, Ch. 8–14.
Mark, Ch. 1–6; Luke Ch. 3–9.
John, Ch. 5.
SERMON ON THE MOUNT
Matthew, Ch. 5–11.
Luke, Ch 6 & 11.

Mary and the baby Jesus
This is a fresco (a painting on a wall in plaster) of the Virgin Mary and the baby Jesus. Both are shown with haloes, a sign that they are sacred figures.

Jesus and His Early Life

THE birth of Jesus is one of the most familiar stories from the Bible. Every December millions of people celebrate the birth of the Messiah, God's anointed Savior. In many cases, though, the religious significance of this event, and what it has meant for Christians since, has been forgotten by many people.

The sources for two of the Gospels, Matthew and Luke, were probably different. The story of the birth of Jesus in the Gospel of Matthew is told very much from Joseph's point of view. Luke's gospel focuses very closely on Mary, mother of Jesus, and on Elizabeth, who was Mary's cousin and the mother of John the Baptist. There is a great deal of detail in Luke's account of the birth of Jesus that relates specifically to Mary. This has led some people to think that Luke's source may have been Mary herself. The writers of Matthew and Luke both agree on the divine part of Jesus's origin, that God Himself was Jesus's father.

There is a huge contrast between the amazing events attending Jesus's birth and the surroundings in which these events took place. The Bible indicates, although does not actually say, that the son of God was born in a stable surrounded by farm animals. He was laid in a manger, from which animals ate. While there, though, He was visited by the magi—wise men and astrologers from the east, from Babylon or Arabia. The Bible tells us that these men followed a new star to find the baby Jesus. Elsewhere, a great chorus of angels announced the birth of Jesus to some shepherds.

When His parents presented Jesus in the temple, as was the custom, they met Simeon and Anna, two prophets whom God had told of the Messiah's birth, who proclaimed Him the Savior of all the people of the world.

After the events surrounding His birth in Bethlehem, Jesus returned with Mary and Joseph to their home town of Nazareth. This was a small, unimportant town in Galilee, although it was close to several of the main trade routes for the Roman Empire. Jesus spent about the first thirty years of His life there.

Jesus's mission properly began with His baptism in the river Jordan. He was baptized by His cousin, John the Baptist. At the baptism, God gave a sign to everyone present that Jesus was special. The Holy Spirit descended to Jesus in the form of a white dove, and the voice of God announced that Jesus was His son. These messages from God said two things. God announced to the world that Jesus was the son of God. He also introduced Jesus to the world as His servant. God was saying that Jesus was the person sent by Him to deliver the people of the world from sin and evil.

Before Jesus could begin His ministry, He had to undergo a test. He went into the wilderness around the Jordan valley and was tempted three times by Satan. The temptations of Jesus explored the idea of what it was to be the Son of God. Jesus's replies to Satan's various challenges strengthened His knowledge of His role and what He would have to do. When Jesus refused to turn stones into bread to eat, He was putting His trust in God to provide what He needed to survive. Jesus says that we should all forget about obtaining earthly goods. We should trust God to provide us with what we need. Satan also told Jesus that He should throw Himself off of the roof of the temple. Jesus refused to put God to the test in this way. Jesus showed that He did not need to put God to the test in order to trust Him.

There is also another important point that the writer of the Bible makes in this story. Jesus proved that He had learned the lessons that God had been trying to teach the Israelites since the time of the Exodus. When Moses was leading the Israelites out of slavery in Egypt, they spent 40 years wandering in the desert before they were allowed to enter the Promised Land. They had not learned to trust God in every way. The answers that Jesus gives to Satan's temptations come from the book of Deuteronomy. They show that He has learned these lessons and is ready to begin His ministry.

This map shows the area of Jesus's birth and early life. You can see Nazareth, from where Mary and Joseph set out on the long journey to Bethlehem, where Jesus was born. Jerusalem is where Jesus was presented in the temple and where Simeon and Anna prophesied His great role.

Bethlehem

The Manger Square in Bethlehem is believed to be the place of Jesus's birth. The ancestors of King David lived in Bethlehem. Joseph was a descendant of David, born in Bethlehem, so he had to return there for the Roman census, in which the Romans counted the population.

A Son for Elizabeth

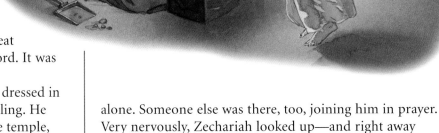

IN the days when King Herod ruled the land of Judea, there was a priest named Zechariah whose wife was Elizabeth. They both tried to live faithfully by the laws of the Jewish religion, but they had one great sadness in their life. They had reached old age without having any children. Still, they always tried to make the most of any happy occasion that came along. One of these occasions was when Zechariah was chosen to be the priest allowed to enter the sacred holy place in the great temple in Jerusalem and burn incense to the Lord. It was a great honor.

The day of the festival arrived and Zechariah dressed in his splendid ceremonial robes, his hands trembling. He could hear his fellow priests singing outside the temple, leading the crowd of worshipers in prayer.

> 66 *They were both righteous before God.* 99

Eventually, Zechariah stood before the incense altar in the holy place itself. With his eyes cast humbly downward, the aged priest began to burn the sacred incense. And as he spoke aloud the holy passages he had learned by heart, Zechariah suddenly had the strangest feeling. He was not alone. Someone else was there, too, joining him in prayer. Very nervously, Zechariah looked up—and right away crumpled to the floor with fear. An angel was standing to the right of the altar!

"Don't be afraid, Zechariah," the angel said. "I have come to tell you that your prayers have been answered. You and your wife are going to have a son, whom you must call John. He will bring great happiness not only to you, but also to many other people. The Lord will love him dearly and will send His Holy Spirit to fill your son's heart even before he has been born. Through John, many souls will turn to God. He will prepare the people for the Lord's coming."

The angel Gabriel
A 14th-century stained-glass window shows Gabriel, the angel who announced the news of John's birth. He also told Mary she would have Jesus. Gabriel's name means "Mighty man of God," and he is one of only two angels named in the Bible (the other is Michael, the warrior angel). He is an archangel who stands in God's presence and takes only special messages into the world.

MOST PEOPLE WOULD FIND IT HARD TO BELIEVE AN ANGEL. THE MESSAGE OF THIS STORY IS THAT GOD EXPECTS HIS PEOPLE TO BELIEVE WHAT HE SAYS, WHICH TODAY IS WRITTEN IN THE BIBLE. ∾

Wailing (Western) Wall
This huge wall in modern Jerusalem is a place of prayer for Jews. It is all that remains of King Herod's temple after the Romans destroyed it. People often leave papers with prayers on them tucked into the gaps between the stones.

Zechariah was totally stunned. "But . . . Why . . . How . . ?" he stuttered. "We're too old to have children. How can this be true?"

"I am Gabriel," the angel exclaimed, and Zechariah cowered in terror. In heaven, the angel Gabriel stood at the side of God Himself. "I have been sent by the Lord to bring you this good news," he said. "Because you don't believe what I say, you will be struck dumb until these things come to pass." And he vanished.

Outside the temple, thousands of worshipers were waiting for Zechariah to finish burning the sacred incense and come out of the temple. They waited and waited. Murmurs began to run through the crowd. "Where's the priest? Maybe he's fallen ill. Shouldn't somone go and check?" Elizabeth started to get worried.

Then a shout went up from the people at the front: "Here he comes!" And everyone saw the shape of the elderly priest emerging from the shadows of the temple out into the sunlight. The cheering crowd fell quiet, waiting for Zechariah to speak. Although the priest's lips moved, no sound came out of his mouth. The puzzled men and women looked at each other. What had happened to Zechariah in there? They watched as the priest moved his hands back and forth, silently demonstrating that he had seen a vision from heaven but could no longer speak. The people were stunned.

As they stood there, gasping in shock, Elizabeth pushed her way through the throng to her husband's side. And quietly, she led him away from all the fuss.

Not long afterward, Elizabeth discovered she was expecting a baby. She knew she'd be the talk of the town if people discovered that such an old woman was having a baby. So she tried to keep in the house, out of sight, where she kept her joyous secret to herself. The couple wouldn't let anything spoil their happiness.

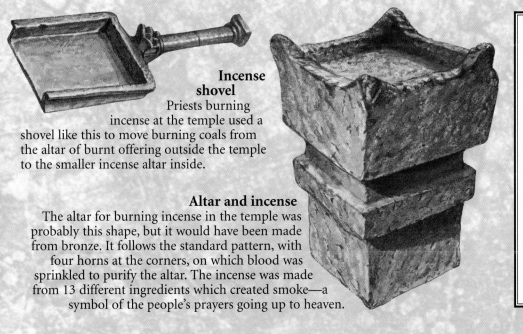

Incense shovel
Priests burning incense at the temple used a shovel like this to move burning coals from the altar of burnt offering outside the temple to the smaller incense altar inside.

Altar and incense
The altar for burning incense in the temple was probably this shape, but it would have been made from bronze. It follows the standard pattern, with four horns at the corners, on which blood was sprinkled to purify the altar. The incense was made from 13 different ingredients which created smoke—a symbol of the people's prayers going up to heaven.

❖ **ABOUT THE STORY** ❖

This happy story about a couple having their prayers answered illustrates what the Bible generally teaches about prayer. God did not give them what they asked for just because they were holy people and He thought they deserved it. He answered because the birth of John the Baptist was part of His bigger plan for the world.

A Son for Mary

ABOUT six months after Zechariah's vision in the temple, God sent the angel Gabriel on another important mission. This time his message was for Elizabeth's cousin Mary.

Mary lived at home with her parents in the region of Galilee, in a town called Nazareth. She was engaged to Joseph, a carpenter who was descended from the great King David, the greatest king of Israel. Every day, as Mary swept and cooked, she looked forward to when she would marry and have a home of her own.

One day, Mary was doing her chores as usual when a light suddenly flooded the room where she was working. She looked up and saw a beautiful man standing in front of her, his face and clothes bright with radiance.

> **‘You will bear a son, and you shall call His name Jesus.’**

"Hello Mary," the man said. "Know that God is with you; I am His messenger, the angel Gabriel. I have come to tell you that the Lord has chosen you above all other women for a very special blessing."

Even though Gabriel had spoken gently, Mary was still petrified. She was always careful to follow God's laws, but she had never expected the Lord to take any notice of a village girl. Priests and elders were far more important than she was, and they didn't have angels suddenly appearing in their kitchens.

Gabriel saw the fear on Mary's face.

Nazareth
In Jesus's day Nazareth was a small and obscure town. It was in the north of Judea, overlooking the fertile Plain of Esdraelon. The Church of the Annunciation, on the site where Mary is thought to have seen the angel, is in the center of the picture.

MARY'S RESPONSE TO THE ANGEL WAS DIFFERENT FROM ZECHARIAH'S. SHE DID NOT KNOW HOW IT COULD HAPPEN, BUT HER FAITH WAS FIRM. SHE HAS BEEN A MODEL FOR FAITH EVER SINCE. ❧

Annunciation
When the angel announced to Mary what God intended to do, it was called an annunciation. The event is marked by a service in many churches, on March 25.

"Don't be afraid," he said kindly. "God loves you. He's going to send you a son, whom you must call Jesus. He will be ruler over all the Lord's people, and His kingdom will have no end."

Poor Mary was even more confused. Nervously, she whispered to the angel, "How can I have a child? I'm not married yet."

"God is going to send His Holy Spirit to you, to grace you with His own Son," the angel replied. "Remember that nothing is impossible for the Lord. Indeed, your cousin Elizabeth has also been blessed and is going to have a baby—even though she's past the age for having children."

Mary was astounded. "How wonderful!" she gasped. As she thought of what the angel promised her she told herself, "It's not right to be afraid, Mary. If the Lord has indeed selected you for this special gift, you should accept it with joy and give thanks for it." With her heart thumping, she said. "I am ready to serve the Lord. Let everything happen to me just as you have said." Gabriel smiled at her and disappeared.

Once the angel had gone, Mary's first thought was to congratulate her cousin. She packed a bag and set off.

Mary couldn't wait to embrace her cousin. "Hello!" she cried as she got closer. "Congratulations!"

As Elizabeth heard her cousin's voice, she felt as if her baby had jumped up inside her to greet Mary. Elizabeth suddenly knew that Mary was pregnant and that the baby would be God's own son. "Mary, you are the most blessed of all women!" Elizabeth exclaimed, throwing her arms around her. "And what an honor to have the mother of my Lord come to visit me!"

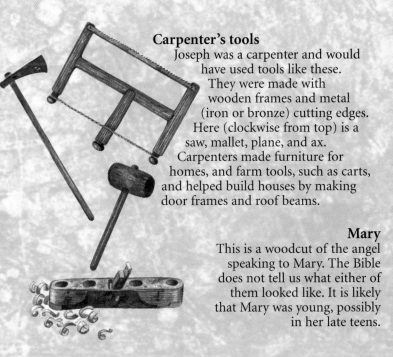

Carpenter's tools
Joseph was a carpenter and would have used tools like these. They were made with wooden frames and metal (iron or bronze) cutting edges. Here (clockwise from top) is a saw, mallet, plane, and ax. Carpenters made furniture for homes, and farm tools, such as carts, and helped build houses by making door frames and roof beams.

Mary
This is a woodcut of the angel speaking to Mary. The Bible does not tell us what either of them looked like. It is likely that Mary was young, possibly in her late teens.

❧ **ABOUT THE STORY** ❧
The birth of Jesus was carefully planned by God. He decided exactly when, where, and how Jesus would be born. Christians see in this story a sign that Jesus really was the Son of God. Because He had no human father but was conceived by the Holy Spirit, Jesus was both fully divine (from His heavenly Father's side) and fully human (from His mother's side).

The Birth of John

MARY stayed with Elizabeth for three months. She was, no doubt, a great help to her older cousin when Elizabeth was heavily pregnant with her unborn baby; and, of course, the two women shared the amazing secret of how they had each been blessed by the Lord. However, Mary began to worry that she had been away from home too long, and eventually the day came when she sadly told Elizabeth that she must say goodbye. Not long after Mary had gone, her cousin gave birth to a baby boy, just as the angel Gabriel had told Zechariah she would.

Like all proud parents, Elizabeth and Zechariah thought they would burst with happiness. Their friends and relatives gathered around to help them celebrate. "What are you going to call him?" someone asked, as they all took turns in cuddling the tiny bundle.

"Oh, they're sure to name him Zechariah, after his father," said a family friend, tickling the child under the chin.

"Yes," a relative agreed. "After all, it's the tradition to name him after the father."

"Well maybe they might like to name him after another member of the family," butted in one of the baby's many uncles, while he grabbed the child out of someone else's arms. "For instance, they might like to name him after me!"

"Wait! Wait!" Elizabeth laughed, holding up her hand for silence. She could see that a family argument was about to break out. When everyone was quiet, she said very firmly, "We're going to name him John."

"JOHN!" everyone repeated in shock. "Why on earth are you going to name him John?"

The argument began all over again.

"The first boy is always named after his father . . ."

"There's not a single person in the entire family who's named John..."

Elizabeth stood her ground.

"I'm sorry," she said, smiling, completely unfazed. "He's going to be called John, and that's that."

Writing
Most people at this time wrote on a wooden board covered with a layer of wax, which was written on with a stylus, a pointed wooden stick. The wax could later be melted and smoothed over, ready for use again. Parchment and papyrus were too expensive for most people.

Scribes
In Biblical times, not everyone could read and write. Scribes were employed to write letters and business documents. Their main job, however, was to copy out the religious texts and teach them to the people. They also taught in the schools attached to local synagogues.

She took her baby back into her own arms, where he lay quite content and peaceful.

The relatives and friends wouldn't give up.

"What does Zechariah think?" they urged.

"Surely he can't be happy about this John business?" Elizabeth sighed.

"Why don't you ask him yourself?" she suggested.

Everyone looked at each other, slightly embarrassed.

"He might not be able to speak," Elizabeth said loudly, getting a little red in the face, "but he hasn't lost the ability to think or write."

66 *'He shall be called John.'* 99

The friends and relations found a writing tablet and a pen, and crowded around the elderly priest in anticipation.

"WHAT DO YOU WANT HIM TO BE CALLED?" one of them yelled in Zechariah's face.

"He's not deaf, too, you know," Elizabeth murmured.

Slowly and carefully, in big, clear letters, Zechariah wrote out, "His name is John."

There was utter commotion as the relatives and friends read Zechariah's words.

"Well, I don't believe it!" one remarked.

"John!" another spluttered. "John!"

"Yes," said Zechariah, above the hubbub. "His name is John." There was a gasp of astonishment as all heads turned to look at the priest. His eyes widened and he clapped his hands over his mouth in surprise. "I can talk!" he whispered. "My voice has come back!" he shouted.

"Thanks be to God!" And he grabbed hold of the laughing Elizabeth and whirled her around, dancing and singing.

After that, there wasn't a single person in the whole of the hill country of Judea who didn't get to hear of the child who had been born so late to Elizabeth and Zechariah and of the miracle of how the priest's voice had returned. Everyone knew that the Lord must have had a hand in the amazing events, and they waited in awe to see what kind of man the child would grow up to be.

Jewish motifs

Jesus was born and raised as a Jew, and He worshiped in the Jewish synagogue. This mosaic depicts several Jewish motifs. In the center is the seven-branched candlestick (the menorah). Also shown here is a shofar (a ram's horn, bottom right), which priests blew to mark the start of the Sabbath and other holy days. Above it is an incense shovel.

Benedictine faith

When Zechariah could speak again, he uttered a prophetic poem about the ministry of his son, John. This poem is called the Benedictus, and is still sung in some church services today. Later, Saint Benedict founded the Benedictine order of monks and nuns, shown here.

The Birth of Jesus

WHEN Mary told Joseph that she was expecting a baby, he was very worried. They weren't yet married, and there was sure to be a scandal. That night, Joseph had a vivid dream. An angel said, "Joseph, don't be afraid to take Mary as your wife. The baby growing within her is the Son of God. He is the Savior whom the prophets said would one day come to save everyone from their sins. When the child is born, name Him Jesus. Raise Him as if He were your own son." Joseph awoke much comforted.

As the time drew near for the baby to be born, another problem arose. The Emperor Augustus Caesar ordered a census. This meant that every man had to go to where he was born, together with his family, to be put on a register.

Joseph had to travel to Bethlehem, a long way from Nazareth. Mary was heavily pregnant. It was not a good time for her to be traveling.

By the time they arrived, the city was full to bursting. There wasn't a single room to be had. Joseph and Mary trudged from place to place, exhausted, dirty, and starving. And Mary began to feel that the baby was on its way.

Bang! Joseph thumped on the door of an inn.

"We haven't any room," said the burly innkeeper from behind the door.

"Wait!" Joseph yelled. "Please! We just need a tiny corner somewhere, somewhere warm and dry. It doesn't matter where. My wife's about to give birth!"

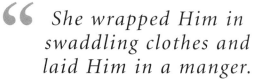

> **❝** *She wrapped Him in swaddling clothes and laid Him in a manger.* **❞**

The innkeeper said, a little more gently, "All my rooms are completely full. I can offer you the stable, if you don't mind the animals. You're welcome to stay there if you like."

Augustus
The emperor who ruled at this time was Augustus. His real name was Octavian. He became the first emperor of Rome in 27 B.C., when he was given his name. He was a great administrator and ordered several censuses. His aim was to govern the entire empire from Europe to Judea firmly but fairly.

JOSEPH DID WHAT GOD WANTED, BUT HE HAD TO DO WHAT THE AUTHORITIES WANTED, TOO. GOD MADE SURE THAT DESPITE THE EMPEROR'S ORDERS, HIS SON WOULD BE BORN SAFELY. ◆

Mary, mother of Jesus
The Bible tells us very little about the Virgin Mary. Like Joseph, she was descended from David. Many Christians believe that she remained a virgin throughout her life. She is regarded as the most important of all the saints.

Joseph accepted the offer gratefully, so it was in the innkeeper's stable, with the oxen, sheep, and chickens looking on, that the Savior of the world was born. Mary had no crib in which to lay her precious bundle, so she nestled Him among the straw of a manger from which the animals fed. There the baby Jesus stayed. He was safe and warm and sheltered, and He had His loving mother and father at His side.

Joseph

In New Testament times an engagement between two people was considered as binding as marriage itself. The only way to break it was to get a divorce. It was also thought to be sinful if someone had a sexual relationship before they were married. So Joseph probably thought Mary had been unfaithful to him. The angel told him it was a miracle, and so he loved Mary and cared for her.

✦ ABOUT THE STORY ✦

The story of Jesus's birth is very moving. It reveals important truths about God's plans for the world. Jesus was born in a borrowed room, not in a king's palace, even though He was the "King of kings," before whom everyone should bow in honor. It teaches that Jesus came into the world to show God's love for people who feel they have nothing. God has known the same sadness that they know.

The Visit of the Shepherds

WHILE Bethlehem was full to bursting with people, the fields around the city were quiet and empty, except for a few shepherds and their flocks. As usual, the men were spending the night under the starry sky, taking turns at sleeping and watching, so that no sheep would go astray, stolen by wolves or even bears. It was a cold and lonely job. They had only the dying flames of the campfire to keep them warm. Apart from its flickering and the pale glow of the moon and stars, all was calm, all was still.

Suddenly the night sky above blazed as if it were on fire. It was like trying to look into the full glare of the

Praising God
In churches today, choirs sing hymns, psalms, and songs as part of worshiping God. Music is a powerful way of praising Him. The pictures of heaven given in the Bible describe angels and people singing God's praises.

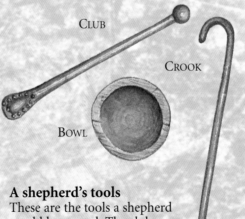

CLUB

CROOK

BOWL

A shepherd's tools
These are the tools a shepherd would have used. The club was for fighting off attacking wolves. He also had a food bowl from which he could eat. The crook was used for rescuing lost sheep.

A shepherd's cloak
Sheepskins would have been made into coats. These were to keep shepherds warm as they stayed up to guard their sheep.

scorching desert sun. The shepherds fell back, trying to shield their eyes, as high overhead a figure appeared.

"Do not be afraid," came its voice, speaking clearly into the mind of each of the shepherds. "I have news that will bring great joy to everyone on earth. Today in Bethlehem, the city of David, a Savior has been born who is Christ, the Lord. You will find Him wrapped up in swaddling clothes and lying in a manger."

> 'To you is born this day a Savior, who is Christ the Lord.'

The sound of countless singing voices filled the air. The heavens were filled with angels.

"Glory to God in the highest," they sang, "and peace to His people on earth."

Then suddenly the singing died away and the light faded. The dazed shepherds were left staring up at the sky. The gleaming moon and stars now seemed only an echo of the real beauty of the heavens, which they had glimpsed for a while and which had now disappeared.

The shepherds hurried off to Bethlehem, leaving only a couple of men behind to guard the flocks. They were excited. The prophets had spoken of a Christ, or Messiah, whom God would send to save the world from its sins. Had this most amazing person now been born?

The shepherds searched from place to place in the packed town until they heard the crying of an infant coming from a stable behind an inn. The shepherds found Mary and Joseph huddled over the manger, attending to a baby wrapped in swaddling clothes.

"It is indeed the Savior! Christ, the Lord!" the shepherds gasped, approaching the little family and falling on their knees. They told the startled parents about the visit from the angels and what they had said. When the shepherds had paid their tributes and gone, singing praises to God as they went, Mary and Joseph began to wonder and marvel at everything that had happened.

Medieval nativity
Many pictures have been painted of the first Christmas. This one shows the shepherds together with the wise men. Mary and Jesus have haloes around their heads. Artists used this device to show people who were specially blessed by God.

❖ **ABOUT THE STORY** ❖

Shepherds were despised by most people. They were thought to be liars and couldn't give evidence in court. Only people with no hope became shepherds. This story reminds readers that God has shown Himself specially to people whom everyone else despises and who think they are not good enough for God. The good news of Christianity is for everyone, regardless of background.

Jesus is Presented in the Temple

WHEN their baby was eight days old, Mary held a naming ceremony according to God's laws. From then on, the baby was called Jesus, just as the angel had told Mary He should be. Then, according to the custom, Mary and Joseph traveled up from Bethlehem to the temple in Jerusalem to present Jesus to the Lord and to offer a sacrifice of two doves or pigeons.

Now there lived in Jerusalem an old man whose name was Simeon. Simeon had always done his best to lead a good life and was well known by everyone in the city to be a very holy man. As the people of Jerusalem watched him make his way to and from the temple every day, his lips moving in constant prayer, they never dreamed that he had a precious secret. The Holy Spirit had promised Simeon that, as a reward for his faithful, lifelong service to God, he would not die before he had seen with his own eyes the Messiah who would save the world. Simeon felt he had been blessed with the highest of honors, and he looked forward with his whole heart to the moment that he would meet his Savior.

> 'Mine eyes have seen thy salvation which thou hast prepared in the presence of all peoples.'

When Mary and Joseph arrived in the temple with Jesus, Simeon was already there. That morning, the Holy Spirit had once again spoken to him, telling him that

❖ ABOUT THE STORY ❖

To most people, Jesus was just another baby. To those who were trying to look at the world through the eyes of faith, He was someone special. Even today, some people, like Simeon and Anna, are gifted with a kind of spiritual second sight that helps them to discern God's purposes behind events. They are called prophets. This event helped Mary and Joseph to know more about Jesus.

Mary weeps
When Mary took Jesus to the temple, Simeon prophesied that she would suffer much grief because of what would happen to Jesus.

Taking Jesus to the temple
The Jewish law said that after 40 days a woman who had a son must offer a sacrifice at the temple. The proper sacrifice was a lamb and a pigeon, but poor people were allowed to bring two pigeons. The ceremony dates back to Old Testament times, when eldest sons used to have to become priests. Then when the Levites took this role, the Israelites would symbolically "buy back" their sons from God, from the priesthood, by making a sacrifice, as Mary does here.

today was the great day when God's promise to him would be fulfilled. With his heart pounding in his breast, Simeon had prepared himself with great haste and hurried to the temple as fast as he could. And as soon as the old man laid eyes on the baby, he knew who He was.

"May God almighty bless you," Simeon cried, holding out his trembling arms to hold the child. "I have long dreamed about this day. Now I can die in peace, for my eyes have seen the one who will save the world. This child will be the glory of Israel and the light of hope for all the peoples of the earth."

Simeon turned to the stunned parents. "This child is a sign from God, but many will not listen to His message," the old man said to Mary. "Because of this, a great sadness will pierce through your heart like a sword," he continued. "However, He will also win many hearts for the Lord."

While Simeon was speaking, a woman even older than Simeon shuffled up. It was Anna, the prophetess. She had spent much of her life in the temple, devoting herself to fasting and prayer.

"Allow me the blessing of holding my Savior," she said. A curious crowd was beginning to gather around the family, and Anna lifted her voice aloud, thanking God for allowing her to see the holy child and telling everyone that the infant was the hope of the world.

As soon as Mary and Joseph had made their offering, they said goodbye to Simeon and Anna and hurried away from the eyes of the temple worshipers. They were more than a little embarrassed by all the fuss and naturally felt bewildered by the strangeness of everything that had happened since their son's birth.

Simeon and Anna
Simeon and Anna were people of faith who were expecting God to do something special. They didn't know what to expect, but prompted by the Holy Spirit they recognized Jesus.

The journey
The distance from Nazareth to Bethlehem was about 80 miles. Mary and Joseph walked there. It does not say in the Bible that Mary rode on a donkey, but it is quite likely that she would have. There were well-trodden tracks between towns, but no paved roads. Bethlehem was a short distance from where the temple was in Jerusalem.

The Wise Men Find Jesus

FAR away in the east, some learned priests were puzzled to see that a strange star suddenly appeared one night in the sky. Not only was it a star they had never noticed before, but it shone brighter than any other. The wise men hurried off to consult their writings. They agreed that the brilliant star was an unmistakable sign. The Savior had been born. Now all they had to do was find Him.

The wise men spread out their maps and plotted a route from the position of the star. Finally, they chose

gifts for the child who was King of the whole earth. Then they mounted their camels and set off across the desert.

News reached King Herod that strangers from the orient were searching Jerusalem. "They're looking for a child that has been born king of the Jews," the king's spies told him.

"Are they, indeed?" murmured Herod, stroking his beard thoughtfully. After all, *he* was king of the Jews. Somewhere in Judea, a rebellion was brewing. He kept calm and summoned the chief priests and scribes to a meeting. Herod pretended that he was curious to learn more.

"Where do your scriptures say that the Christ child is to be born?" Herod asked innocently.

"The prophets say that the Messiah will be born in Bethlehem," the priests replied.

Herod nodded, interestedly. He had the answer that he needed.

As soon as the priests and scribes had gone, the king called for the most trusted officers in his army.

"Find these wise men from the east," he ordered, "and bring them to me. Only do it in secret, or the people will really start to take notice of these rumors."

Soon, the wise men were ushered into the presence of the king of Judea. They had heard that Herod was a ruthless, harsh ruler and were worried. However, Herod was politeness itself.

"When exactly did this star appear?" the king asked. The wise men told him all they knew about the child.

The magi
Most pictures show three wise men, or magi, because they brought three gifts, although this number is not used in the Bible. It is likely that there were more than three, as people tended to travel in larger groups. They were learned priests—not kings, as is sometimes suggested.

Astrologers
The magi were also astrologers. In ancient times, astronomy (the study of planets) and astrology (giving advice based on the stars) were practiced by the same people. The Jews were not allowed to use astrology—God alone was their guide.

The wise men did indeed find Jesus in Bethlehem. The star shone biggest and brightest over the town and led the travelers to where Mary and Joseph were now staying. They were surprised at the arrival of the splendidly dressed guests, just as the wise men were to find the holy family in humble surroundings. They had no doubt, though, that the baby was the king of all kings. They bowed their heads to the floor and paid tribute, then they unlocked their jeweled caskets and offered Mary their gifts of gold, rarest frankincense, and myrrh.

The night before the wise men set off on their return, they had a dream which deeply disturbed them. "Herod must not be told," they agreed. They took a different route home, so that the evil king could not find them.

In turn, Herod seemed most helpful.

"Try Bethlehem instead of Jerusalem," he suggested.

The wise men bowed down and thanked Herod for his generous help. There was no time to waste.

"Oh, by the way," Herod added, "when you have found the child, would you be so kind as to tell me where He is? I must of course go and worship Him myself."

> " *They offered Him gifts: gold and frankincense and myrrh.* "

"Consider it done, O King," the wise men agreed. As soon as the door closed behind them, Herod thumped his fist down on his throne.

"As soon as I know where this 'king' is, I will make sure He is killed!" he snarled.

Casket and gifts
The gifts brought by the magi may have been in a casket like this. The gold was the sign of royalty, frankincense was a sign for a priest, and myrrh was a sign of death and burial.

Arabia
This is the town of San'a in Yemen. The Bible tells us that the magi came from the east. The most likely places were Arabia or Babylon.

❧ **ABOUT THE STORY** ❧

The wise men were gentiles (non-Jews). Their appearance in only Matthew's Gospel is of great significance to Christians. The message is that Jesus has come into the world for all peoples. Matthew, in fact, is the most Jewish of the Gospels, so this story is a reminder of Jesus's wider ministry. This event is celebrated in many churches as the Feast of Epiphany (January 6).

Escape to Egypt

MARY and Joseph marveled at how far the wise men had traveled to see their son. So many strange things had happened since He had been born. Maybe the departure of the wise men would mark an end to all the amazing and unusual events for a while. . . .

That night, Joseph once again dreamed that an angel came and stood by his side.

"You must take Mary and the baby and hurry away from here at once," came the angel's urgent message. "Flee into Egypt, and stay there until I come to tell you it is safe to return. King Herod of Judea is going to search for the child. He is determined to kill Him."

Next morning, Joseph gently shook Mary awake and told her to get Jesus ready. He lifted his wife and her precious child on to the donkey, and the family crept away unnoticed through the quiet streets of Bethlehem.

Meanwhile, in Jerusalem, King Herod was waiting for the wise men to return. Every day, he grew more and more frustrated and more and more angry.

"Surely those wretched astrologers must have found the child by now?" he'd bellow at his trembling advisers.

The days turned into weeks, and Herod grew more and more furious. Finding his rival, the baby Christ, was top of his agenda. The thundercloud-faced king could think of nothing else. How could he enjoy life, knowing that rumors were spreading about another king of the Jews? Besides, if the wise men were right, and this baby really was the Messiah spoken of in the scriptures, He would soon have supporters up and down the country. And that would leave Herod at serious risk of losing his throne.

One sunset, as yet another day ended with no word from the wise men, King Herod finally snapped. "Bring me the general of the royal army!" he roared.

The burly army commander was at once ushered in.

"Order your men to go through every single household in the Bethlehem area and find every male child under two years old," Herod spat, "then kill them all."

A gasp went around the throne room.

The blood drained from the general's face, and he fell to his knees before the ruthless, cruel monarch.

"But . . . but . . . sire, surely . . ." he stuttered, falling silent as Herod bent down to whisper in his ear.

"If I hear that there is even one male child under two years old left alive, I shall hold you personally responsible," hissed the king, and he swept away to his private chambers, leaving the army general groveling miserably on the cold palace floor.

> ❝ *Herod is about to search for the child, to destroy Him.* ❞

Soon, the sound of screaming rose up over Bethlehem. No one could escape the heartbreaking shrieks that tore the air. Panicking parents ran desperately to and fro, trying to secrete away their tiny sons. The soldiers marched like machines into every possible hiding place. They trampled over those who threw themselves to the ground and begged for them to have mercy. They turned deaf ears to pleading and crying of men and women beside themselves with grief.

At last, when there was not a single male child under the age of two left in the whole of the area around Bethlehem, Herod was satisfied. So much, then, for the supposed Messiah, king of the Jews!

In fact Jesus was long gone. Joseph kept Him and His mother safe in Egypt until the angel told him that Herod had died and it was time to return home to Judea. So finally the family returned to the quiet town of Nazareth in the remote district of Galilee, where Jesus grew up far away from the evil eyes of Herod's son, King Archelaus.

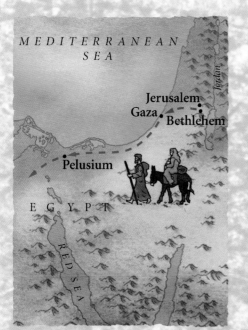

The fact that Jesus eventually returns to Israel, from Egypt, to save the people there echoes the way that the Israelites had fled Egypt with Moses hundreds of years before. ❧

Flight into Egypt
The Gospel of Matthew tells us that as soon as Joseph was told by the angel that Jesus was in danger, he took his family out of Israel to Egypt. It was a long and difficult trip for the family to make, especially as Jesus was so young.

❖ **ABOUT THE STORY** ❖

Herod the Great is known to have been a violent and cruel man, who was greatly afraid of rivals. He even had two of his own sons put on trial, convicted, and executed because of an alleged family plot against him. There is no record outside the New Testament of this event (which was confined to Bethlehem), but it would be typical of Herod to order it.

Lost and Found

In the sleepy town of Nazareth, Jesus grew up just like all the other children. Mary and Joseph taught Him to obey all the laws of their religion and made sure that He learned all the teachings of the holy scriptures.

Every year, Mary and Joseph traveled to Jerusalem to celebrate the great festival of Passover, as all Jews tried to do. One year, when Jesus was 12 years old, the family went as usual to share the wonderful experience of praising God in the temple at this important time of the year.

When it was time to go home, Mary and Joseph found a crowd of travelers planning to go their way. Jesus disappeared among them. Like all children His age, He

didn't want to walk by His parents' side. He wanted to talk with His own friends. Mary and Joseph weren't worried. They knew their son was sensible enough to keep close by.

After the first day's journey, when the tired, dusty travelers were getting ready to make camp for the night, Jesus was nowhere to be seen.

"Jesus! Jesus!" called Mary and Joseph, at the tops of their voices. The boy didn't come running.

The anxious couple hurried from group to group.

"Has anyone seen our son?" they asked. "He has very dark eyes; He's about this high; He's very gentle and well-mannered; a quiet, thoughtful boy."

Everyone just shook their heads.

Joseph looked very serious. Mary was close to tears.

"There's nothing more we can do now," the carpenter told his wife, putting his arm around her. "First thing in the morning, we'll retrace our steps."

Neither Mary nor Joseph managed to sleep for worry. Anything could have happened to Jesus. What if He had been kidnapped by bandits or eaten by wild animals? It didn't bear thinking about.

> ❝ *All who heard Him were amazed at His understanding and His answers.* ❞

As they went back to Jerusalem, Jesus's parents grew more anxious. There wasn't a single sign as to what had happened to Him. The boy had just disappeared.

People milled everywhere in the narrow streets, jostling

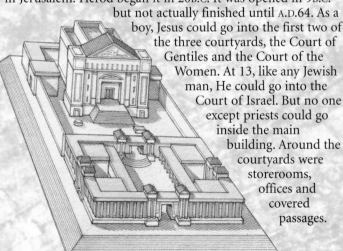

Herod's temple
This was the greatest of all three temples which had been built in Jerusalem. Herod began it in 20 B.C. It was opened in 9 B.C. but not actually finished until A.D.64. As a boy, Jesus could go into the first two of the three courtyards, the Court of Gentiles and the Court of the Women. At 13, like any Jewish man, He could go into the Court of Israel. But no one except priests could go inside the main building. Around the courtyards were storerooms, offices and covered passages.

Bar and Bat Mitzvah
When Jewish girls reach the age of 12 they have their Bat Mitzvah; Jewish boys have a Bar Mitzvah aged 13. This is a ceremony when, in the eyes of their religion, they become adults, and take on the religious duties of a Jewish adult.

was going on in one of the porticoes. They could see elders and priests, deep in discussion. They tiptoed forward. Then Mary's voice rang out loud and clear.

"Jesus!" she cried, pushing her way through the learned men to where Jesus stood in the middle of them.

"Please excuse us," Joseph explained. "We've been looking for Him all over the place."

To his utter astonishment, the leaders all shook his hand.

"We cannot believe your son's understanding of the scriptures," they told him. "And He has raised searching questions that few people ask."

Meanwhile, Mary's relief at finding her son was giving way to anger.

"Jesus, we have been worried sick!" she scolded. "How could you just go off on your own and leave your father and me wondering where you were?"

"You should have known that you would find me in my Father's house," Jesus said, calmly.

shoulder to shoulder. It was looking like an impossible task. Several times they thought they saw Jesus, but each time it turned out to be another boy about His age. They couldn't leave without their precious son. They would hunt high and low until they found Him, hopefully alive and well. By the third day the only place the desperate parents hadn't searched was the great temple itself.

Wearily, Mary and Joseph climbed the great stone steps and entered the huge courtyard. Some type of meeting

Mary was taken aback at Jesus's strange answer, but she didn't have the time to puzzle over His mysterious words. All she wanted to do now was get back home safely. Later, she remembered Jesus's strange reply. And, of course, she hadn't forgotten the angel, the shepherds, and the wise men, Simeon and Anna in the temple. It was all very mysterious indeed . . . .

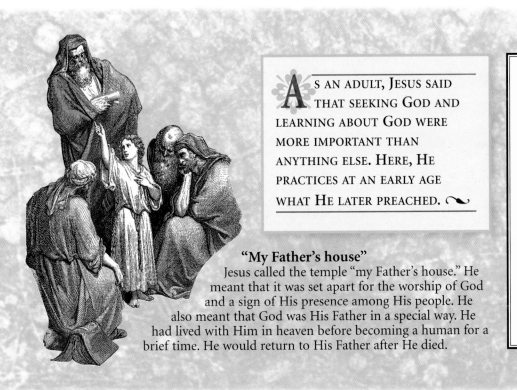

AS AN ADULT, JESUS SAID THAT SEEKING GOD AND LEARNING ABOUT GOD WERE MORE IMPORTANT THAN ANYTHING ELSE. HERE, HE PRACTICES AT AN EARLY AGE WHAT HE LATER PREACHED.

"My Father's house"

Jesus called the temple "my Father's house." He meant that it was set apart for the worship of God and a sign of His presence among His people. He also meant that God was His Father in a special way. He had lived with Him in heaven before becoming a human for a brief time. He would return to His Father after He died.

⟡ ABOUT THE STORY ⟡

We know little about Jesus's boyhood, and nothing about how He looked or how He behaved. Some legends were made up in the 3rd and 4th centuries, but none of them can be traced any earlier. This story shows that Jesus was aware of His special relationship with God from an early age. It also shows that He learned to obey His parents in His preparation to obey God.

Jesus is Baptized

JESUS's cousin, John, grew up to devote his life entirely to God. When he was a young man, he went off on his own into the wilderness around the river Jordan. John just wrapped a rough camel skin around him and ate locusts and honeycombs that he found in the wild.

When John was around 30 years old, a change came upon him. Instead of keeping himself to himself, he began to preach to all the peoples who lived near the river.

"I have heard the word of God!" he would shout. "You must think about your sins and be truly sorry for them. I hear you say that you're Abraham's descendants, God's chosen people. I tell you that God could raise these very stones up to life, if He wanted. Beg the Lord's forgiveness and be good. For the day is coming when the Lord will judge sinners."

> ❝*I have baptized you with water; but He will baptize you with the Holy Spirit.*❞

People began to travel to the Jordan to hear what John had to say. All kinds of men and women came: common folk, noblemen, priests, tax collectors, even Roman soldiers. No matter who they were, John's message was the same. He said people should turn back to God, be kind, not cheat or lie, and not hurt anybody with harsh words or violence.

Every day, people would line up by the river Jordan, eager to be forgiven for their wrongdoings and wanting to make a new start. One by one, John would take them into the river and submerge them, blessing them as they rose up from the water cleansed of their sins.

As the weeks passed, rumors began to spread among the people of Galilee.

"Maybe this John is the Messiah spoken of by the prophets . . ." people would murmur.

"Surely this holy man is the Christ!" exclaimed others.

John was always very clear about the truth.

❖ ABOUT THE STORY ❖

This event marks the beginning of Jesus's public ministry. Through it He received confirmation that He was indeed the Son of God, and He received the spiritual power He needed to do His work. His baptism was also a way of identifying with the people He came to die for. He was saying that He was willing to take people's sin on His shoulders, which He did on the cross.

Baptism
Baptism is a ceremony in which a person is submerged beneath water, or sprinkled with water, as a sign that they want to follow Jesus and turn away from their sins. Most churches use it as the main ceremony to make someone a church member.

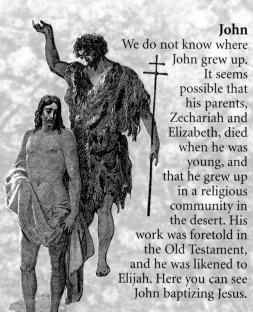

John
We do not know where John grew up. It seems possible that his parents, Zechariah and Elizabeth, died when he was young, and that he grew up in a religious community in the desert. His work was foretold in the Old Testament, and he was likened to Elijah. Here you can see John baptizing Jesus.

"I am not the Messiah, or Elijah, or any other prophet. I am merely one voice crying out in the wilderness, trying to prepare the way for the Lord," he said. "I'm baptizing you with water, but there is one coming soon who will baptize you with the fire of the Holy Spirit. He is much greater than I—so great that I'm not even fit for the job of cleaning His sandals."

When Jesus himself arrived among the crowds at the banks of the Jordan, John knew who He was immediately, and he told everyone who was there.

"Here He comes!" he cried, falling on his knees. "The one God has promised us! The one who will take away the sins of all the world!"

Jesus laid a hand gently on his cousin's arm and looked deep into his eyes.

"Will you baptize me too, John?" He asked.

"My Lord," John gasped. "I can't baptize you! It should be you who baptizes me!"

However, Jesus insisted.

"We should each of us do what God has given us to do," He said quietly.

And so John led Jesus down into the Jordan.

At the very moment that John blessed Jesus as He rose from the waters, the two men heard a mighty thunderclap. John looked up to see the clouds of the heavens parting, and a dove came gliding down, bathed in heavenly light. John knew that the Holy Spirit was descending on his cousin. Then they heard a voice that seemed to come from everywhere and nowhere all at once.

"This is my beloved Son," the voice said, "with whom I am well pleased."

Locusts and honey

Locusts are large grasshoppers which can breed into great swarms. They are very nutritious and are still eaten today. Wild bees made nests in rocky places. John could collect their honey.

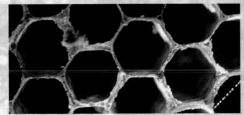

Sadducees

Most Sadducees were priests, but not all priests were Sadducees. They were a group within Judaism. As a group they were very snobbish and came mostly from the upper classes. They despised ordinary people. In Jesus's time, they were the major group in the Sanhedrin, the Jews' ruling council. However, they often had to follow the Pharisees because the latter were popular with the ordinary people. They accepted only the written laws of the Old Testament, and not all the extra ones the Pharisees made up. They did not believe in life after death, or that God could or would guide a person's life. The Sadducees died out after the temple was destroyed by the Romans in A.D.70. No one is sure how they started, whether as a political, religious, or aristocratic group.

Tempted in the Wilderness

JESUS knew He was the Son of God, the Messiah the prophets had said would come to save the world from its sins. Now He had to prepare for the job He had been sent to do.

Led by the Holy Spirit, Jesus went into the wilderness, where He could be on His own to pray. There He talked to God for 40 days and 40 nights, asking for guidance in the difficult days that lay ahead. He ate nothing, and as He grew weak with hunger and exhaustion, the devil came to Him in His thoughts.

"If you really are the Son of God," Satan whispered, "why don't you turn these stones into bread?"

Jesus knew this would be wrong on several counts. First, He had heard the voice of the Lord calling Him His Son. He knew He should have faith that this was true, not try to work a miracle to prove it. Second, eating was far less important than obeying God. Jesus realized that His body would die if He didn't eat, but His body would die one day anyway. It was far more important to look after His soul by not doing anything that would offend His Father in heaven. Besides, He should trust God to look after Him. After all, long ago, Moses had led the starving Israelites through the desert. He had trusted the Lord, and God had sent them food from heaven.

Jesus summoned up His strength.

"No," He told the devil. "People can't live on bread alone; we need to listen to the words of God to survive."

Satan was annoyed. However, he tried not to let it show. Instead, he put a picture of the holy city of Jerusalem in Jesus's mind. It was as if Jesus were standing right on the top of the great temple, looking down on the streets and houses all around. Balancing so high up made Jesus dizzy, and His head began to whirl and spin.

"If you really are the Son of God," Satan challenged, "don't be afraid to fall off. The angels will come and catch you. They'll make sure you don't even bruise a single toe."

It was a very tempting thought. Why struggle to do things the hard way, fighting Satan, when there was a quick solution? Jesus knew it would be wrong. His life as the Messiah was going to be dangerous, sad, and lonely. There would be no easy way out. His Father in heaven wanted Him to live as a human, to show people the right way to God—even if it was the most difficult way of all.

❧ **ABOUT THE STORY** ❧

Jesus was tempted in the same way as everyone else. The first temptation was to put the satisfaction of His own needs and desires before God's will. The second was to take a short cut to do God's work, rather than do it in God's way. The third was to grab power over people for Himself. The message is that we should not be concerned just with the result, but also with how we get there.

The Judean Desert
This area is wild and inhospitable. There are oases (for water), but it is hot in the day and cold at night, and there is little shelter. Jesus was here about six weeks. The desert is often thought of as a place of testing because it is a place of extremes.

JESUS RESISTED TEMPTATION BY QUOTING FROM GOD'S WORD, WHICH IS A GOOD WAY OF DEALING WITH IT. IF THOUGHTS AGREE WITH THE BIBLE, THEY ARE FROM GOD; IF NOT, THEY COME FROM THE DEVIL. ❧

wonders of the world. Images of golden palaces, splendid temples, and treasure houses overflowing with the riches of the earth arose in Jesus's mind. There were magnificent armies of brave-hearted warriors and rows of gleaming chariots led by prancing horses. There were fleets of ships laden with exotic cargoes from mysterious lands...

"Take a good look!" urged Satan. "All this can be yours. I will give it all to you—if only you will bow down and worship me."

Jesus knew that the devil was indeed mighty, for he had hold of many people's hearts. Those who turned to Satan to make them powerful ended up dishonest, selfish, and cruel. They ruled by crushing others and kept themselves happy by making others miserable. Those who followed the Lord might not become rich or famous, but they would find love and happiness and be truly at peace.

> **''** *'You shall worship the Lord your God, and Him only shall you serve.'* **''**

Besides which, Jesus knew that all kingdoms of the world will one day fade to dust and that only the kingdom of God will last forever.

"No," He told the devil, in disgust. "Get away from me! People should worship only the Lord God."

Satan nearly exploded with frustration. He had tempted Jesus with all he had. Raging wildly, the devil disappeared. And as Jesus sank down in the sands of the desert, utterly worn out, angels came to look after Him.

"No," He told the devil, firmly. "It is wrong to put God to the test like this. The easiest thing to do is by no means always the best."

Satan was furious, but he didn't give up. Instead, he whisked Jesus's thoughts away to the highest mountain in the world. As if Jesus were an eagle, flying high up in the skies, He could see the whole earth spread out below Him. How beautiful His Father had created everything! Waving fields of crops grew out of pink and brown soil. Wide carpets of green grass and sweet-smelling forests covered plains and hills. Deserts glowed yellow, and ice caps shone blue-white. Rivers rippled and sparkled down to seas as broad as the skies above. The devil showed Jesus all the

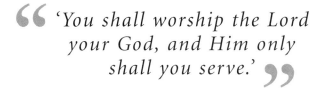

Satan
Satan is often pictured with horns (like a raging bull) and a forked tail (like a snake's tongue). These are symbols of what he is like. He is vicious in attitude and poisonous in intent. The Bible tells us very little about Satan. It seems he was an angel in heaven who became jealous and proud. He rebelled against God and was thrown out. Now he seeks to oppose God and His people in any way he can. He is not so powerful as God, however, and Jesus came to destroy the grip Satan has on people.

The First Miracle

JESUS left Judea and traveled back to Galilee. It was time to begin teaching the people what they had to do to enter the kingdom of God. Several of John the Baptist's followers went along with Jesus, wanting to help. As soon as Jesus arrived home, He and His mother had to go to a wedding in Cana. Weddings were always big, important celebrations and often lasted several days.

Perhaps the steward in charge of the wedding reception hadn't ordered enough wine for such a large feast. Or maybe the guests were drinking more than usual. Whatever the reason, Mary noticed halfway through the wedding reception that the wine had almost run out. While the guests were all munching their way through each delicious course, nervous, red-faced servants were scurrying off with empty wine jars.

"Look. There's no more wine left," Mary quietly said to her son.

Jesus was concerned. He knew how embarrassing it would be for the bride and groom if they had nothing to offer their thirsty guests to drink.

"I'm sorry, but I can't do anything about it," He whispered back. "The time is not yet right for me to show the powers my Father has given me."

Mary just held His hand and nodded, reassuringly. Then she turned to the servants nearby.

"Excuse me," she said, politely. "I couldn't help noticing that you're almost out of wine. My son can help you. Just do exactly as He says."

Jesus looked at His beloved mother and smiled. Then with a sigh, He said to the servants, "Fill your empty jars up to the brim with water."

> ❝ *The steward of the feast tasted the water now become wine.* ❞

Very puzzled, they hurried off to carry out his instructions. And soon they were back, struggling under the weight of their full urns.

"Now draw out some of the water into a goblet," Jesus told them, "and take it to the steward for tasting." (It was the custom for the steward to check every jar that came out of the cellar, to make sure that the wine was good.)

Well, the servants were mystified. They were sure that their boss would think they had gone crazy when they took him water to test, pretending it was wine. They didn't dare refuse to carry out one of the guest's instructions. And besides, there was something about the man's kind eyes and His mother's gentle manner that made them trust that everything would be all right.

Now the steward was an expert wine

Cana
This was a small village north of Nazareth. We are not sure of the exact site today. The town pictured may be built near it.

Water jars
Water jars were usually used for the ceremonial washing of people's feet. It was the custom to wash a visitor's feet when they came to your house; they wore open sandals. Many Jews also insisted on ritual washings before they ate, as a religious act.

taster. He knew all the tricks of his trade, such as serving the best wine first and bringing out the cheaper wine later, when the guests were less aware of what they were drinking. When he drank this time from the servant's goblet, he was amazed. This new wine was even better than the wine they had served at first! Before the servants could explain, the steward hurried off to congratulate the groom on his good taste and generosity.

Jesus had worked the first of many miracles He was to perform throughout His life. His followers had seen Him do the impossible, and they believed more strongly than ever that He truly was the Son of God.

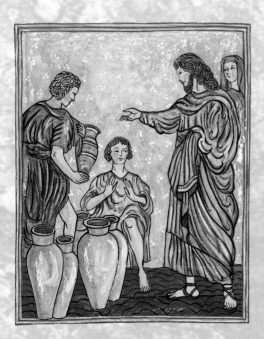

Mary's words—"Do exactly as He says"—are advice that everyone can follow. In order to live in God's way, Christians believe that we have to do everything He says.

Wine tasting
This shows the steward tasting the wine. Wine in the New Testament can also stand for Jesus's blood, which He shed on the cross for the sins of the world. It is significant that Jesus's first miracle involved wine, as if looking forward to His greater miracle of salvation.

❖ ABOUT THE STORY ❖

Jesus sometimes said that His teaching was like new wine, or that He came to bring to people the new wine of the kingdom of God. He meant that He brought the new life of the Holy Spirit to people who would follow Him. As with many of His teachings, Jesus illustrated His words by His miracles. God's new life is plentiful, like the supply of wine at Cana. There is plenty of it.

Followers Flock to Jesus

JESUS began to travel around Galilee, teaching from synagogue to synagogue.

"Beg the Lord to forgive your sins," He urged, just like His cousin John the Baptist. "For the time is near when the doors of God's kingdom will be thrown open. The Holy Spirit has sent me to bring the good news that captives will be set free, the blind will see, and the poor will no longer have to suffer."

Everyone who heard Jesus was amazed at the way He spoke. He didn't simply read out the Scriptures, as the scribes did. He interpreted them as if He were sure He knew what they were all about.

Jesus's actions were pretty astounding too. Jesus was preaching one day in Capernaum, when a madman suddenly flew into a crazy fit.

"I know who you are," the madman yelled at Jesus. "You're the Holy One of God! What do you want with us? Have you come here to destroy us all?"

Jesus remained calm. He said firmly, "Be quiet!" He stared at the madman. "Leave him!" He commanded.

At once, the man crumpled into a heap on the floor. At Jesus's command, the demons left him.

❧ ABOUT THE STORY ❧

There was something "different" about Jesus. It was not just what He said, nor was it just what He did—there had been miracle workers before. He was in a class apart, and people could see it. However, He wouldn't explain it. Jesus silenced the one person who really knew—the madman. He wanted people to learn to trust Him in the ordinary things of life.

The miraculous catch of fish
This had a special impact on Peter. He knew that in the daytime fish went to the bottom of the lake where the water was cooler. If Jesus had the power to make the fish come into the net, He could do anything. The miracle spoke to Peter in terms he understood.

The worshipers were left in shock.

"Who on earth is this man?" they whispered.

Reports spread like wildfire about what had happened. Even though it was nearly dark, everyone who heard about the captivating stranger with the special powers came at once to find Him. Sick and injured people came flooding from the nearby towns and villages to be healed by Jesus.

> ‘ *I know who you are, the Holy One of God.* ’

He laid His hands on them, filling them with a sense of forgiveness and hope, curing each and every disease.

"You will stay with us, won't you?" the people pleaded.

"I'm afraid I can't," Jesus explained. "I must move on to other places. I have to tell everyone how they can find happiness by turning to God. It's what I was sent to do."

One day, Jesus was preaching to a crowd on the beach when He noticed Peter and Andrew, who were fishermen, washing their nets. Jesus jumped into their boat and asked them to take Him a little way offshore. There He sat and spoke to the people from a safe distance.

When Jesus finished preaching, He asked Peter to steer the boat into deeper waters and to lower his nets.

"Master, we fished all night last night and caught nothing," Peter protested. "Since it's you who's asking, we'll try again."

When the brothers tried to pull up their nets, they were so heavy with fish that they could hardly lift them. They had to call to James and John, in another boat, for help.

When the two boats were nearly sinking under the weight of the catch, Peter knelt at Jesus's feet.

"Lord," Peter said, "I'm not worthy to be one of your followers. I didn't really trust you. I didn't really believe that we'd catch anything."

"Don't be afraid," Jesus said. "From now on, all of you are going to be catching people instead of fish."

The men left behind everything they had and dedicated their lives to following Jesus.

Jesus and the disciples

A disciple is someone who learns from another person and seeks to do what they say and live how they live. There were many disciples of Jesus. He chose 12 of them to do special work for God.

Fishermen

Many people who lived around the Sea of Galilee were fishermen. They fished from boats at night, or waded into the waters in the day to throw nets over the smaller fish in the shallows by the shore, in the same way as the fishermen shown here. The Sea was well stocked with many kinds of edible fish that were sold locally.

Demons

Some people who seemed insane, or mad, were thought to be possessed by demons. People believed demons to be beings who wanted to stop God's work.

Jesus the Healer

PEOPLE far and wide got to hear about Jesus. So many men and women came to see Jesus that the synagogues weren't big enough to fit them all in. With everyone lining up to be healed, Jesus could hardly find a moment to Himself to go off and pray. The authorities began to grumble at how whole towns would grind to a halt when the exciting new preacher arrived. Everyone would lay down their tools and go off to hear Him talk.

Jesus didn't mean to cause trouble. He was just concerned to spread His message to as many folk as possible and help all those who were in need.

In one city, a leper crept up to Jesus one day and knelt at His feet. "Lord, I know that if you want to, you can cure me," the poor man begged, his skin crumbled and deformed with the terrible disease.

"Of course I want to," said Jesus, gently. "Be clean." And Jesus reached out and touched his skin.

The leper was shocked. After all, his deadly disease was so infectious that most people ran off screaming if they saw him coming. Then he realized that Jesus was smiling at him. The leper looked at his fingers. He felt his face. He peered down at his legs. He couldn't believe it! He was cured! His skin was smooth and healthy! Weeping with joy, he thanked Jesus over and over again.

"Don't tell anyone about this," Jesus said. "Go straight to the priest and make an offering of thanks to God."

The overjoyed leper couldn't contain himself. He went leaping around the streets on his brand new legs, waving his healthy arms in the air, telling everyone he met about how the wonderful Jesus had cured him.

So Jesus's reputation spread even farther afield, and even more people came traveling to see the extraordinary man. Instead of going to towns, Jesus began to preach in the wide open spaces of the countryside, where there was room for everyone.

On another occasion, Jesus was preaching in a private house to a crowd that included many important teachers of the law. Priests, elders, and Pharisees had come from towns and cities all over Galilee and Judea, and even from the great city of Jerusalem itself, to question Jesus. They wondered who He really was. A trickster? A prophet with healing powers like Elijah and Elisha? Could He possibly be the Messiah, as so many people were claiming?

> " *Great multitudes gathered to hear and to be healed of their infirmities.* "

As usual, there wasn't even standing room inside the little house. People were crammed together so tightly that they couldn't even raise a hand to scratch their nose. Others spilled out into the passage that led to the street.

While Jesus spoke, four latecomers began struggling to push their way inside. Their job was made even more difficult because they carried a friend of theirs on a stretcher, a man who was paralyzed. The ranks of spectators were too dense. There was only one thing to do.

Sweating with the strain, the men carried their friend up the outside stairs onto the flat roof of the house. They tied ropes to the stretcher and removed some of the roof covering. Then, very slowly and carefully, they lowered the stretcher through the gap and down into the room where Jesus was teaching.

Jesus was extremely moved at the friends' faith and at the plight of the paralyzed man.

"Take heart, my son," he said, "your sins are forgiven."

All the Pharisees and Saducees present were horrified. It was one thing to have the power of healing, but how could anyone have the power of forgiveness? Only God had that! It was blasphemy!

Jesus soon put a stop to their grumblings.

"I know just as well as you that anyone can say, 'Your sins are forgiven,'" He said. "After all, no one can see whether they really have been or not. To prove to you that God has granted me this power and has healed this man's soul, I shall heal his body, too."

Jesus turned again to where the man lay stiff and still on his stretcher.

"Rise up and walk," He commanded.

To everyone's amazement, the man immediately stood up and rolled up his stretcher. Then, praising God, he hurried off to show his family, with his grateful friends cheering and slapping him on the back.

The priests, elders, and Pharisees didn't dare say a single word more. How could they? What they had just seen was truly astonishing. In fact, everyone agreed they had never seen anything like it before.

JESUS COULD SEE THAT THE MAN HAD A DEEPER NEED THAN JUST TO HAVE HIS BODY HEALED. EVERYONE NEEDS FORGIVENESS FOR THEIR SPIRITUAL "SICKNESS"—THE SIN THAT KEEPS THEM AWAY FROM GOD. ᐁ

Pharisees
They were a group of powerful religious leaders who believed that the only way to be right with God was to keep every one of His laws all the time. Pharisees were sincere people, but they hindered others' faith, so Jesus often criticized them.

❖ ABOUT THE STORY ❖

This story shows that Jesus wasn't out to get lots of publicity; His main concern was for the people He helped. Jesus's miracles were not a way of seeking attention, He wanted what was best for people. Jesus knew that people might be attracted to Him by miracles. He also knew, though, that such things would not make them want to trust their lives to God, which was what He wanted.

Matthew Is Called

JESUS was walking down a road one day with His many disciples when He looked into an open window and saw a man working at a desk. The man was Levi, later known as Matthew, and he was working in the tax office.

At that time, Judea was under the rule of the Roman empire. The Jews hated everything to do with the conquering nation and its army. They had to pay the Romans in taxes, and the people who collected the taxes for the Romans were seen as traitors. As a result, if you became a tax collector, people you had been friends with for years suddenly stopped talking to you. Even members of your own family didn't want to know you any more. Complete strangers would shout at you in the street, calling you names.

Matthew was one of these hated tax collectors. And while many citizens in the town had taken the day off to see Jesus, Matthew knew he wouldn't be welcome among the crowds of the city. He stayed indoors, busily hunched over his tax records.

Matthew was trying hard to concentrate on his work, when he suddenly felt that someone was watching him. The hair bristled on his neck, and he swung around. Matthew found himself looking straight at a stranger who was staring in at him through the open window—a stranger with the kindest face and deepest, darkest eyes he'd ever seen. Matthew knew it was Jesus.

"Follow me," He said.

Matthew didn't need telling twice. Without a word, he got up out of his chair. He didn't even close his books or put away his pen. He just left everything exactly where it was and hurried off eagerly to join Jesus's disciples.

That night, Matthew insisted that he repay Jesus's kindness by having Him to stay at his house. It was his way of showing how much Jesus meant to him. When

Women disciples
There were also female disciples following Jesus. They looked after the practical needs of the twelve. They also listened to and learned from Jesus.

Metal cup
Most ordinary people drank out of pottery cups or out of small bowls. Silver cups like this would be used only by rich people and in the temple.

Tax collectors
Tax collectors were in charge of collecting a wide variety of taxes for the Romans, which they used to pay for their empire.

it. Surely, they thought, Jesus should be sitting down to eat with us, rather than with the common folk? And not just peasants, but tax collectors! Sinners!

The Pharisees grew even more annoyed when Jesus told them off for their moaning.

"Those who are well have no need of a doctor," He explained. "It is those who are ill who need to be healed. I have not been sent to look after good people; it is sinners who have most need of me."

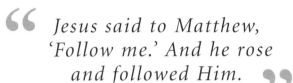

> ❝ *Jesus said to Matthew, 'Follow me.' And he rose and followed Him.* ❞

"We try so hard to live good, strict lives!" they protested. "Our followers often fast and pray, as do the disciples of John the Baptist. We never see yours doing the same. Your followers always eat well and drink merrily, as if they're at an eternal banquet! What's it all about?"

"Would you expect guests at a wedding not to celebrate while the bridegroom is present?" Jesus scolded. "There will be plenty of time for fasting when the bridegroom is taken away from the guests."

Jesus's mysterious answer infuriated the Pharisees all the more. Even His disciples didn't really understand. They didn't mind too much. Jesus often seemed to talk in riddles. He always seemed to know more than He was letting on. His followers realized that He explained everything He thought they needed to know. They trusted that the rest would all unfold in its own good time.

Jesus had invited him to go along with His followers, Matthew hadn't wanted anyone to notice him. He hadn't jumped up and down for joy, shouting aloud for all to hear. Inside, his heart was dancing. And he was sure that Jesus somehow knew how he felt.

Matthew threw the greatest feast that he could offer Jesus and His disciples. He didn't really have any friends of his own to share the joyous occasion with, so he invited other tax collectors along instead. For the first time ever, Matthew's house was full of guests enjoying themselves— and he loved it.

When the Pharisees got to hear of it, they were very jealous! The Pharisees were devoutly religious and considered themselves better than other people because of

The Roman Empire
Jesus lived in Galilee under the rule of the Roman Empire. This was the largest empire in the world at the time. Emperor Augustus brought stability to the empire and secured the borders.

⟡ ABOUT THE STORY ⟡

Jesus was known as a friend of tax collectors and people who were regarded as sinners. To have a former tax collector as one of His inner circle of disciples made Him even more odious to the religious leaders, who regarded such people as beyond God's help. Jesus said He came to call all sorts of people to follow God, and this was shown in His choice of disciples.

The Faithful Centurion

JESUS befriended many people who were despised by other Jews. One day, He helped an officer in the Roman army.

It all began when a group of elders came hurrying up to Jesus when He was preaching one day in the town of Capernaum.

"Sir, we have been sent to find you by a Roman centurion," one began.

"He has a loyal servant whom he's grown to love like his own son," interrupted another.

"But the servant is very ill," butted in yet another.

"You really should help him out," another elder added. "Even though the centurion is a gentile and an enemy of Israel, he's always been very good to us Jews. He even helped to build our synagogue . . ."

> "*He is worthy to have you do this for him, for he loves our nation, and he built us our synagogue.*"

Even before they had finished talking, Jesus was already striding along on His way to the centurion's house.

Jesus had very nearly reached the centurion's house when some people came dashing out of it.

"We have a message for you," they told Jesus. "Our friend says he's not worthy to have you honor his home with your presence, and that is why he never dreamed of coming to see you himself. He begs you not to trouble yourself any further. Instead, he says that if you simply say

Chemists
Although Jesus healed many people, most of the time people had to rely on the medicine of the time. Chemists used herbal remedies for everything, because there were no drugs. Some of these may have been useful, but others were not. Many chemists were con-men and would just cheat the people.

JESUS OFTEN USED HIS MIRACLES TO TEACH SOMETHING ALSO. HE SAID PEOPLE SHOULD TRUST GOD AND ACCEPT HIS WORD. THAT IS WHAT FAITH IS ALL ABOUT, TODAY AS WELL AS THEN.

Surgical instruments
Compared with modern standards, Roman surgery was very crude, but for the time it was well advanced. The bronze instruments shown here are (from top to bottom) forceps, a spoon, a spatula, and a scalpel.

the word of command, his servant will be healed. After all, he's a centurion. He's used to giving orders and finding that everything then happens just so!"

Jesus's face lit up with happiness.

"I tell you, I haven't found such faith among any of you Jews," He told the crowds who were following Him. "There will be people from far-off nations who are allowed to enter the kingdom of heaven, while many from the nation of Israel will be left outside in the darkness, to howl and gnash their teeth in despair."

Jesus turned away, and the centurion's friends began to hurry back to the house. They found the servant was completely recovered, just as if he had never been ill.

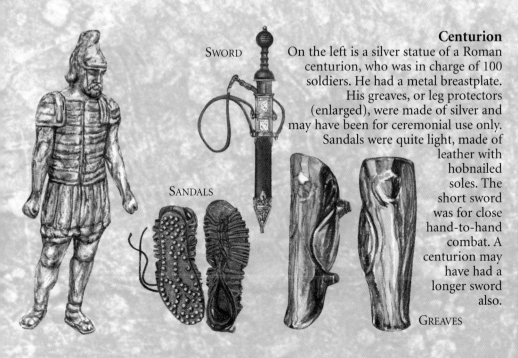

Centurion

SWORD

SANDALS

On the left is a silver statue of a Roman centurion, who was in charge of 100 soldiers. He had a metal breastplate. His greaves, or leg protectors (enlarged), were made of silver and may have been for ceremonial use only. Sandals were quite light, made of leather with hobnailed soles. The short sword was for close hand-to-hand combat. A centurion may have had a longer sword also.

GREAVES

❧ ABOUT THE STORY ❧

This story is told to show Jesus's character and His spiritual authority. He only has to say a word, and all creation responds. Here, a man is healed. On a later occasion, a storm was stopped. The Jews knew God had created the world by speaking words of command. There was only one conclusion they could come to. Jesus was God in human form, with all the authority of God.

Trouble Begins to Brew

Day by day, as Jesus's friends grew in number, so did His enemies. Jesus first came up against opposition in Nazareth. You might think that the people of His hometown would be proud of the famous local boy. When they heard Him preaching in the synagogue, telling them all kinds of new things they should and shouldn't be doing, they were irritated and envious.

"Where on earth did He get all this wisdom and the knowledge to do all these amazing things?" they scoffed.

"He's only the son of Joseph the carpenter, after all. We know His family: Mary, His mother, and all His brothers and sisters! He's just a normal person like us!"

Jesus was deeply saddened by their lack of belief. There was nothing He could do but turn His back on Nazareth. The people had wasted their chance to hear His message.

Elsewhere, Jesus couldn't help offending other people because His teachings were so new and fresh. The priests and elders, Sadducees and Pharisees, had spent their lives studying the ancient scriptures, but Jesus often presented them in a very different light.

"It's all right to eat all kinds of food," Jesus preached. "It's not what goes into people that is unclean, but what comes out of them, such as evil thoughts, pride, violence. You don't have to stick to all the traditional washing rituals, either. They don't cleanse your soul, as the Pharisees believe they do. They only cleanse your body."

> **But they were filled with fury and discussed with one another what they might do to Jesus.**

Of course, the holy men who had been doing their best to follow these laws for years, believing they were doing the right thing, were furious to hear Jesus telling them it wasn't necessary. And sometimes He even criticized them openly, saying that they had lost sight of what God's commandments were really all about and that they were just practicing meaningless traditions.

What annoyed the Jewish leaders most was the way in which—in their eyes—Jesus broke the laws of the Sabbath. One Sabbath morning, some Pharisees were with Jesus and His disciples walking through a wheatfield. Now even though no Jews were allowed to eat until later in the day, Jesus's hungry followers were pulling the heads off the stalks and eating the grain.

"Don't you remember what David once did when he was desperate for food?" Jesus told the angry Pharisees. "He ate the holy bread that only priests are allowed to eat. You should make sure you remember that the Sabbath was made for people, not people for the Sabbath."

Jesus regularly healed people on the holy day. The Jewish elders considered this to be work and therefore a sin. On one occasion, He healed a crippled woman who had been bent double in terrible pain for 18 years.

"None of you would think anything of untying a donkey or ass on the Sabbath to let it drink," Jesus explained, "so shouldn't I set this woman free from her bonds?"

Another time, Jesus healed a man who had a dreadfully deformed and paralyzed hand.

"Do you think it's right to do good or evil on the Sabbath?" He challenged the fuming holy men and scribes. "Do you think

that on God's holy day we should save life or destroy it?"

One Sabbath, Jesus went to the pool of Bethesda, where lots of sick and injured people used to gather in the hope of a miraculous cure. It was said that now and again an angel would stir up the water, and then the first person to plunge into the pool would be cured. Jesus knew that one crippled man in particular had been waiting by the pool for a long time. For whenever he saw ripples on the water, he couldn't drag himself to the pool fast enough and someone else always beat him there. Jesus was filled with pity and simply said, "Pick up your bed and walk." To the man's delight, he found he could do exactly that. Many of the Jews who saw and heard about the miracle weren't so pleased. They were sure that His healing on the Sabbath was breaking God's commandments. Jesus's answer annoyed them even more. "My Father doesn't stop working on the Sabbath and neither do I," He told them.

"How dare He call God His Father!" the priests and elders gasped, totally outraged. "It's blasphemy!"

Jesus just shrugged.

"It is God my Father who has given me the authority to perform miracles such as these, to raise the dead to life and to judge sinners. I warn you that the day is coming soon when everyone will hear the voice of the Son of God calling them to be judged—even the dead will come forth to be either rewarded or punished."

The Jewish leaders were fuming, but Jesus carried on.

"You search the scriptures to find out how to win eternal life. Even though Moses wrote that I would be coming, you refuse to follow me. If you don't believe Moses, how do you expect to believe what I am telling you?"

So it was that many of the priests and elders, Pharisees and Sadducees, became Jesus's enemies. Little by little, more and more of them began to gather together in secret to plot ways in which they might get rid of Him . . .

JESUS DID NOT BREAK GOD'S LAW, BUT HE DID BREAK THE RULES PEOPLE HAD ADDED TO GOD'S. HIS ACTION REMINDS PEOPLE TO CHECK THAT THEIR TRADITIONS DON'T STOP THEM FROM KNOWING GOD. ∿

Pool of Bethesda
Bethesda was like a health spa. The pool is probably one of two which can be seen near St. Anne's Church in Jerusalem today. Legend said that the first person to enter the pool after it was touched by an angel would be healed.

❖ ABOUT THE STORY ❖

The Sabbath (the seventh day of the week, our Saturday) is special for the Jews. God was said to have rested from creation on the seventh day. People were commanded to rest and remember God on that day. Jesus was later raised from the dead on Sunday, the first day of the week, and for Christians Sunday has become their "Sabbath." Jesus said the day was for everyone's benefit.

The Apostles Are Appointed

THERE came a time when Jesus said He needed to be alone for a while. Everywhere He went, people clamored to see Him. So eventually Jesus went on His own up a mountain to pray. All night long the disciples waited for Him to return. At last they saw the familiar figure of Jesus striding toward them.

Jesus called out 12 names: the brothers Peter and Andrew, James and John, Matthew the tax collector, Philip, Bartholomew, James, Thaddaeus, Thomas, Simon the Zealot, and Judas Iscariot. Then He took the puzzled men away from the rest of the disciples, where He could speak to them in private.

"I have something very important to ask of you," Jesus said, seriously. "I need

you to help me carry out my mission. I want you to split up and go off on your own into the countryside. Preach my message as you go. Tell all the people that the kingdom of heaven will soon be here. I am going to give each of you special powers. I want you to heal the sick as I do, to raise people from the dead for me, to cleanse lepers, and to cast out demons from those who are possessed by evil."

The 12 men looked at each other anxiously.

"Furthermore, I want you to do all this for nothing," Jesus continued. "You mustn't take any payment from anyone. I don't want you to take anything with you—not even a bag with a

THE APOSTLES HAD TO RELY ON GOD FOR EVERYTHING. TODAY, WE TEND TO ASK GOD ONLY FOR WHAT WE CAN'T GET OURSELVES. THIS STORY ENCOURAGES US TO RELY ON GOD AND NOT TO WORRY. ❧

The 12 apostles
This mosaic from Italy is one artist's attempt to show what the 12 apostles looked like. The word "apostle" means "one who is sent." With the exception of Judas Iscariot, they all became leaders of the Christian Church after Jesus died.

change of clothing or a spare pair of sandals. You must rely on finding good people in the towns you visit who will put you up and look after you."

The friends all nodded, listening very carefully.

"It will not be an easy job," Jesus went on. "You have already seen the problems I face. If anyone refuses to listen, don't get dismayed. Just go on your way and shake off your disappointment, just as you shake the dust from your shoes. However, be wary all the time. I know that I'm sending you out like sheep heading straight for a pack of wolves. There will be people who will hear you and follow you, but there will be others who make up their minds to hate you because you are my representative. They will try and arrest you, and they'll haul you before royal courts to order you to stop spreading my message. Don't be afraid. At times like these, the Holy Spirit will give you courage and tell you what to say. You shouldn't fear people, because they can hurt only your body, not your soul. Have great fear of the Lord, for He can destroy both your body and soul in the fires of hell. My Father in heaven will be looking after you all the way."

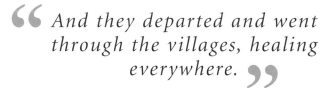

> *And they departed and went through the villages, healing everywhere.*

Jesus was pleased to see that the 12 men He had chosen looked determined.

"Don't think that I have come to bring peace on earth," He told them. "I have come to bring a sword that will carve up the righteous from the wicked. Anyone who does not take up his cross and follow me, bearing the responsibilities that go with this, will not find heaven. If you give up your lives to me—even perhaps dying for my sake—you will be given new lives."

From that day onward, the 12 men were known as the apostles. And for several weeks, they went out on their own around the countryside, teaching and healing. And when they returned, they were full of the wondrous miracles they had been able to perform in Jesus's name.

❧ ABOUT THE STORY ❧

Jesus spent much of His time with the 12. He gave them more teaching than the rest of the disciples, and He trained and equipped them to take over His mission when He died. Despite all their experience with Jesus, they still didn't fully understand His mission until after His resurrection. Then it became clear, and they were ready for their special work.

The Sermon on the Mount

ONE day, Jesus went up a mountain so everyone could hear Him.

"Blessed are all those people who realize that God is missing from their lives, for heaven will be theirs. Blessed are those who are full of sorrow, for they will be comforted. Blessed are the gentle, for they will be given the earth. Blessed are those who hunger and thirst for goodness, for they will receive what they desire. Blessed are those who are merciful, for they will have mercy shown to them, too. Blessed are those with pure, true hearts, for they will see God. Blessed are those who strive for peace; God considers them His own children.

> **"** *'If anyone strikes you on the right cheek, turn to him the other also.'* **"**

Blessed are all those who are made to suffer because they are trying to do right, for theirs is the kingdom of heaven. If others mock you and make your life miserable because you follow my teachings, you should rejoice and be glad, for you will win a wonderful reward in heaven! You are the light of the world, so shine like beacons to lead others to God."

The crowds were amazed at Jesus's words.

"Don't think that I'm telling you to forget the law or abandon the teachings of the prophets," Jesus continued. "I'm not. You need to pay more attention to them than ever. The law says that you should not kill anyone; I'm

Church of the Mount of Beatitudes
This church is built where Jesus is believed to have preached the Sermon on the Mount. The sayings that begin with the word "Blessed" at the beginning of the sermon are known as Beatitudes.

The Lord's Prayer
Jesus gave this prayer as a model, rather than simply a prayer to be recited. In it are all the main elements of prayer. It addresses God as Father, who can be trusted to provide all we need. It worships Him and puts His will first. It seeks forgiveness and thinks well of others. It asks for God's protection, as well as for His provision of our basic needs.

∾ THE LORD'S PRAYER ∾

OUR FATHER WHO ART IN HEAVEN,
HALLOWED BE THY NAME.
THY KINGDOM COME,
THY WILL BE DONE,
ON EARTH AS IT IS IN HEAVEN.
GIVE US THIS DAY OUR DAILY BREAD;
AND FORGIVE US OUR TRESPASSES,
AS WE FORGIVE THOSE WHO
TRESPASS AGAINST US;
AND LEAD US NOT INTO TEMPTATION,
BUT DELIVER US FROM EVIL.
FOR THINE IS THE KINGDOM, THE POWER,
AND THE GLORY, FOR EVER.

AMEN.

telling you that you shouldn't even argue with anyone. The law says that you shouldn't go off with another person's husband or wife; I'm telling you that you shouldn't even think about it. If what you can see is leading you to sin, then gouge out your eyes. It's better to lose part of your body than have your whole body burned in the fires of hell because you have sinned. The law says that you are entitled to take revenge on someone who wrongs you. I'm telling you that you should do nothing to get your own back. In fact, if someone hits your right cheek, turn the left toward them so they can strike that too. The law says love your neighbors and hate your enemies. I'm telling you to love your enemies, too. You should be kind and generous to all people, no matter who they are."

The crowds looked up at the preacher in awe.

"Now," Jesus went on, "many people like everyone to know that they give money to the needy, and they go every day to the synagogue, making sure that everyone knows about it. God will not reward these people in heaven, for they have already received the admiration of those on earth. Don't show off your good works and boast about them. Do your fasting and giving to charity in secret, not so everyone knows, and when you pray, use these simple words . . ."

And Jesus taught the crowds to pray.

"Also, don't bother with wealth. The riches of this world can easily be stolen or turned to rust. Instead, build up the treasure of good thoughts and deeds that thieves can't get and that won't decay. And don't worry about what you're going to eat or wear. If you put your efforts into searching for God, He'll make sure that you're looked after."

Jesus stretched His arms out to the hundreds of people who were patiently listening, entranced.

"Everyone who follows these words of mine will be like a wise man who builds his house on rock, so it stands firm. Anyone who hears what I say and yet takes no notice will be like a fool who builds his house on sand. The winds will blow it down, and the rains will wash it away."

Solid foundation
Jesus wanted to make sure that people knew that those who built their "house," or life, on the foundation of faith in God will be safe and secure.

Andrew and James
Andrew had been a disciple of John the Baptist before he became one of the apostles. James is believed to be the brother of John. They, like Peter and Andrew, seem to have been fishing partners.

➤ **ABOUT THE STORY** ➤

The Sermon on the Mount was probably not given all at once. Jesus repeated this teaching on different occasions throughout His ministry. He needed to, as it was very different from what people had been taught then. It is still different from what most people do today. It says that God's kingdom is far more valuable than all the riches in the world.

The Parables of the Kingdom

IN His preaching, Jesus told many stories, or parables, to the people.

"Imagine a person walking down a field, scattering grain onto the earth," He said one day. "Some of the seeds will land on the pathway and won't sink into the soil. The birds will swoop down right away and peck them up. Some of the seeds will fall onto rocky, stony ground. They'll start growing very quickly, but as soon as the sun comes out, they'll be scorched and wither away, because they don't have any deep roots. Other seeds will fall into thorny patches of weeds. The brambles and briars will grow faster than the grain and choke it. The seeds that fall onto good soil will grow up tall and strong into a plentiful crop."

The listening crowds looked up anxiously at Jesus, waiting for Him to explain what it all meant.

Jesus just said, "Now everyone go away and work out what the story means."

Later in the day, when the disciples were alone with

Jesus, they questioned Him about how He had handled the crowds.

"Jesus, why do you tell the people parables and then leave them to try to understand for themselves?" the disciples asked. "When you're with the 12 of us in private, you always explain everything."

Jesus sighed. "You have been given the gift to understand all the secrets I tell you about the kingdom of heaven," He explained. "Other people, who haven't been privileged in this way, wouldn't understand. So I teach them through stories. This way, the more carefully they listen and the harder they try to understand, the more they will get out of them and the closer they will get to the kingdom of heaven. For many of them look at me, but they don't really see who I am. They listen to me, but they don't really hear what I'm saying. They think they're taking in my words, but they don't really understand."

And He explained to the disciples what the parable of the sower meant.

> 66 *And He told them many things in parables.* 99

"The seed is the word of God. The pathway stands for those who hear the word of God but who don't take it in. The devil will swoop down right away and steal the message away from them. The rocky ground represents those who pay attention to the word of God and take it on board for a short while. Because the message hasn't sunk deep enough into their hearts, any difficulties that arise will overcome them, and they will give up on it. The weeds

are those who hear the word of God but who are either too worried about their daily problems or simply too busy having a good time to do anything about it. The good soil stands for those who absorb the word of God deep within themselves. They give it a place to grow, and over time they bear good fruit."

Jesus explained other parables to the disciples. He told a story about a sower whose enemy had secretly planted weeds among his crops. When the sower's servants saw the shoots appear, they asked him if he wanted them to go and pull them out. The sower was worried that they'd get confused and pull the good plants out with the bad ones. "Leave it till harvest time," he told them. "Then I'll tell my reapers to pull out the weeds first and burn them, leaving the grain to be safely gathered in." Jesus explained that the sower was the Son of God and the field was the world. The seeds were people who loved God and the weeds people who opposed God. He said that at the end of time, the Son of God would send His angels to cast the bad people into hell, leaving the good people to live happily in the kingdom of heaven.

Once, Jesus compared the kingdom of heaven to a grain of mustard. "It is a small seed," He said, "but it will grow into a massive bush, and birds will nest in its branches."

Other parables showed how determined people had to be to enter the kingdom. They needed to be like a pearl merchant who sees the most precious pearl of all and sells everything he has in order to buy it. Or a person who discovers buried treasure in a field. He covers it up again, and he rushes away to sell everything that he owns, just so that he can buy the field. God's kingdom is like the treasure: you must want it more than anything else.

Jesus warned everyone to listen hard to the stories He told. "No one goes out to buy a lamp and then covers it up or puts it under the bed, so its light is hidden," He said. "So having come to hear me, make sure you don't ignore my teachings. For what I am telling you everyone will one day know to be the truth."

Sower's bag
Farmers sowed their seed by hand. They plowed the soil then walked up and down throwing handfuls of seed from the bag slung over their shoulder. Usually, they then plowed the field again, or drove animals over it, to push the seed into the soil.

Grain sieve
Grain was always sifted in a shallow basket like this before being ground to make flour for bread. Some weed seeds might be mixed in with it and would poison the bread. Some weed seeds were picked out by hand and the contents of the basket shaken so that any remaining seeds which were smaller than the grain, would drop out of the holes.

❧ **ABOUT THE STORY** ❧

These parables build up a picture of what the kingdom of God is like. It isn't something that could be illustrated in one simple picture. Together the parables show that it is God's rules working in people's lives. Therefore the kingdom of God can be anywhere. It grows as more people learn to serve God and influence others for good. It is worth more than anything else because it lasts forever.

Jesus Stills the Storm

JESUS was exhausted. He'd been preaching all day by the Sea of Galilee to crowds that were bigger than ever. His throat was hoarse and His legs and back were aching. He'd already tried to tell the people that He'd finished for the day.

Even though it was now growing dark, it was obvious that many didn't want to go home. They were still lurking around in groups, waiting to see where Jesus was going next, so they could follow Him.

"Let's sail over to the other side of the lake," Jesus said to His disciples. "We might be able to be on our own there for a while."

They splashed along the seashore to their boat and pushed off, raising the little sail. As the boat cut through the waters, Jesus sank into a deep sleep down at the back of the boat, rocked by the rise and fall of the waves and lulled by the swish of the sea.

While Jesus dreamed, the disciples were horrified to notice dark clouds racing across the sky and heading straight for them. Before they'd even had time to furl the sail, the wind began to whip up around them. It wailed and howled, stirring up the waters into great peaks that tossed the little boat into the air and then plunged them down toward the depths.

> ❝ *'Why are you afraid, O men of little faith?'* ❞

Of course, Peter, Andrew, James, and John were used to storms like this. They were fishermen and had often been caught in them.

"Don't worry," Peter called out cheerfully, "it's just a little breeze. Nothing to be afraid of!"

He showed them how to tie the sails down and how to bail out the water which splashed over the side and made their feet cold.

However, it wasn't just a little breeze. It was the most horrendous storm they had ever known. It was as if a giant hand were shaking the boat, trying to make it sink.

"I'm scared!" shouted one of the disciples.

"I can't swim!" cried another.

Soon, even Peter was terrified. Some clung onto the sides of the boat and the mast for dear life, drenched by the waves that came crashing onto the deck, threatening to wash them overboard. Others were thrown to and fro as they rushed back and forth, trying desperately to bail out the water that swamped the boat. Through it all, Jesus went on sleeping, undisturbed.

"Master! Master!" the terrified disciples cried, their voices nearly drowned out by the screaming of the gale. "Wake up! We're all going to drown!"

Jesus opened one eyelid and sat up. He yawned and stretched, then stood up in the front of the boat to face the full force of the storm.

"Peace!" He thundered, reaching His arms up toward the black, raging skies.

"Be still!" He shouted, stretching His hands out over the billowing waters.

At once the howling died away, the wind dropped, and the sail hung limply in the still air. The sea suddenly flattened into a glassy mirror, its surface barely disturbed by a single ripple. The clouds were blown from the evening skies, until a still, starry night hung over the peaceful little boat.

Jesus turned to face the trembling disciples.

"Why were you afraid?" He asked the astounded men, as they cowered away from Him in complete awe. "You have so little faith."

Then He lay down once more and drifted off to sleep, just as if the danger had never happened.

As the disciples stirred themselves from their shock and turned the boat back on course for the far shore, they couldn't stop whispering about what they had witnessed.

THE DISCIPLES FORGOT ONE IMPORTANT FACT: GOD WOULD NOT LET HIS SON PERISH IN AN ACCIDENT BEFORE HIS WORK WAS COMPLETED. INSTEAD OF PANICKING, THEY SHOULD HAVE TRUSTED GOD.

Storm on the Sea of Galilee
The Sea of Galilee is surrounded by steep hills. During the afternoon, the hot air which rises off the lake cools over the hills and can form storm clouds. This then rushes down the steep hills and whips up the lake into a boiling cauldron.

❖ ABOUT THE STORY ❖

Jesus teaches two things through this extraordinary storm. One is that He trusted the disciples to look after the boat, which is why He was asleep. The second is that He showed Himself to be Lord of creation. He has complete power over natural forces. The message is that with Jesus "on board" a person's life, there is nothing to fear.

Legion and the Swine

THE disciples sailed across the calm waters and landed safely on the far side of the Sea of Galilee. They were all looking forward to taking a well-earned rest.

As they walked up the shore, a wild man suddenly came screaming out of the stillness. He was naked and filthy, his skin covered with wounds where he had cut himself. The locals had tried to tie him up, but the man had just burst out of his chains. He lived among the tombs of the town's burial ground, haunting them like a demon. Everyone in the area said that he was possessed, taken over by evil spirits.

The madman came racing toward Jesus and flung himself at His feet. He seemed to know His name.

"Jesus, Son of the Most High God, what do you want with me?" the madman slobbered.

Jesus knew that it wasn't the man himself who was really speaking; it was the demons inside him.

"What is your name?" Jesus demanded.

"Legion," the demons inside the madman replied. "For there are whole legions of us inside of him."

Jesus began to tell the evil spirits to get out of the man

Demon possession
People at the time believed that sometimes evil spirits took over a person's life. Examples have been seen in many cultures. Casting out demons is known as exorcism. This is a sculpture of a demon leaving someone's mouth.

Burial ground
Most cultures respect their dead. This is a Middle Eastern burial ground. The one Legion lived in was probably a network of underground caves.

put on clothes and was sitting calmly by Jesus's side. The townspeople couldn't understand what had happened. Who was this stranger to command evil spirits like that?

> ❝ *The whole herd rushed down the steep bank into the sea and perished in the waters.* ❞

"Keep away from us!" the nervous locals yelled. Jesus sighed and picked Himself up and went back to the boat.

Legion ran after them. "I can't thank you enough! Please, take me with you," the grateful man begged.

Jesus took his hand. "Go back to the home you once had," He said. "I want you to tell everyone how much God has done for you."

and leave him alone. "Don't send us into hell!" shrieked the demons. "Let us live somewhere else, such as in those pigs."

Jesus looked at the snuffling animals nearby.

"Go!" He commanded the demons.

At once, the pigs began to grunt in terror. Then they galloped wildly down the slopes to the cliff edge and dived to their deaths on the rocks below.

The petrified herdsmen fled in terror. Soon they were back, with anxious townspeople. Legion had washed and

Monastery at Kursi
The exact site where this story took place is unknown, but this Byzantine monastery at Kursi was built where tradition said Legion had been cured.

Demon mask
This terracotta mask comes from Babylon. It shows the giant Humbaba. Masks like this were the Babylonians' way of trying to keep the demons away.

❖ **ABOUT THE STORY** ❖

To the Jews, pigs were unclean animals. The demons' going into a herd of pigs was a clear sign that the spirits were unclean, or evil. It was perhaps also a rebuke to the people for not living their lives according to the laws of God. The reaction of the townspeople was one of guilt. God's presence among them was unsettling. They preferred the devil they knew to the God they didn't.

Healed by Faith

ONE day, a synagogue leader named Jairus pushed his way through the hundreds of people surrounding Jesus and knelt down at the surprised preacher's feet.

"Master," he pleaded, ignoring those jostling him from all sides. "My little daughter is only 12 years old, and she is dying." He looked up at Jesus with a tear-stained face. "I beg you to come and lay your hands on her to make her well again."

Jesus immediately stood up and set off after Jairus. And as usual, the massive crowd went with Him, surrounding Him on all sides, pulling and elbowing each other out of the way to be as close as possible to the great teacher.

They hadn't gone very far when, without any warning, Jesus suddenly stopped and spun around. The startled crowd fell silent.

"Who touched me?" He said, scanning the rows of anxious faces. "Who reached out and touched my robe?"

The people hung their heads and waited for the person to step forward.

"Master," said Peter quietly, "there are people pressing in on you from all sides. You are struggling to walk along because everyone's pushing you back and forth. How can you ask who has touched you?"

"Somebody in particular reached out for me," Jesus

explained. "I felt power go out of me."

Jesus's eyes singled out a woman in the crowd.

"Don't be afraid," He said. "Come here." And the people fell back to let the trembling woman through.

> ❝ *'The girl is not dead, but sleeping.'* ❞

The woman had been ill for 12 years with a painful disease. She had been to many doctors in the hope of a cure, but, if anything, they had made her worse. Yet she had great faith in Jesus. She had truly believed that He had the power to cure her. Even if she couldn't get to see Him or speak to Him, she had been determined to get close enough to touch Him, for that, she felt, would be enough. As the crowds had pushed and shoved around Jesus as He walked along, the woman had seized her chance. She had pressed her way forward as near to Jesus as she could, then thrust her arm out between the people in front of her. Her fingers had just scraped the edge of Jesus's robe.

"My daughter," Jesus said to the woman, gently. "It is your faith that has made you well."

All this time, Jairus was waiting anxiously. Please hurry up, he was thinking, or it will be too late. Just as Jesus was finishing speaking to the woman, Jairus saw one of his servants approaching. His heart sank.

"My lord," the servant said gently. "Don't trouble the preacher any further. I'm afraid that your daughter is dead."

Jesus had overheard. He put His hand on the heartbroken Jairus's arm.

"Don't worry," He said. "Trust me. She'll be all right."

When Jesus, Jairus, and the crowd of followers reached Jairus's house, the mourners were already there, weeping and wailing outside.

"Don't be so upset," Jesus told them. "The girl isn't dead at all. She's just in a deep sleep."

The mourners scoffed at His kind words. Some of them even laughed. Jesus paid no attention. Taking only Jairus and his wife, and His three friends Peter, John, and James, He made His way to the room where the body lay, stiff and cold. Tenderly, Jesus held the little girl's hand.

"My child," He whispered, "it's time to get up now."

The girl opened her eyes wide and sat up on the bed.

Even though Jesus told the overjoyed parents not to tell anyone what he had done, it wasn't long before news of the miracle was all over the countryside.

Jesus and hope
This mosaic shows Jesus wearing a blue robe. The artist showed Jesus wearing blue because it is the color of hope. This is because it resembles the sky. It was this faith and hope that Jesus liked and admired, and wanted people to have.

◆ ABOUT THE STORY ◆

The sick woman demonstrated her true faith in Jesus. She knew that if she touched Him she would be cured. But she delayed Jesus so much that Jairus's daughter was dead before Jesus got to her. Some people would say that Jesus got His priorities wrong. By doing what He did, Jesus meets the needs of young and old equally.

The Death of John the Baptist

JOHN the Baptist was thrown into prison by King Herod Antipas of Judea because he had criticized the king's marriage to his niece Herodias. The marriage broke the law of Moses because the couple were related, and they had both had to divorce their partners in order to marry.

John was all alone in prison, and his mind was troubled. He sent his followers to ask Jesus if He really was the one the world was waiting for.

"Tell John everything you have seen," Jesus told John's disciples. "The blind see, the lame walk, lepers are healed, the deaf can hear, the poor are cheered in spirit, and the dead are raised to life."

He paid tribute to the great preacher.

"John the Baptist is the greatest person ever born," He told them, "but many people have refused to listen to him, just as they now fail to listen to me."

King Herod's new wife had tried to make King Herod execute John. Herod did not dare kill such a righteous man, no matter what he had said.

One day, the king threw a great banquet, and his daughter, Salome, danced for him.

Herod clapped his hands in delight.

"That was wonderful," he gushed. "What can I give you to say 'thank you'? Anything you want. You just name it."

Greek dancers
Dancing was a favorite pursuit at banquets in ancient times. Salome's dance followed in a long tradition that went back hundreds of years. This is a painting from a vase of Greek dancers, from 500BC. Salome's dance has often been portrayed in music and dance since. A composer named Richard Strauss wrote a whole opera called *Salome*.

Symbol of Rome
The eagle, seen here on a round base, was the symbol of the Roman Empire.

Wedding statue
This Roman relief shows the bride and groom holding hands while a third person reads out the legal contract.

The best the king could do was to return John's body to his followers. His horrified disciples buried him and then told Jesus the news.

> ❝ *Herodias had a grudge against him, and wanted to kill him.* ❞

Herod couldn't forget what he had done. And when news came to him of a strange preacher who healed the sick and raised the dead to life, Herod trembled. He thought that perhaps Jesus was John the Baptist risen from the dead.

"Anything?" asked Salome, her eyes opening wide. She dashed off to tell her mother.

"Mother says that I should ask you for the head of John the Baptist," Salome murmured, when she called back.

Herod gasped. He'd made a promise in front of all his guests. He'd have to keep his word, and he ordered John executed. Later that day, Salome took her cruel mother the head of John the Baptist on a plate.

HEROD PAID THE PRICE FOR HIS OWN FOLLY. HE SHOULD NEVER HAVE PROMISED SALOME "ANYTHING." MAKING RASH PROMISES IS RARELY A GOOD IDEA. THINGS CAN HAPPEN TO MAKE US REGRET THEM. ❧

The harp
The harp was a popular instrument throughout Biblical times and would have been played at Herod's banquet. However, the instrument used in Biblical times was more properly called a lyre, because it had fewer strings than a harp.

❖ ABOUT THE STORY ❖

The coming of John the Baptist was foretold in the Scriptures. People were looking for Elijah, as the Scriptures had said, but Elijah was reborn as John. The fate that John meets foreshadows the death of Jesus Himself. John is executed because of the silly dislikes and jealousy of one person. Jesus is a victim of the jealousy and dislike of a whole group of people.

Jesus's Time and Place

LIFE in Judea at the time when Jesus lived was dominated by the occupying Roman army. Soldiers were everywhere, patrolling the streets to keep law and order, since there was no police force.

The soldiers had wide powers. They could order people to do anything for them. Ordinary people could be told to feed soldiers or give them somewhere to sleep. If soldiers were marching somewhere, they could force people to carry their bags, or they could just walk into their homes and take an ox-cart or pack animal.

The Romans had an efficient system of government. Ruling over the whole empire was the emperor (called Caesar in the Gospels, which was a title rather than a name). Jesus was born during the reign of the great emperor Augustus, who organized the empire with great efficiency. The emperor during Jesus's ministry was Tiberius. He was a bad emperor. He hardly ever went to Rome and lived a life of indulgent luxury and splendor.

Each province and district had a senior Roman official in charge, usually appointed directly by the emperor. Two such governors are mentioned in the Gospels: Quirinius was in charge of the province of Syria, and Pontius Pilate, who was prefect of Judea, sentenced Jesus to death by crucifixion. From records outside the Gospels we know that Pilate was a cruel man.

The Romans allowed the Jews some freedom and the right to have kings in various parts of Judea. All of these were members of the Herod family. Herod the Great had started to build the temple in Jerusalem for the Jews. He died about the time Jesus was born, and his area was split between three of his sons, all of whom are named in the Gospels: Herod Philip, Archelaus, and Herod Antipas. They had limited, but real, powers to govern aspects of life.

The Roman occupiers were hated. The Herods, though, were thought to have more sympathy with the Romans than with their countrymen, and they were too powerful to displease. However, the people who collected taxes for the Romans from merchants and ordinary householders were despised and seen as traitors.

The greatest critics of tax collectors were the Pharisees, a group of about 6,000 men. They were very traditional in their beliefs and practices. Jesus often came into conflict with them because they taught that the only way to be right with God was to practice all the tiny laws which they said were contained in the Scriptures. The Pharisees were very fussy. Jesus said that they had lost sight of the real meaning of the law. They were so busy sticking to all the little laws that they ignored all the big ones.

Sometimes allied with them were the Sadducees, who were a snobbish group of leaders, mostly priests, who accepted only the written laws of the scriptures, not the

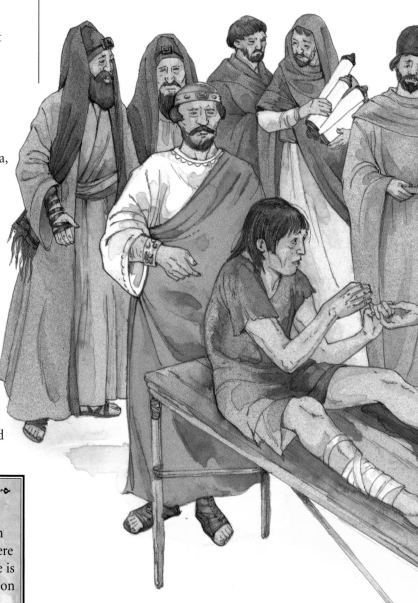

❧ PEOPLE AT THE TIME OF JESUS ❧

This picture shows Jesus healing a paralyzed person (center). Watching him are a number of people whom we encounter in the Gospels. From left at the back there are two Pharisees and two Sadducees. In the blue robe is a tax collector. Roman soldiers stand at the back, and on the far right are two Essenes. In the foreground are a king (left), such as Herod Antipas, and a Roman emperor (right).

others which the Pharisees had added. Unlike the Pharisees at the time, they did not believe in life after death.

Other religious groups existed in the area but are not mentioned directly in the Gospels. Among them were the Essenes. They were scattered in monastic communities all over Judea, but their most famous community was at Qumran, near the Dead Sea, where the Dead Sea Scrolls were found. They had a strict rule of life. It is sometimes thought that John the Baptist grew up among the Essenes, but there is no direct proof of this.

Dead Sea Scrolls

The "Shrine of the Book" is in a museum in Jerusalem where some of the Dead Sea Scrolls are kept. They were found in 1947 in caves near Qumran, by the Dead Sea, and were the library of the community that once lived there. The scrolls contain ancient copies of all the Old Testament books except the Book of Esther.

Roman worship

This is the temple of Castor and Pollux, the twin gods who the Romans believed helped them win battles. The Romans worshiped many gods and built temples to them through the empire.

Gladiators in Rome

The Roman Emperors were famous for putting on grand shows for the Roman citizens. This is the Colosseum, where the Romans made men called gladiators fight wild animals and each other.

The Apostles

Jesus had many disciples. The word means "one who learns." They were people who followed Jesus around the countryside whenever they could. They thought about His teaching, watched His actions, and tried to live in the way He taught. At some point early in His ministry, Jesus selected 12 particular disciples to become an inner core that He would teach to become leaders in the church.

Later, they were called apostles, which means "one who is sent." They were Jesus's agents sent into the world to spread His teaching. At least some of them, such as Peter and Matthew, had been called as individuals first. Jesus taught the apostles privately, and restricted some of His more significant miracles (such as the stilling of the storm) to them alone.

Within the circle of 12, there was an even smaller inner circle of 3: Peter, James, and John. We do not know much about the backgrounds of the apostles, but certain things do stand out.

Peter's birth name was Simon, which means "stone" in Greek. He was dubbed Peter (the rock) by Jesus. He was the spokesman of the group. Peter often opened his mouth before thinking, and as a result sometimes offended people. Passionate, impulsive, and dedicated, he seems to have been the sort of person who would be your friend for life if he liked you.

He was a fisherman from Lake Galilee, and owned a boat which Jesus used

PETER

from time to time for transportation and also as a floating pulpit when he preached to large crowds by the lakeside. At the crucifixion, Peter denied ever knowing Jesus. Filled with remorse, he was forgiven, and became the leader of the first Christians. He also became the first disciple to take the Gospel to non-Jews. He was martyred in Rome by the emperor Nero about A.D.66. It is believed that he was the source of information behind Mark's Gospel.

The brothers James and John were also fishermen of Galilee and may have been partners with Peter and his brother Andrew. James and John were nicknamed "Sons of Thunder" by Jesus. On one famous occasion, they were angry at being rejected by a village. They asked if, by using their new spiritual powers, they should call down some judgment on the people there. Jesus took this opportunity to teach them more about the gentle ways of God.

John, it is believed, wrote the fourth Gospel, the *Book of Revelation*, and the three New Testament letters attributed to him. After Jesus's death he was an elder in the church in Ephesus in Turkey. He was later exiled to the prison island of Patmos in the Aegean.

JOHN

JAMES

ANDREW

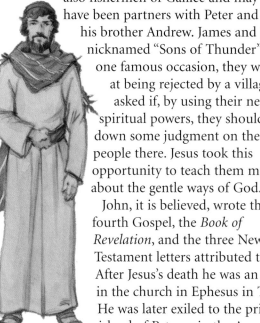

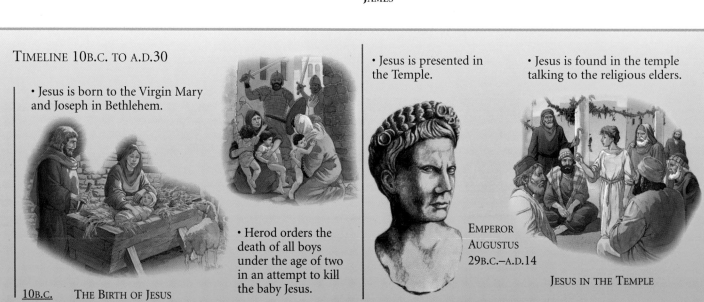

TIMELINE 10 B.C. TO A.D. 30

• Jesus is born to the Virgin Mary and Joseph in Bethlehem.

• Herod orders the death of all boys under the age of two in an attempt to kill the baby Jesus.

10 B.C.   THE BIRTH OF JESUS

• Jesus is presented in the Temple.

EMPEROR AUGUSTUS 29 B.C.–A.D.14

• Jesus is found in the temple talking to the religious elders.

JESUS IN THE TEMPLE

JUDAS

MATTHEW

James was to become one of the first Christian martyrs, executed by King Herod in about A.D.43. He is not the same James as the one who later led the church in Jerusalem and wrote the New Testament letter bearing his name.

Andrew, Peter's brother, was not one of the inner circle but deserves a special mention. He comes across as the most gentle and caring of the disciples. It was Andrew who first brought Peter to Jesus. "Come and see!" he'd cried excitedly to his (probably elder) brother. It was Andrew who saw the possibility of using the five loaves and two fish to feed the 5,000. And it was Andrew who, with Philip, brought some non-Jews to Jesus, too. He was a man of vision. It is believed that he was crucified in Asia Minor in about A.D.60.

Matthew was a tax collector, also called Levi, and he gave up his despised job to become a disciple. He did not, however, become the treasurer of the group. That job fell to Judas Iscariot, who became infamous later as the one who

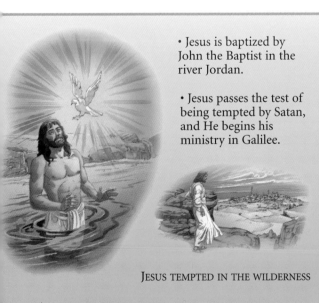

PHILIP

THOMAS

THADDEUS

handed Jesus over to the rulers. Why he did this has remained a mystery. The Gospels indicate he was prompted by the devil. We know that when he saw that Jesus was to be executed, he gave back the money he had been paid to betray him and committed suicide.

Thomas, known as the doubter, was missing from the group when Jesus first appeared to them after the resurrection. He refused to believe their stories. Only later, when he was able to see and touch Jesus for himself, did he believe in His resurrection. The experience was life-changing; it is believed that he went on to form the church in India.

Little is known of the others. There is even some confusion over their names in the Gospels (like Peter, many of them seem to have had more than one name). They were Bartholomew, another James, another Simon (also called "the Zealot"), Thaddeus (also called Judas), and Philip.

BARTHOLOMEW

SIMON

JAMES

• Jesus is baptized by John the Baptist in the river Jordan.

• Jesus passes the test of being tempted by Satan, and He begins his ministry in Galilee.

JESUS TEMPTED IN THE WILDERNESS

• Jesus perform His first miracle, turning water into wine at the wedding in Cana.

THE FIRST MIRACLE

JOHN THE BAPTIST EXECUTED

• John the Baptist is executed by Herod at the request of his step daughter, Salome.

A.D.30

THE MAN OF MIRACLES

Jesus explains the Christian way of life through parables and miracles

The Man of Miracles

JESUS spent much of His time in Galilee, the northern part of the country, where He had grown up. He worked his way southward, possibly visiting Jerusalem briefly several times. Here you can read about some of His teaching and miracles in Galilee, and then in Jericho and elsewhere.

Among the outstanding things He did were feeding 5,000 people with just five loaves and two small fish; walking across the choppy waves of the sea; appearing to three of His disciples in His heavenly glory; and raising Lazarus from the dead.

Much of His teaching was in parables: simple stories based on everyday events which contained deep truths about God and His plans. Jesus used parables because it was easier for the people around Him to understand what He was saying in the form of a story. Some of Jesus's most famous stories are included here: the good Samaritan who cared for a stranger; the lost sheep that was found by a loving shepherd; the prodigal son who came home to say he was sorry; the proud Pharisee and the humble tax collector; and the unmerciful servant who didn't do to others what had been done to him.

Jesus's teaching remains as relevant today as it was 2,000 years ago. Among the subjects He covered were how to handle money and possessions, how to regard people we don't like, what God's plans are for life after death, and how to get ready to meet God.

Jesus was a legend in His own time. People didn't know what to make of Him. Some thought He was just a great prophet; others thought He was one of the past

Jesus Christ
This painting of Jesus shows Him with a halo, a bright circle of light, around His head. Haloes like this first appeared in art in the 400s. The circle symbolizes perfection.

Judea and the Sea of Galilee
Jesus spent about three years traveling around Galilee, teaching and healing the people that He found. He performed many miracles on and around the Sea of Galilee, such as walking on water and feeding the 5,000 people.

prophets come back to life. He was watched with great interest because people in first-century Judea did believe that the promised Messiah, God's specially chosen servant, would come to them soon.

Jesus's followers were called disciples. Jesus had chosen twelve of these as His special companions, who are sometimes called apostles. One day, when Jesus was talking to His 12 disciples, He asked them who they thought He was. Peter, who acted as spokesman for the group, blurted out, "You are the Christ! The Son of the living God!" He got it right, although he hadn't worked it out for himself. Jesus said that it had been specially revealed to him by God.

However, even Peter and the others didn't really know exactly what that meant. The Messiah they expected was a military liberator who would chase the Romans out of Judea and set up a Jewish state which would be the envy of the world. The Romans had conquered all of Judea as part of their great empire, and they had left soldiers to keep the people of Judea in order. Some rich people made the best of the presence of the soldiers. Also, tax collectors were employed to collect money for the Romans, but this meant they were hated by the normal people. Most people resented the presence of the Romans, and wanted them out of their country. When Jesus arrived, saying He was the Messiah people expected Him to rid them of the Romans, but that was not Jesus's aim.

Jesus set about showing them, as well as explaining to them, who He really was. Soon after Peter's "confession," Jesus took Peter, with James and John, up a mountain where He was "transfigured" or transformed in front of their eyes. He glowed with heavenly glory. "That's the kind of Messiah I am," He was saying. "God's Son from heaven, not a soldier from earth."

When He fed the 5,000 with five loaves and two fish, He was demonstrating that as the Son of God He was also the Creator of all things and could provide what people needed. It was a lesson in both religion and faith. And when He walked on water, He was showing that nothing on earth was beyond His power to control.

His healing miracles showed that God cared for people in every part of their lives. With His raising of Lazarus from the dead, He showed that death is not the end. Even this doesn't defeat God. There's something more to come.

Some people were so offended by the way Jesus wanted to change the old traditions and reinterpret the law of God that they dismissed Him as a trickster and a false teacher. Jesus was saying that important people had been misinterpreting the teachings of the Bible for generations. Although most people struggled to understand Him, no one who really watched Him or listened to Him with an open mind was ever quite the same again. And Christians today would say that hasn't changed down the centuries, either.

The woman from Samaria
The Samaritans had been hated by the Jews since the time of the Exile, when the Samaritans had taken over the sacred city of Jerusalem. Jesus, though, preached to Samaritans as well, extending the word of God to everyone.

❖ THE MAN OF MIRACLES ❖

Here you can read the stories of Jesus's teaching and miracles throughout Galilee, and in Jericho

FEEDING THE FIVE THOUSAND
Matthew, Ch. 14; Mark, Ch. 6; Luke, Ch. 9; John, Ch. 6.
JESUS WALKS ON WATER
Matthew, Ch. 14; Mark, Ch. 6.
JESUS'S MINISTRY IN GALILEE
Matthew, Ch. 16–25; Mark, Ch. 9 & 10; Luke, Ch. 10-19.
OPPOSITION TO JESUS GROWS
John, Ch. 6 & 7.
LAZARUS RAISED FROM THE DEAD
John, Ch. 11.
JUDGMENT DAY
Matthew, Ch. 25.

Jesus and the Sea of Galilee

THE Sea of Galilee and the region that surrounds it are where Jesus spent much of His time, preaching to the people of the area and teaching them about the new ways that He wanted them to live their lives.

The Sea of Galilee is actually a lake, through which the river Jordan flows. This supply of fresh water made the Sea of Galilee home to great numbers of fish, such as carp and tilapia, also known as Saint Peter's fish. The fishing grounds in the Sea of Galilee were famous throughout the Roman Empire, so the people of Galilee were able to export a lot of their catch, they would sell it to other countries. The Sea of Galilee is 692 feet below sea level and is surrounded by steep hills. This means that fierce storms can start on the lake at almost any time. Jesus and His disciples were sometimes caught out on the lake in these storms, but Jesus was miraculously able to calm the waves and get everyone safely to shore.

The fact that Jesus grew up in Galilee is reflected through all the Gospels. Many of His miracles and His parables relate to the type of work that ordinary people at this time would have done and relate to the kinds of agriculture that would have been familiar to people at the time. Not only is Jesus drawing on the kind of experiences He would have had growing up, but He is telling His stories using characters and places with which His audience is familiar. When Jesus performed a miracle and fed 5,000 people with five loaves of bread and two fish, the fish that He used were almost certainly tilapia or carp, caught by local fishermen in the Sea of Galilee.

Throughout Jesus's parables we see a similar situation. He talks about agriculture, about farmers and vineyards, and He uses the relationship that the Jews had at the time with people like the Samaritans to make His point. Ever since the time of the Exile, the Jews had hated the Samaritans, who were the people that the conquering Babylonians had moved to the sacred city of Jerusalem. Jesus uses this in His parable of the good Samaritan. He chose someone that His hearers believe will not help the injured man in order to make the point that race and color do not matter in God's kingdom, that the hated Samaritan who helped is more the man's neighbor than the priest and the Levite who did not.

Jesus's ministry in Galilee was a mission of preaching and healing. He healed a wide range of problems, including paralysis, blindness, and leprosy; He cured people who were possessed by "demons" and even raised people from the dead. There were many people at the time who claimed to be able to cure people of these problems; Jesus was different, not only in that He could genuinely cure them of their illnesses but also in that He did not use the sort of elaborate rituals that many people would have used to try to impress the audience. Jesus's power and authority over evil are unquestionable, so a single word of command was enough.

Jesus is also remarkable in that most of the miracles that He performed were not in order to show how powerful He is. He pities people for their suffering, and because He is the Messiah, the son of God, He is able to cure these people miraculously. When He is not healing people He is still helping them, such as when He feeds 5,000 people with five loaves and two fish, or when He calms the storm, or even when He turns water into wine at the marriage in Cana. He is not reserved about this; He helps miraculously because He is the Christ.

There are, though, exceptions to this. When Jesus walked across the water to reach His disciples, He was not helping anyone. But in this case He was teaching His disciples. He was making it clear to them who He was and making it clear to Peter that faith can achieve anything.

We can see on this map the areas in which Jesus performed miracles, and some of the people He healed and the events in His life.

Roman influence

The influence of Rome runs through the whole of the New Testament. Jesus was brought up during the occupation, and was crucified according to Roman law. Although there were problems with the Romans, as far as the people of Judea and Galilee were concerned, these rulers gave them a great deal. Their buildings were very advanced for the time; for example, this is a magnificent Roman amphitheater. By A.D.200 the Romans had built over 50,000 miles of roads through their empire.

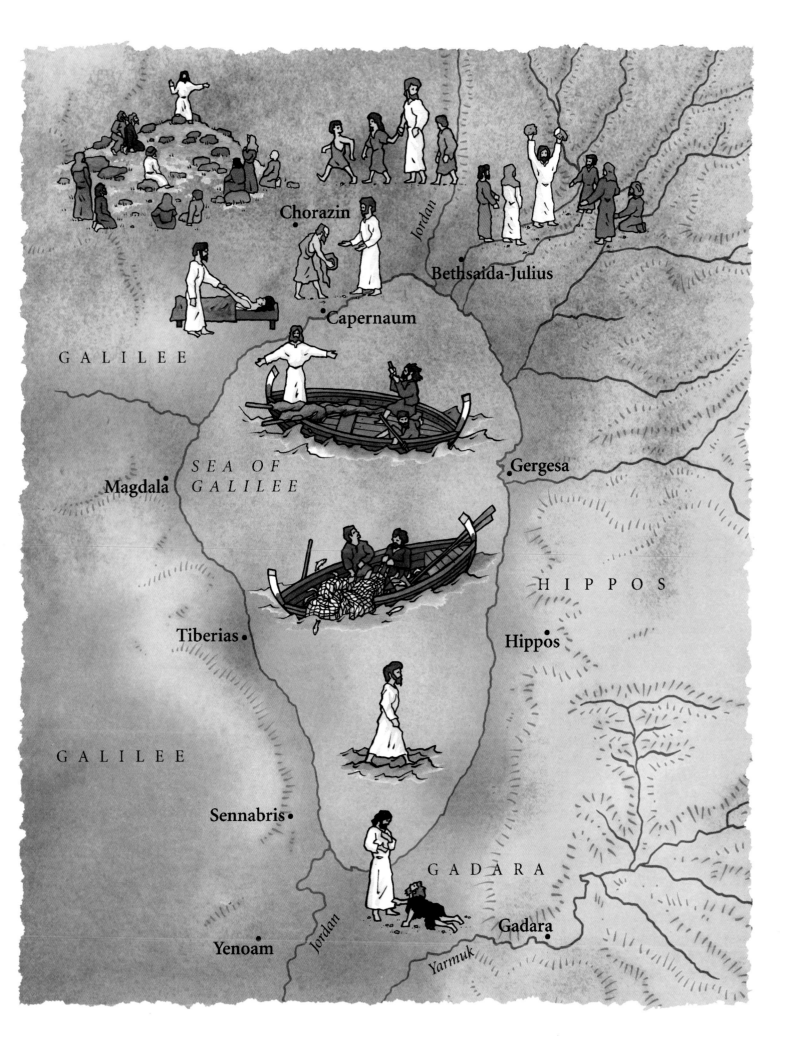

Chorazin

Bethsaida-Julius

Capernaum

GALILEE

SEA OF
GALILEE

Magdala

Gergesa

HIPPOS

Tiberias

Hippos

GALILEE

Sennabris

GADARA

Yenoam

Gadara

Jordan

Yarmuk

Feeding the Five Thousand

THE twelve disciples had accompanied Jesus on His travels for many months. They had also spent several weeks in pairs on the road. Without Jesus present, they taught His message, healed lepers, and cured diseases. By the time they rejoined their master, they were exhausted.

Times were even more trying for Jesus. The crowds grew bigger every day. However, many of the Pharisees and Sadducees refused to accept Jesus's teaching. They longed to get Him out of the way. Finally, on top of everything else, Jesus's cousin, John the Baptist, had been executed after spending several months in King Herod's dungeons.

One day Jesus and His 12 friends got into a little boat and sailed away from the crowds across the Sea of Galilee toward the quiet northern shore. They all urgently needed some rest and some peace and quiet.

At last it was peaceful! The sounds of the crowds were blown far away by the wind. Jesus and the disciples could hear nothing but the comforting swish of the sea, the gentle flap of the sail, and the friendly cries of the seagulls.

However, the hundreds of people on the shore weren't going to be put off. On foot and on donkeys, they set off at once racing around the coast, joined by others they saw on the way. By the time Jesus's boat reached the far shore, to his surprise He found a massive throng waiting in anticipation for Him.

Instead of getting angry, Jesus just sighed.

"Look at them milling about," He said gently. "They're like sheep without a shepherd."

As the disciples guided the boat in, the people started clamoring for Jesus to heal them. Even though Jesus was tired, He agreed to stay, and the crowd settled down. Putting His exhaustion aside, Jesus began to speak . . .

Jesus was still preaching to the huge crowd when it began to grow dark.

"Master," said the disciples, "it's getting late now, and we're a long way from anywhere. You should tell everyone to leave and find some food and a place to stay."

"You give them something to eat," Jesus replied bluntly.

The disciples looked at each other anxiously. They thought there must be over five thousand people listening to Jesus. How were they going to be able to feed them?

"We have only 200 denarii between us," they protested.

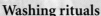

Washing rituals
The Pharisees had many religious ceremonies. This is one of the ritual baths they used for washing as a sign of spiritual purity. Jesus taught that people became pure by saying sorry to God and by living His way, not by taking part in ceremonies.

Popular catch
The carp fish, shown above, was one of the main fish living in the Sea of Galilee at this time, so it was a fish often caught by fishermen. It may well have been the kind of fish Jesus had in the story.

Loaves and fish
This ancient mosaic shows the kind of loaves and fish Jesus might have used. The picture reminded people that Jesus could provide for all their physical needs. It also reminded them that anything offered to Him, however small, could be used by Him to do good.

"Even if we find somewhere to buy bread, we would need a fortune to be able to buy enough food for everyone here. There won't be anywhere near enough to go around."

"All we've got at the moment is what this lad has brought with him," Andrew added, guiding a young boy with a basket through the crowd. "Five loaves of bread and two fish. But they're not going to go very far among this many people!"

"Tell everyone to sit down," Jesus said quietly, taking the basket from the boy. When everyone was settled, He said a blessing over the loaves and the fish and broke them into

> " *Taking the five loaves and the two fish, he looked up to heaven, and blessed and broke the loaves.* "

pieces. "Now share them out among the people," He instructed His disciples calmly.

To everyone's utter astonishment, there was more than enough bread and fish to satisfy everyone. It soon became clear that there would be enough leftovers to fill 12 whole baskets.

Baking bread
In Bible times, fire was usually lit inside the stone oven rather than underneath it. When the stones were hot, the fire was raked out and dough placed on the sides (sometimes even on the outside) of the oven, where it baked. The bread came out looking like flat rolls, or fat pancakes.

Fishing nets
The fish Jesus used were caught in the Sea of Galilee. Fishermen either dragged nets behind their boats or cast them from the shore.

❖ **ABOUT THE STORY** ❖

Jesus was the host at this gathering, and took the responsibility of feeding all of the people. His miracle reminds us that Jesus, the Son of God, is the Creator and Sustainer of all things and that we are dependent on God for all our needs. It also reminds people that Jesus not only cares for the spiritual needs but also our physical needs.

Jesus Walks on Water

THE news rippled through the crowd that Jesus had used only five loaves and two fish to feed them.

"A miracle! Jesus must be the prophet that was promised to us,"came the delighted cries. "Let's make Him our king!"

The people began to shout for Jesus to speak again. So Jesus turned back to the disciples huddled around Him.

"They're obviously not going to let me go for a while," He said to his 12 friends, kindly. "Why don't you start back without me?"

"But Lord, how will you . . . ?" the disciples protested.

"Don't worry, I'll catch up," Jesus reassured them.

Wearily, the friends went down to their boats, climbed aboard, and sailed away from the crowds.

Eventually people went home. Jesus wanted to talk to His Father, so He climbed into the hills to pray.

Meanwhile, the disciples were in trouble. A strong wind had blown their boats off course, into the choppy open waters. The night grew darker. They lost sight of the shore and the stars. They felt lost and afraid. As they searched for the glimmer of the dawn, they saw a pale glow in the darkness which lengthened into the white form of a man.

"It's a ghost!" the disciples cried, shrinking away in fear.

Then a familiar voice called to them above the gusting wind and the crashing waves.

"Don't be afraid!" it said. "It's me, Jesus!"

The disciples didn't know what to think. So many strange things had happened to them recently! Nothing was as it seemed any more.

Fishing boat
Boats like this were used on the Sea of Galilee. They were powered by a single sail and by oars. They were large enough to carry about a dozen men.

Sea food
This plate from Roman times is decorated with images of sea foods. People using decorations like this shows how important the sea was to people in Biblical times. Not only was it used for food and water, but also for transportation and trade.

PETER LEARNED AN IMPORTANT LESSON: HE COULD DO WHAT JESUS WANTED WHEN HE HAD COMPLETE FAITH IN JESUS AND TRUSTED HIM ENTIRELY. PEOPLE NEED GOD'S HELP TO DO HIS WILL. ❧

Anchor
Just as an anchor stops a ship from drifting, so God's promises to us are firm and secure. They will keep us safe from harm.

Peter peered forward, squinting through the darkness. "Lord, is it really you?" he cried. "If it is, tell me to come to you across the water."

"Come! Come!" Jesus's voice floated across to them.

> **When they saw Him walking on the sea they thought it was a ghost.**

Peter swallowed hard and stood up. Gingerly, he made his way to the edge of the rocking boat and looked down into the swirling water. Then he lifted his head and focused on the white shape in the distance. "It is Jesus, my friend," he said to himself. "Jesus has told me to come to Him." Peter stepped out of the boat.

The other disciples couldn't believe it. Far from plunging into the depths, Peter was walking away from them on the water! Step by step across the tossing waves he went, as steadily as if he were strolling along the sand on the shore, not walking across the sea itself in a storm.

But when Peter looked down at the seething water beneath him, his courage suddenly deserted him. "Help me, Lord!" he yelled in a panic. "I'm sinking!"

Jesus reached out a hand and heaved Peter up. "You have such little faith in me! Why did you doubt me?"

Jesus put His arm around His friend and guided him back to the boat. Instantly, the waves and wind fell calm. The other disciples in the boat had seen it all.

"Lord!" they cried, falling at Jesus's feet. "We know you truly are the Son of God!"

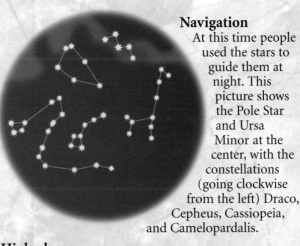

Navigation
At this time people used the stars to guide them at night. This picture shows the Pole Star and Ursa Minor at the center, with the constellations (going clockwise from the left) Draco, Cepheus, Cassiopeia, and Camelopardalis.

High places
Mountains and hills in Judea provided many places to go to, to pray alone. It is not likely that the Jews felt they were nearer to God in high places, but that mountains reminded them of God's power.

ABOUT THE STORY

This is one of Jesus's strangest miracles. Most of His miracles helped people by healing or feeding them. This one is meant to teach the disciples about Jesus. No one can walk on water, and only God could overrule the laws of nature. Hence Jesus was showing them, in a way they could not doubt, that He was God in human form.

Peter the Rock

ONE day Jesus and His disciples were on the road to Caesarea Philippi. For once, there was no one else around and they could talk freely. Jesus seized the opportunity to have a very important conversation.

"I sometimes call myself the 'Son of Man,'" Jesus said, as they tramped along the dusty path. "What do people think I mean by that? Who do people think I am?"

The disciples shrugged.

"Some say you are John the Baptist . . ." one began.

"Or the great prophet Elijah come back to us . . ." interrupted another.

"Or one of the other prophets from the old days, like Jeremiah," suggested another.

Jesus shook His head and sighed.

"But who do you think I am?" He asked quietly.

Peter replied without a moment's hesitation. "You are the Christ, the Son of the living God!" he said.

Jesus smiled.

"You have been blessed, my friend," He told Peter. "My Father in heaven has helped you to understand this."

Jesus rested His hand on Peter's shoulder.

"You are Peter the rock," said Jesus, "the rock on which I will build my church—a church that nothing will be able to destroy, not even death. Peter, I will give you the keys to the kingdom of heaven, and whatever laws you lay down on earth will stand in heaven, too." Jesus looked around at the little group.

❖ **ABOUT THE STORY** ❖

When Jesus called Peter "The Rock," he was playing on the meaning of Peter's name, which is "stone." The message he and the others preached was like a "rock," strong and firm. Peter also became the first leader of the church and the first disciple to preach to non-Jews. Peter was an effective foundation upon which the church could be built.

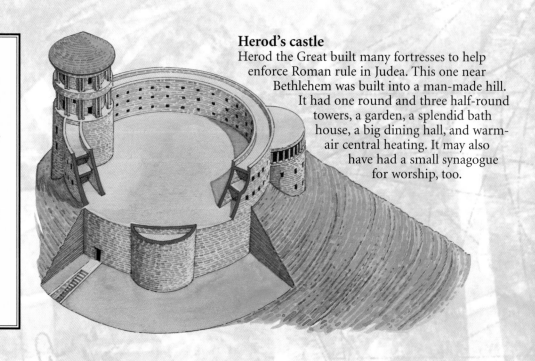

Herod's castle
Herod the Great built many fortresses to help enforce Roman rule in Judea. This one near Bethlehem was built into a man-made hill. It had one round and three half-round towers, a garden, a splendid bath house, a big dining hall, and warm-air central heating. It may also have had a small synagogue for worship, too.

"It is most important that you tell no one that I am the Christ. No one at all. But since you all know who I am, I should tell you what is going to happen to me."

Jesus's tone was deadly serious. He breathed a deep sigh.

"The time is coming soon when I will have to go to Jerusalem, and things will become extremely difficult there. The elders and the chief priests and the scribes will make a great deal of trouble for me, and I will have to go through a lot of suffering. Eventually, they will even put me to death." The disciples gasped. "But," Jesus said, holding up His hand to silence them before they could protest, "on the third day after my death I will be raised back to life again."

> ❝ *And He began to teach them that the Son of Man must suffer many things.* ❞

Peter couldn't get over what Jesus had just said.

"God forbid, Lord!" he cried, absolutely horrified. "Such dreadful things should never happen to you!"

Jesus drew Himself up, straight and determined.

"To take an easier way would be to give in to the devil's temptations," he explained. "Peter, you are seeing things through human eyes. You aren't seeing them as God does."

Peter sadly hung his head.

"Now," Jesus announced to all the friends, His voice kind but firm. "Anyone who wants to follow me is going to have to sacrifice all their pleasures and comforts. They will have to be prepared to face danger and hardship, pain and suffering. To follow me even to the death, if need be."

Jesus looked at the disciples' anxious faces.

"But I tell you this," He assured them. "Anyone whose main concern is to keep safe and content will lose the chance of eternal happiness. Yet anyone who gives up their life for the sake of me and my teachings will live forever in heaven. For what good is it if you win the whole world, but lose your soul in getting it? And what could be more precious to someone than their soul? Believe this—the Son of Man will one day come again in heavenly glory, and everyone will then be repaid for all they have done."

As they walked on, the disciples' minds were perplexed and their hearts heavy with dread at what Jesus had warned lay ahead.

Jesus and His disciples
This carving depicts the moment when Jesus told the disciples that He would be killed and then raised in Jerusalem.

Peter and the keys
This painting shows Jesus giving Peter the keys of heaven. This shows that the disciples had the "key message" which enabled people to find God.

Herod's coins
The Romans allowed the Jews to mint their own coins. These were minted by either Herod the Great, Herod Agrippa, or Herod Antipas. Usually Jewish coins had pictures of plants or man-made objects on them.

A Vision of Glory

ABOUT a week after Jesus's solemn conversation with the disciples, He asked Peter and the brothers James and John to go with Him up a mountain to find a quiet place to pray. They left the other disciples at the foot of the slopes with a bustling crowd. The four friends reached a peaceful spot and settled down to pray.

Peter, James and John were so wrapped up in their prayers that they had no sense of time passing. It could have been minutes, it could have been hours.

As Jesus prayed, His face turned toward heaven. He was utterly motionless, like a living, breathing statue. It was as if He was present only in body and not in spirit; as if He couldn't hear the birds wheeling and crying overhead nor the wind gently ruffling His hair.

When the three disciples had finished praying they turned to watch Jesus, not daring to move or speak. They waited and waited . . . and still Jesus went on praying. After a while, Peter, James, and John felt as if they were sinking into a trance themselves. Then something seemed to stir them. They shook themselves awake to an amazing sight.

Jesus's face began to shine with an inner glow. It grew lighter and lighter until it was more radiant than the sun.

His robes began to glisten and gleam—brighter and brighter until they were a dazzling white. While Peter, James, and John shielded themselves from the glare, two other glimmering figures appeared. Jesus opened His eyes and stood up to talk to them.

To the three disciples' astonishment, they realized that the heavenly newcomers were Moses and Elijah—the mighty lawgiver and the greatest of the prophets! They heard them discussing with Jesus the terrible trials He was to face in Jerusalem—what He was going to suffer and the way He was going to die. And as Peter, James, and John watched and listened—totally transfixed—they saw the great prophets Moses and Elijah start to move away, gradually beginning to fade into the distance.

> ❝ *His face shone like the sun, and His garments became white as light.* ❞

"Master!" Peter cried out urgently, not wanting the magnificent vision to end. "It's wonderful that we're here. Allow us to make three shrines—one for you, one for Moses and one for Elijah . . ."

Mount Tabor
This is one possible site of Jesus's transfiguration, where He appeared as a heavenly being to Peter, James, and John. There was a town on its top even in Jesus's day, so it wouldn't be easy to be alone there. Some scholars think that the transfiguration happened on the more remote Mount Hermon.

PETER WANTED TO BUILD SHRINES BECAUSE HE WANTED TO KEEP THE FIGURES ON EARTH. HE HAD TO REALIZE THAT SPIRITUAL EXPERIENCES CANNOT BE PRESERVED.❧

As he was speaking, a cloud surged above them, blotting out the luminous skies and throwing darkness over the ground. A voice boomed down from heaven, saying, "This is my Son, my Chosen One; listen to Him!"

At the sound of the almighty voice, the three disciples fell on their faces in terror. When it had finished speaking, they felt the cloud's shadow lifting from over them. They felt Jesus's gentle touch upon them and heard His familiar voice saying, "Get up. Don't be afraid."

When Peter, James, and John looked up, Jesus was alone—just a seemingly ordinary man, as before.

As the three stunned disciples followed their master down the mountain, Jesus told them not to tell anyone at all what they had seen and heard, not until He had risen from the dead.

Peter, James, and John were bewildered. There were so many things that the three of them didn't understand.

"What do you mean, you will 'rise from the dead'?" they asked Jesus. "Besides, why should the Son of Man suffer and be condemned to death? And why does it say in the scriptures that Elijah must return before all this is to happen?"

"Elijah's return is to prepare the way for the Son of Man—and in fact he has already been here," Jesus explained. "But the people did not recognize him. They

did to him exactly what they liked, just as they will do to the Son of Man." At last the three apostles realized with a shiver that Jesus was speaking of John the Baptist.

Jesus with Moses and Elijah
Moses gave the Old Testament law to the Jews, and Elijah was the greatest prophet of the Old Testament. Jesus came to complete their work.

John the Baptist
John the Baptist was Jesus's cousin, who prepared the way for the coming of Jesus. He was executed when Herod promised his stepdaughter anything she wished after she danced for him. Her mother told her to ask for John's head because he had criticized her marriage to Herod.

❖ **ABOUT THE STORY** ❖
Jesus had taught that He came from heaven, and this incident showed the disciples what heaven was like. It helped them to believe that He really was the Son of God, as Peter had declared a few days earlier. They saw the purity and holiness of heaven as a bright light. Visions of God's holiness often make people realize just how sinful they actually are.

Moving Mountains

JESUS, Peter, James, and John came down from the mountain to find a noisy crowd surrounding the disciples who had remained behind at the foot of the slopes. The companions hurried to find out what was going on. Suddenly Jesus was swamped by people all shouting at once.

Jesus raised His hands and motioned for everyone to be quiet. Then He spoke. "Will someone please tell me what you are squabbling about with my disciples?"

An anxious-looking man immediately stepped forward. "Teacher, I came with my son to find you. He's ill. It's like there's an evil spirit in him which suddenly throws him to the ground. He foams at the mouth and jerks horribly, then stiffens like a board. I asked your disciples to cast out the evil spirit from my son, but they couldn't."

Jesus looked around at the nine embarrassed and deeply puzzled disciples. Thanks to Jesus's gift of healing powers, they had been able to perform many miraculous cures by themselves. But each disciple had tried to heal this particular boy, and no one had had any success.

"My faithless friends! How long must I put up with you?" Jesus scolded. "Now bring the child to me."

Jesus had barely laid eyes on the boy when he collapsed.

"How long has he been like this?" Jesus asked.

"From childhood," the boy's father sobbed. "It's very dangerous, too. It's like the evil spirit wants to kill him! My son has fallen onto the fire and even into water."

The child moaned and tossed.

"I beg of you," the upset man continued, "if it's possible to do anything, please help us."

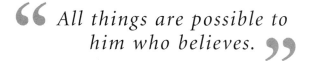

> **❝** *All things are possible to him who believes.* **❞**

"My friend," Jesus replied, "anything is possible if you only have faith."

FAITH IS NOT SOMETHING YOU CAN MEASURE IN THE SAME WAY AS WE CAN MEASURE LENGTH OR WEIGHT. FAITH IS SIMPLY TRUSTING GOD TO WORK IN HIS WAY. THE BOY'S FATHER ASKED JESUS TO HELP HIM TO PUT HIS TRUST IN GOD.

Lunatics

The Romans (but not the Jews) believed that the moon affected people's minds. They called mentally ill people "lunatics" after the Latin word for moon, "luna." As the moon got bigger, so people got madder, they said. The boy in the story may actually have been suffering from some kind of epilepsy.

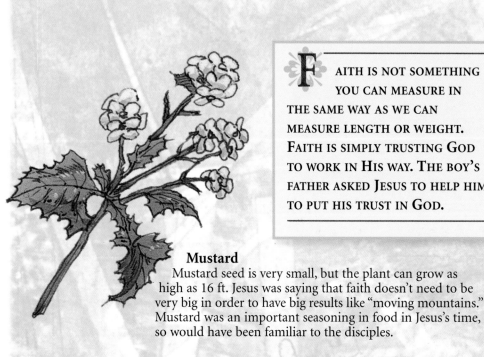

Mustard

Mustard seed is very small, but the plant can grow as high as 16 ft. Jesus was saying that faith doesn't need to be very big in order to have big results like "moving mountains." Mustard was an important seasoning in food in Jesus's time, so would have been familiar to the disciples.

Everyone fell silent as Jesus stepped closer. He bent down and took the boy's hand in His own. At once, the child's fingers quivered. Then they tightened around Jesus's grasp. Finally, he opened his eyes, and Jesus helped the dazed child to stand up.

While the crowds were still with them, the disciples said nothing to Jesus about the healing. But as soon as they were on their own, they asked Jesus why He could cure the boy when they couldn't.

"It's because you have so little faith," Jesus explained. "Even if you had faith the size of a mustard seed, nothing would be impossible for you. You would be able to move mountains."

The father's eyes lit up with hope. "I believe you can help my unbelief!" he cried.

Jesus turned to the writhing body of the boy.

"Spirit! I command you to come out of him!" He ordered, sternly. "Never enter him again!"

Immediately, the boy began to thrash more violently than ever. Fits convulsed him, his arms flailed in the empty air, and his legs twitched. The onlookers gasped as the boy gave a final groan and collapsed into a crumpled heap.

His father was left motionless with shock, appalled and terrified. But the crowd began to whisper.

"He looks as though he's dead," someone muttered.

Charms
The Romans used lucky charms like this bulla to ward off evil spirits. The Jews did not believe that charms could defeat spirits. Jesus often cast evil spirits out of people to show that God was always more powerful than evil.

Fire
Fire was essential to life, but it was not easy to light, so people kept fires burning all the time. The boy could have fallen in at any time. This model is of an Egyptian fanning a charcoal fire to make it burn brighter.

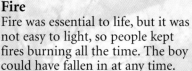

❧ ABOUT THE STORY ❧
Perhaps one reason why the disciples couldn't cast out the evil spirit was that they had come to trust in the powers Jesus had given them, rather than in God himself. Jesus shows that there is no magic involved in healing or helping people. He wants His followers to trust God entirely, and not assume that because they've served God effectively once they can do so again by themselves.

Jesus and the Children

JESUS'S disciples had a lot to learn. While they were following Jesus down the road to Capernaum one day, they began a silly argument.

"Which one of us is the best, then?" was the question that started it all.

"Well," someone piped up, "I've known Jesus the longest . . ."

"Ah, but that doesn't necessarily make you the greatest," someone else quickly protested.

"I reckon it's him," came another voice, "because he's done the most miracles."

"No, no, no," another voice insisted. "I think it's whoever prays hardest . . ."

And so they went on . . . and on . . . and on.

The disciples didn't think that they had been overheard. But when they had reached their destination and had settled into their lodgings, Jesus asked them, "So what were you discussing on the way down here?"

The 12 men fell into an embarrassed silence. None of the disciples could look Jesus in the eye. Some of them shifted awkwardly from foot to foot and began to fidget.

It was as if Jesus had heard every word. Or maybe He just knew what was in all of their hearts.

"If you want to be considered great before God," Jesus said, "you must put others first and yourself last. Here on earth, the greatest people are thought to be those who have the most servants to run around after them. But in the kingdom of heaven, the greatest people will be those who have willingly done the most to help others."

> **'Let the children come to me, and do not hinder them.'**

Jesus reached out to a little child that was running by, and she smiled as He drew her toward Him.

"Look at this simple, earnest child," He said. "Unless you give up your worldly values and become like this little girl,

---

❧ ABOUT THE STORY ❧

There was nothing sentimental about Jesus's attitude to children: He knew they could be as awkward as anyone else. He also knew they could teach people something about trust. He wanted to stop the disciples from discriminating against people. They did not think of children as fully human yet; Jesus accepted them, and everyone else, just as they were.

Capernaum
This was an important town on the northwest shore of the Sea of Galilee, close to where the river Jordan enters it. It was the home of Peter and other disciples and was where Jesus began His ministry. He preached in the synagogue there shortly after He was baptized.

you will never even set foot in the kingdom of heaven. It is those who are selfless and giving like children who are the greatest in the kingdom of heaven. Their angels see God face to face. Always respect those who have a simple, childlike faith. For in doing so you'll be honoring me and my Father. If you sneer and look down on them, you'll end up wishing that you'd drowned yourself in the depths of the sea."

But the disciples didn't remember their lesson for long. Some weeks later, after Jesus had been preaching for the whole day, the disciples saw that some people were bringing their children to Jesus so He could bless them. While some of the little ones were shy and hung back, hiding behind their parents' legs, others ran around boisterously. The disciples began to shoo the children away, feeling sure that, at the end of such a long day, they must be annoying the weary preacher. But Jesus stopped them. "Don't send the children away. Let them come to me," He scolded, "for the kingdom of heaven belongs to them." Jesus bent down among them so the children could wrap their arms round His neck and climb onto His lap. "Unless you are like this—able to give yourselves wholeheartedly—you will never be able to enter the kingdom of heaven."

Children
Jesus used children as an example of faith and trust. Children do not usually have the same worries as adults, and they took Jesus at His word.

God's children
This picture shows that all people are God's "children." That is, He cares for them like a good parent.

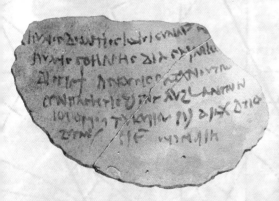

God's provision
This is a receipt issued by a Roman tax collector. Jesus told people not to get worried about money and possessions, but to have the simple faith of a child and trust their heavenly Father to provide for their needs.

The Rich Man's Question

JESUS stood up and drew His robes around Him, ready to take to the dusty road once more. But before He and His disciples were quite ready to set off, a man came running up to them.

"Wait!" he was crying. "I beg you to wait!"

The friends stood patiently while the man dashed up and knelt at Jesus's feet. The disciples were a little surprised, as the man was well-spoken and dressed in what were obviously very expensive clothes. It was strange to see such a wealthy person kneeling to anyone!

"Good teacher," the man panted, trying to catch his breath, "please tell me what I have to do to win eternal life."

"Why do you call me 'good'?" Jesus asked gently. "No one is good but God alone."

The man looked puzzled, so Jesus just answered his question with a kind smile.

"You know the commandments," He said, "Do not kill, do not pursue another man's wife, do not steal, do not lie, respect your father and mother, and love your neighbor as yourself."

"Master, I have tried my hardest to keep all these commandments ever since I was a little boy," the man said.

"Then there is only one other thing you must do," Jesus said, His voice low. "You must sell everything you possess and give every penny of all the money you make to the poor."

Dyeing clothes
Rich people in Biblical times, as today, liked to wear richly colored clothes. Wool (and linen for rich people and priests) was dyed in vats like this.

The eye of the needle
Jesus's humorous saying about a camel passing through the eye of a needle means that people who trust in their wealth or status cannot get into heaven. Only people who trust God—rich or poor—can enter His presence.

The man's eyes widened. Then his face fell, and he bowed his head. "Thank you, master," he said and slowly got to his feet and turned away.

> ❝ *'Sell what you have, and give to the poor, and you will have treasure in heaven.'* ❞

The disciples watched the man trudge off down the road. He was deep in thought, his shoulders slumped and his heart heavy.

Jesus understood that He had just told the man to do a drastic, life-changing thing. He realized that it would be extremely difficult for him to carry out the instruction. Yet He also knew that it was a necessary for him to do to get to heaven. He sighed.

"How difficult it is for those who are wealthy to enter the kingdom of God!" Jesus remarked. "In fact, it is easier for a camel to pass through the eye of a needle than for a rich person to reach heaven."

The disciples were worried. After all, most people worked hard to be comfortably off. Very few people would find it possible to give away all that they owned.

"Surely no one will be saved then?" they asked Jesus.

"There are things that are impossible for people," He replied, "but with God, there is always a way."

As Peter listened and pondered, a thought struck him.

"Lord, we have left everything to follow you—our families, our homes, our possessions, our jobs," he said. "Is this enough?"

"Anyone who has done what you have done will receive a reward a hundred times better than what they have left behind," Jesus assured them, "and eternal life will be theirs."

The color purple
The best and most expensive dye for clothes came from the murex, a shellfish in the Mediterranean. It gave a deep purple color. Only rich people, like the man in the story, could afford it.

Flax
Flax grows in many parts of the world and has blue flowers. The stem of the plant can be soaked in water and its fibers separated and woven to make linen. Linen was more expensive than wool and was woven in several grades from coarse to fine—fine linen was the most expensive.

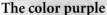

❖ ABOUT THE STORY ❖

This story does not mean that rich people can't go to heaven. Jesus did not discriminate on the basis of wealth. People who have a lot of possessions tend to focus their life on what they have and can get. God then takes second place in their lives. Jesus said that God had to be first. Sometimes that's easier if you have nothing. You then trust Him for everything.

The Good Samaritan

JESUS seemed to know the scriptures and the law of Moses so much better than anyone else. The experts who had dedicated their lives to studying God's teachings were jealous of Jesus, and were always trying to catch Him out.

One day, a lawyer came to Jesus to put him to the test. "Teacher, what must I do to win eternal life?" he asked.

"What does the law tell you to do?" Jesus asked.

"It says to love the Lord God with all your heart and soul," the lawyer replied. "And to love your neighbor as much as you love yourself."

Jesus looked the lawyer firmly in the eye. "Correct," He said. "So there's your answer."

The lawyer wasn't satisfied. "Ah, but who is my neighbor?" he asked smugly.

Jesus answered the question with a story. "A man was traveling from Jerusalem to Jericho," He began, "when bandits attacked him on the road. There was no one around to hear the man's shouts for help. The bandits beat and kicked the man to the ground, until he lay bleeding in the dust. They stripped him of all his possessions and ran off, leaving him for dead."

The lawyer winced at the terrible crime and drew his cloak a little more closely around him.

"Some time later, a priest came along," Jesus went on. "But as soon as the priest saw the dreadfully injured man, he quickly crossed over to the other side of the road and hurried on past, trying not to look."

The lawyer was shocked. How could such a holy man have ignored someone in such need?

"The next traveler to come by was a Levite," Jesus said.

The Levite is sure to help, thought the lawyer. Levites are good people—so good that God rewarded their tribe with the highest positions of office in the temple.

"But the Levite did just the same as the priest," Jesus continued. "He took one look at the naked, bruised body and dashed by on the other side of the road."

The lawyer was appalled. He would have expected such behavior of a Samaritan—one of the hated people who had taken over Samaria when the Jews were sent to Babylon—but not a Levite!

It was almost as if Jesus had read the lawyer's mind.

Oil flask
In Bible times there were no medicines as we have today. When someone was cut, wine was used to clean the wound. Oil was rubbed on the body to ease pain. This jar would have been used to store olive oil, or possibly wine, in someone's home.

The priest and the Levite
Although the story sounds amazing to us—we would expect religious leaders to help someone—there was a twist in it which Jesus's hearers would have understood. Neither of the leaders would dare touch a dead body, because it would make them "unclean" and unable to do their work for a while. They were thinking of themselves, not caring for their neighbor.

"The third person to see the dying man was a Samaritan," Jesus announced.

Well, that's it then, the lawyer thought, making a face. I bet he goes over to see if there's anything to steal and then kicks him when he finds there isn't!

> ❝ *'When he saw him, he had compassion.'* ❞

Jesus said, loud and clear, "The Samaritan was horrified to see the injured man and rushed over at once to help."

The lawyer couldn't believe his ears!

"The Samaritan cleaned the man's cuts and bandaged the wounds. Then he put the man up on his donkey and went to the nearest town. The Samaritan gave an innkeeper some money to look after the man until he was better. 'If you spend more than that,' the Samaritan told the innkeeper, 'I'll pay you back when I next come this way.' Which of these three travelers would you say was the neighbor of the man who was attacked?" He asked.

"The one who helped him," mumbled the lawyer.

"Yes," said Jesus. "Then go and behave the same way."

IT IS ALWAYS EASIER TO DO WHAT WE WANT THAN TO DO SOMETHING THAT IS BETTER FOR OTHERS, BUT IT IS ALSO COSTLY. THIS STORY TELLS US THAT GOD'S WAY IS SOMETIMES THE HARD WAY.

Lawyers

The lawyers who opposed Jesus were also called "scribes." They were people who copied out the religious law and taught it to others. Jesus said that they had failed to apply their own teaching in the way God intended.

❖ ABOUT THE STORY ❖

This parable is probably one of the best known of all of Jesus's stories. People today still talk about a kind person as a "good Samaritan." Jesus wanted people to live out their faith in practical ways. He also implied that we cannot please God just by caring for our neighbor and ignoring God. The two commandments belong together: love God; love others as much as you love yourself.

Joy Over Repentance

FOR centuries, the Jews had always looked up to their religious leaders with the utmost respect. However, these leaders often looked down their noses at the Jewish people.

Jesus's new style of religious leadership was dramatically different. He was often to be found visiting the poor and the sick, laying his hands on lepers, or dining at the houses of the hated tax collectors. He not only walked, talked, ate, and slept among the common folk, he genuinely seemed to enjoy their company, too. And, in turn, He won vast numbers of their hearts. Jesus never turned anyone away—no matter how lowly their position was in society or how hated they were because of their race or job. Jesus even befriended liars, thieves, and vagabonds. Indeed, He often said that He had not been sent to meet good people but to search out as many sinners as possible.

The Jewish leaders hated Jesus for mingling with those they saw to be the dregs of society. They couldn't understand how a holy man could bring himself to mix with sinners, criminals, and down-and-outs. How degrading it was, they thought, to all those who tried hard to uphold the strict religious laws—and degrading most of all, to God.

One day, when a crowd of particularly poor people had gathered around Jesus to hear the word of God, the Pharisees and scribes began to grumble and complain even more loudly than usual. Jesus soon quietened them by telling a couple of stories.

"A shepherd had a flock of 100 sheep," Jesus began. "But when he came to round them up at the end of the day, he saw that one sheep must have wandered off and gotten lost. Without a moment's hesitation, the shepherd left his flock in the sheepfold and went off over the fields to look for the one missing sheep. He searched high and low for a

❖ **ABOUT THE STORY** ❖

Jesus taught that every human being has dignity before God. Indeed, the whole Bible teaches that. People at the bottom of the social pile, despised by others, are said to be of special concern to God. In these stories, Jesus shows that God actively looks for people who need Him and lavishes His love on them, even if they have done wrong in the past.

Beer jug
Most of the people Jesus met drank wine, which was cheap and easy to make from the grapes grown locally. Beer was not widely drunk in Palestine. This beer jug is unusual and perhaps belonged to a rich person.

Silver ingots
In Old Testament times, people used silver ingots like this as money. The value depended on the weight. By New Testament times this was becoming less common for everyday trading, as there were many coins in circulation.

long time, and when he finally heard a lonely bleating he was overjoyed. The shepherd returned home with the stray animal, knocking on all his friends' and neighbors' doors to share the good news with them.

"And there was a woman who owned ten pieces of silver. Then, one night, one of them went missing. Determined to find it, she lit a lamp and searched through the house, sweeping every nook and cranny, turning out every corner and cupboard, shifting every piece of furniture, until she found it. 'Hurrah!' she cried to her friends and neighbors. 'I have found my lost piece of silver!' And they all celebrated with her."

At first, the disgruntled Pharisees and scribes were puzzled at the stories. They didn't see what lost sheep, or a woman losing her money, had to do with them. But their faces grew red with embarrassment when they heard Jesus's explanation.

> 66 *'Just so, I tell you, there is joy before the angels of God over one sinner who repents.'* 99

"Like the shepherd's joy over his one lost sheep, there will be more gladness in heaven over one sinner who repents than there will be over 99 good people who do not need any forgiveness. And like the woman's happiness at finding her single piece of silver, there will be great celebrations in heaven for each and every sinner who repents—no matter how common or humble they are."

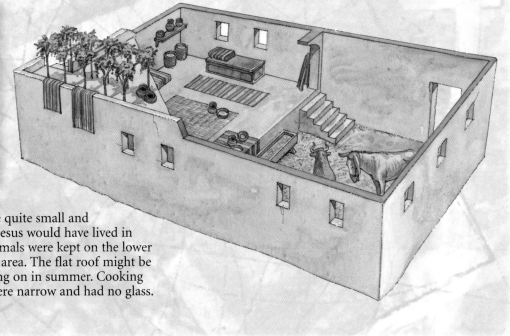

IT IS VERY EASY TO LOOK DOWN ON PEOPLE WHO ARE LESS WELL OFF THAN US OR WHO HAVE "STRAYED" FROM GOD'S WAYS. CHRISTIANS ARE CALLED TO LOVE SUCH PEOPLE JUST AS GOD LOVES THEM. ∾

Palestinian house
Most houses in New Testament times were quite small and often had only one room (on two levels). Jesus would have lived in such a house and visited many others. Animals were kept on the lower level; the family ate and slept in the raised area. The flat roof might be used for drying crops or eating and sleeping on in summer. Cooking was usually done outside. The windows were narrow and had no glass.

The Story of the Prodigal Son

JESUS had a powerful parable for the snooty religious elders about showing forgiveness to sinners. "Once upon a time," He began, "there lived a wealthy farmer. He had two sons who worked beside him on the land and he was content that they would inherit the farm when he died and would look after it well. However, one day the younger son came to him with a proposition.

"'Father, I'm old enough now to choose my own path,' the lad said, 'and I want to go off and see the world.' He shifted about from foot to foot, looked down at the floor, and nervously cleared his throat. 'I was hoping you could perhaps give me my share of the farm now, in cash.'

"The farmer was more than a bit taken aback by this unusual request, but, being a generous man who loved his sons dearly, he agreed. And as soon as the money was in the younger son's hand, he packed his bags and set off, looking for excitement and adventure.

"Unfortunately, the lad wasn't as mature and capable as he had thought. He managed to travel a long way, saw lots of sights, and eventually made it safely to a distant city. But there he fell in with a bad set of friends, who were only too willing to help him squander his money. Before long, the boy had no money left. Of course, the moment the farmer's son hit hard times his "friends" disappeared. He found himself alone and penniless.

"He knew there was nothing else for it but to try to find a job. However, a dreadful famine suddenly swept the country, and everyone tightened their belts. It was no good begging for scraps or rooting for leftovers—there weren't any.

And the only work the boy knew how to do—farming the land—was scarce. The desperate young man was thankful to get a job as a lowly swineherd.

"Every day as the farmer's son drove the pigs out to feed, he had to fight off the urge to eat some of the pig swill for himself. He was miserable and starving.

"'On my father's farm even the hired hands have enough to eat,' he moaned to himself, 'and they still have food left over. Why, oh why did I leave home!'

"Bit by bit, the lad swallowed his pride.

"'I want to go home,' he finally decided. 'I'll go back to my father and beg his forgiveness for being such an arrogant fool. I won't even dare ask him to accept me back as his son, but perhaps he'll take me back as one of his laborers—and that's more than I deserve.'

"The farmer's head had been filled with thoughts of his son every single day he had been away. He had worried over him and missed him, and hadn't stopped loving him for one second. When the landowner saw his child's familiar figure approaching from the distance, he ran to meet him as fast as his aging legs would carry him.

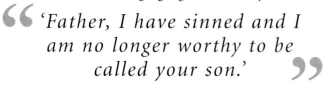

> **'Father, I have sinned and I am no longer worthy to be called your son.'**

"'Father,' the trembling boy wept, as his father enveloped him in a huge bear hug. 'I have sinned against God and against you. I am no longer worthy to be called your son.'

"'Bring out my best robes!' the farmer interrupted, calling to his servants. 'Dress my son in my best clothes! Put my ring on his hand and new shoes on his feet! Bring that calf we were saving for a festival and cook it up into something really special! We're going to celebrate and feast like never before. My long-lost son has come home!'

"While the younger son was filled with repentance and gratitude, his older brother was furious.

"'Father, what do you mean by all this?' he demanded angrily. 'How am I supposed to feel? I have stayed here and worked with you all these years, and you've never thrown a feast for me! But as soon as this loser shows up again, having wasted all your hard-earned money, you give him the best of everything you own!'

"With tears of joy in his eyes, the farmer took his eldest son by the hand.

"'Son, you don't know how much it means to me that you have remained by my side. And everything I have is yours. But today is a day to be glad. For your brother was dead to me and now he is alive; he was lost and now we have found him again!'"

Plowshare
Today, plows have steel "shares,"—the part that digs into the earth and turns it over. In ancient times plows often consisted of the forked branch of a tree, to which an iron share was attached. They were pulled by oxen, often yoked together in pairs. The farmer walked behind, steering the plow by the handle. Plowing was essential to preparing hard soil for the seed.

Signet ring
The ring given by the father to his son was probably like this one, a signet ring. It might have had a family symbol on it. It was a sign of authority and honor, rather than being just a piece of jewelry. Rings were commonly worn by both men and women in Biblical times.

> ❧ **ABOUT THE STORY** ❧
>
> *This moving story is not really about the son at all, but about his father. The older man is always looking for the boy, and when he comes at last, the father is ready to forgive and forget his sins. Jesus meant that as a picture of God. He wants people to come back humbly to Him, and He will forgive whatever they have done that is wrong.*

Heaven and Hell

ALTHOUGH Jesus spoke often about the coming kingdom of God, many people didn't understand what He meant. They thought of the great rulers of the time who had magnificent palaces of gold and silver, treasure houses full of jewels, armies of golden chariots and armored footsoldiers, and ranks of slaves to do their bidding. They pictured Jesus as the proclaimed king of the Jews and at the head of a mighty army, which would come marching through Judea, flags flying, to take charge of the country. The Pharisees once challenged, "So when is the kingdom of God coming, then?"

Jesus replied, "The kingdom of God will not come with great announcements and fanfares, nor will there be anything splendid to see. For the kingdom of God is inside you." Jesus was talking about a spiritual kingdom that exists through life and after death, where both good and wickedness will grow until the end of time. Then God will cast out everything that is evil, leaving only goodness.

Besides not understanding what the kingdom was like, people also found it difficult to accept Jesus's teachings on what they had to do to enter it.

"Everybody wants lots of money, a big house, an important job, and expensive possessions, don't they?" they would wonder. "But Jesus tells us that none of these things are important in the kingdom of God—in fact, they can even stop you from getting there!"

> ❝ *'And at his gate lay a poor man named Lazarus.'* ❞

"Yes," others would agree. "Jesus says that if we want to enter the kingdom, instead of envying those who have lots of servants, we should give our lives willingly to helping others. Instead of trying to get rich, we should give away everything we own to those who are poor."

One day, Jesus told the people a story that He hoped would help them understand before it was too late. "There was once a very rich man who lived in a huge house. Every day he dressed in the finest clothes and dined at a table overflowing with the best food. Each day a wretched beggar named Lazarus would crouch outside the gates of the mansion, dreaming of what it would be like to taste

A triumphant emperor
This is the sort of leader many people expected Jesus to be, a commander of an army riding into a city in a triumphant procession, such as the Roman emperor shown above. Instead Jesus came meekly, riding on a donkey.

Riches
These are Roman coins from the 1st century. The rich man was so greedy that he didn't think about God at all and ended up separated from God in hell.

Judea
Judea was the name that the Romans gave to the area that the Jews called Judah. It was ruled by a Roman governor until after Jesus's death.

some of the rich man's leftovers. Lazarus was all alone, starving, and in rags. He was so miserable he barely noticed the stray dogs who licked his filthy skin or the flies that crawled over his skinny body.

"Eventually, the poor man's suffering came to an end and he died. And as he left the dirt and poverty of his life in this world, angels hurried to carry his soul to heaven.

"Now it so happened that soon afterward the rich man died also—but his soul was taken straight to the fires of hell. As he suffered in torment, the rich man cast his eyes heavenward and saw the beggar standing side by side with the great Abraham, father of the Jewish people.

"'Abraham!' the rich man screamed. 'Have mercy on me and send Lazarus to cool my burning tongue with a few drops of water! I am being burned alive!'

"Abraham remained unmoved and his voice was stern.

"'Son, remember that on earth you surrounded yourself with luxury and comfort, leaving Lazarus in the cold. Now he is being comforted while you suffer. Besides, it's impossible for those in heaven to be cast into hell, and for those in hell to escape to heaven. Hell is an eternal punishment.'

"The rich man groaned in despair. Too late, he began to think of other people.

"'Then please at least send Lazarus to my father's house. I have five brothers, and they're all like me. They need warning, or they'll all end up here!'

"Abraham shook his head.

"'No!' he retorted. 'They have the words of Moses and the prophets. If they don't heed those great people, they won't take notice of any other voice from the dead.'"

WE CANNOT EXPECT GOD TO GIVE US GOOD THINGS IF WE NEVER SHARE OUR GOOD THINGS WITH OTHERS. IN FACT, IF WE DON'T LEARN TO GIVE, WE WILL BECOME GREEDY AND SHUT OFF FROM GOD'S LOVE.

Dogs

In New Testament times, Jews did not have dogs as pets. They roamed the streets and scavenged scraps. People regarded them as vermin and "unclean." So being licked by dogs made Lazarus a complete outcast in Jewish eyes.

❖ ABOUT THE STORY ❖

This story is about having right attitudes to money and people in this life. It refers to life after death in the popular terms of the day. It is not intended to teach us more about eternity than that some people go to be with God and others don't. It does show that we "reap" in the next life what we "sow" in this one, however. It encouraged Jesus's hearers that God loves those who are despised.

Opposition to Jesus Grows

JESUS's preaching was sometimes so bold that it outraged many of the Jews.

"He says to us, 'I have come down from heaven.' How dare He!" many of them exclaimed. "This is just Jesus, after all, the son of Mary and Joseph!"

"He says to us, 'I am the living bread from heaven'!" others scoffed. "What on earth does He mean?"

Even some of Jesus's faithful followers were offended when He said, "He who eats my flesh and drinks my blood has eternal life, and I will raise him up on the last day."

"It's the spirit that's important," Jesus explained, "not the flesh that surrounds it. My words promise life."

After this, many of Jesus's disciples gave up in disgust.

"What about you?" Jesus asked His 12 closest friends. "Do you want to leave me too?"

Peter spoke up determinedly for all of them.

"No, Lord," he reassured Jesus. "You speak to us of how to win eternal life and we believe you. We have all come to know that you are God's Chosen One."

> ❝ *The chief priests and Pharisees sent officers to arrest Him.* ❞

"Yes, and *I* chose you," Jesus reminded them. "But I have to tell you, one of you will turn to evil."

The disciples were shocked, but Jesus would say no more.

By the time of the feast of Tabernacles, Jesus had

❧ ABOUT THE STORY ❧

What made life difficult for the religious leaders was that Jesus was not denying the laws of Moses. He was thinking about them and applying them in a different way. Jesus showed people that the law without love was of no value. He did not break the law but applied it more thoughtfully and more fairly than the harsh and uncaring ways of the Pharisees.

Soldiers

Roman soldiers were based in Judea to keep the peace. The chief priests also had their own guards, and it was probably these who tried to arrest Jesus. However, it was the Romans who finally crucified Him.

❧ ARMOR OF GOD ❧

The apostle Paul described to early Christians the armor that they would need to fight the power of the devil. He described it to them as if it were the armor of a Roman soldier.

Equipment	Meaning
Belt	Truth
Breastplate	Righteousness
Sandals	Gospel of peace
Shield	Faith
Helmet	Salvation
Sword of the Spirit	Word of God

offended so many of the elders that going publicly to Jerusalem was highly dangerous. But he was determined to celebrate the occasion properly. When the news spread that Jesus, a wanted man, was preaching openly in the temple, the Jews were amazed.

The chief priests and the Pharisees ordered his immediate arrest as a rabble-rouser. But the officers came back empty-handed.

"Where is He?" cried the chief priests and Pharisees. "Why haven't you brought Him to us?"

"He's an extraordinary man!" the officers answered sheepishly. "We've never heard anyone speak like Him. The crowds love Him. Everyone's talking about Him and wondering what He means! But even though He speaks strangely, He hasn't done anything wrong. What can we arrest Him for?"

The chief priests and Pharisees decided they'd have to trick Jesus into openly defying one of the laws and then He'd *have* to be arrested.

Next day, Jesus was teaching in the temple when the scribes, priests, and Pharisees strode in to talk to Him.

"Teacher," they said to Jesus, dragging forward a frightened woman. "This woman is a sinner. She has been seen with another woman's husband. Now, the law of Moses says she should be stoned to death. What do you think we should do with her?"

Jesus stood up and faced the hostile officials. "Let him who has never sinned throw the first stone," He said.

Jesus's answer completely thwarted the authorities. He hadn't interpreted the law of Moses as they did, but His answer hadn't broken it either. After all, all of them had sinned in some way; they were only human. Lost for words, they stormed out.

Holy Communion
In this service, Christians eat bread and drink wine, which symbolize Jesus's body and blood, reminding people of Jesus's death on the cross for their sins.

Pens
These pens come from Roman times and may have been the kind used by the scribes in Judea. Scribes wrote letters for people and also copied the scriptures.

Bull sacrifice
The Jews sacrificed a bull in the temple once a year to show they were sorry for their sins. The New Testament says that "the blood of bulls" cannot take away people's sins; only Jesus can do that.

Ungrateful Lepers

WHEREVER Jesus went, His fame as a healer spread before Him. One day ten figures, tattered and misshapen, stumbled into the path ahead. They stood a little way off and held up their hands. The disciples realized that the group was infected with leprosy.

"Jesus, master, have mercy on us," the lepers moaned.

"Go and show yourselves to the priest," Jesus said.

Filled with hope, they did what He told them. The lepers hadn't gone far when they felt their skin tingle. They looked at each other in disbelief. Trembling, they felt the smoothness of their skin. They were cured! Weeping tears of happiness, they ripped off their bandages and danced with joy. They were cured!

❝ *Then said Jesus, 'Were not ten cleansed? Where are the nine?'* **❞**

Some time later, Jesus and His disciples saw a stranger running toward them.

"Thanks be to God who healed me!" the man wept.

The astonished disciples realized he was one of the lepers, now totally cured.

"You're a Samaritan, aren't you?" said Jesus. "Tell me, where are the other nine I healed? Are you the only one who's come back to give thanks and praise God?"

❖ ABOUT THE STORY ❖

When the man came back, Jesus told him that his faith had made him well, that is "whole." He was healed not only in his body but in his spirit because he had come to worship God. Jesus healed people because He cared about their physical needs. But He also cared about their spiritual requirements and their life as a whole.

Lourdes

Healing is a mysterious thing. Even doctors don't always know why some people get better and others don't. Christians believe that people who are ill should pray for God's healing as well as go to doctors. Some make pilgrimages to special places such as Lourdes (seen here) where they believe God sometimes performs special miracles of healing.

The Power of Prayer

JESUS often said how important it was to pray—and He didn't just mean reciting long verses in the temple. He meant having private conversations with God about everyday worries and asking for personal guidance. This was a new idea for many people.

"If your child asked you for a fish or an egg to eat, would you give them a snake or a scorpion?" He said. "Of course not! Well, if you give good gifts to your children, think about all the wonderful things your heavenly Father knows how to give you if you only ask Him!"

> ❝ *And He told them a parable, to the effect that they ought always to pray and not lose heart.* ❞

Jesus realized that some people would misunderstand Him, and would expect to pray for something one day and have it the next. So He told a story to show that people should never stop talking to God, even if they felt their prayers weren't being answered.

"There was once an arrogant judge who had no respect for either God or people. He simply didn't care if justice was being done or not. However, every day a good woman would come to his house and bang on the door.

"'I am being wronged by my neighbor!' she would yell. 'Please come with me and consider the case, then you can give me a just verdict.'

"Day after day the judge ignored her. But she still turned up. 'She's never going to give up!' the judge finally burst out. 'She's going to plague me for ever!' And he went and sorted out her problem for her—just so she wouldn't bother him again."

Jesus told His disciples, "The woman was so determined that even the corrupt judge gave her what she wanted. So imagine how much faster the heavenly Father will respond to the pleas of those He cares for."

Votive hand
The Romans often sought healing by visiting the temple of their favorite god. They would make offerings to the god and say a prayer. Sometimes they would leave a model of the part of the body they wanted to be healed, such as this hand. This was called a votive offering. Some people left models of ears, which we assume was because they were deaf.

Physician and child
On this marble tombstone a doctor is seen examining a child. Medicine in the first century was very crude. On the ground is a cup for collecting blood, possibly taken to try to cure the child.

> ❖ **ABOUT THE STORY** ❖
>
> *Jesus taught that prayer isn't about trying to make God do what we want Him to do but about finding out what God wants us to do. Jesus showed that God always wants the best for people—that is, by getting to know and trust God even when life is difficult. God may know that wealth or healing is best for someone, but Jesus didn't promise that either were ours by right.*

The Pharisee and the Tax Collector

THE Pharisees had been brought up from birth to think that they were special—different from common Jews and way above the likes of foreigners. And none of the lessons that Jesus taught through His stories managed to get through to them. The Pharisees took great pride in the way in which they carefully observed every single rule of the faith, and it blinded their eyes, sealed their ears, closed their minds, and hardened their hearts. When Jesus preached how good people should befriend sinners and forgive them, the Pharisees merely scoffed. When Jesus taught that the wealthy should give all they had to the poor—even if they were ungodly, undeserving people—the Pharisees just sneered. It was impossible to shake their confidence in the righteousness of their own beliefs and habits.

Still, even though the Pharisees were Jesus's worst enemies, He never gave up trying to warn them about how they were falling unwittingly into sin.

"Once upon a time," He told His disciples, "two men went into the temple to pray. One was a Pharisee . . ."

The Pharisees in the crowd looked smug. How good we are, they thought, making sure we pray at all the right times!

"The other man was a tax collector," Jesus went on.

The Pharisees bristled. How dare a Roman-loving traitor venture into the holy temple—the house of God, they thought.

Jesus saw the Pharisees' self-satisfied faces change to looks of disgust, but He went on regardless.

"The Pharisee strode straight into the center of the temple, in full view of everyone. He made a great, solemn show of lifting his eyes and arms up toward heaven and then he began to pray out loud.

Ceremonial washing
Jewish rituals in the first century often involved ceremonial washings as a symbol of being cleansed from sin. There was a large laver bowl in the temple, and probably smaller ones like this were used both in the temple and elsewhere. Jesus taught that people needed to purify their hearts, not their hands, if they were to know God, and that meant doing God's will and not just performing ceremonies.

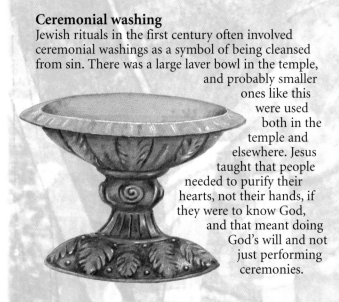

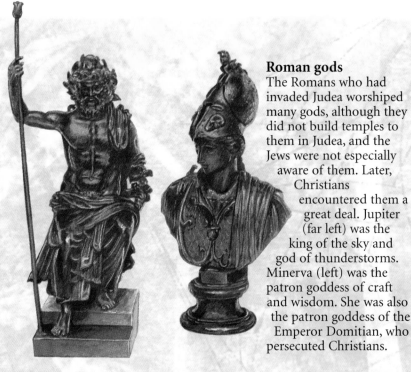

Roman gods
The Romans who had invaded Judea worshiped many gods, although they did not build temples to them in Judea, and the Jews were not especially aware of them. Later, Christians encountered them a great deal. Jupiter (far left) was the king of the sky and god of thunderstorms. Minerva (left) was the patron goddess of craft and wisdom. She was also the patron goddess of the Emperor Domitian, who persecuted Christians.

'God, thank you for making me different from everyone else,' he announced. 'Thank you for lifting me above all the liars, thieves, and scoundrels. I fast twice a week, I give a percentage of all I earn to charity, and I'm glad about it. God, thank you for making me better than people like that no-good tax collector who crept in with me,' he cried.

"The tax collector was hiding behind a pillar in the farthest, darkest corner of the temple. He didn't dare venture out where anyone might see him. He hung his head and wrung his hands. His heart was heavy with the anguish of wrongdoing and the burden of regret.

"'Oh Lord, I am a sinner,' he whispered, looking at the floor in shame. 'I beg you to have mercy on me.'"

> ## 'But the tax collector would not even lift up his eyes to heaven.'

Jesus paused for a moment and looked around at the waiting faces of the crowd. He saw that the Pharisees were scowling, angry at how he had portrayed them as pompous, conceited windbags to everyone that was listening. But nevertheless, He looked them straight in the eye and He finished the story.

"I tell you, that day it was the tax collector who went home blessed by the Lord," Jesus said. "For all those who set themselves high will eventually fall, and all those who consider themselves lowly will be raised up."

The Pharisees stood up, fuming with cold rage. They turned on their heels and stalked off, their elaborate robes swirling out behind them.

Animal sacrifices
Many ancient religions offered sacrifices of animals. The Romans did it only occasionally, but butchers often slaughtered meat using special pagan ceremonies, and this caused the first Christians real problems of conscience. This sacrificial knife would have been used to slit animals' throats. It has an ornate lion's head on the handle.

Seat of Moses
Synagogues often had a stone seat at the front called the "Seat of Moses". The scribe who taught the law of Moses sat there, and in a sense was sitting in Moses's place. This ancient seat was found in a synagogue in Chorazin, in Galilee.

❖ ABOUT THE STORY ❖
This is an important parable because the attitude of the Pharisee is one which still exists in our society today. Jesus is saying that it doesn't matter how good a particular person is, they can never be good enough for God. This is because everyone has sinned in some way. Jesus told people not to compare themselves with others, but with God instead.

Martha and Mary

JESUS and His disciples were gradually drawing nearer to the capital city, Jerusalem. The 12 friends brooded on the awful things Jesus had told them would happen to Him when He got there.

One of the villages Jesus stopped at on His way to Jerusalem was Bethany. A woman named Martha invited Jesus to come and stay at her house.

Martha made sure that Jesus and His friends were cool and comfortable, and at once set about serving the weary people with refreshments. As she bustled in and out, carrying in jugs of wine, pitchers of water, drinking goblets and plates of nibbles, another young woman crept out of an inner room and quietly sat down.

> ❝ *Mary sat at the Lord's feet and listened to His teaching.* ❞

"Mary, come and give me a hand!" Martha hissed at her sister, as she deposited another tray of food among the hungry guests. But Mary just shrugged and turned back to

Jesus, listening intently to every word He had to say.

Martha stood there, hands on hips, more than a little bit annoyed. She too would like to sit with the great preacher and chat. But if she did that, everyone would be left hungry and thirsty. After all, someone had to get the

dinner . . . The dinner! She remembered with a shock the pot she had left boiling over the flames and hurried back to attend to it.

Martha made trip after trip to and from the kitchen, carrying in course after course of delicious food and taking out load after load of empty cups and plates. When the final morsel was laid on the table, she went to join Jesus and His friends. But how left out Martha felt by then! The disciples were deep in a conversation she couldn't follow; she had no idea what they were talking about or laughing at. And there was scarcely room for her to sit down at the very edge of the group!

Martha had been determined to show Jesus and His friends the very best hospitality she could provide—but in doing so she'd hardly seen anything of the great preacher she so admired. She looked at her lazy sister sitting there at Jesus's feet, gazing up at Him in awe! Martha's face was flushed, her arms were aching, and now her lip began to tremble.

"Lord!" she burst out sobbing. "Don't you care that my sister has left me to do everything? Why don't you tell her to get up and help me?"

While Mary hung her head in shame and the disciples fell into an embarrassed silence, Jesus got up to comfort the poor woman.

"Martha, Martha," he soothed, "you have

concerned yourself with preparing and cooking all these different dishes when we only needed one to satisfy our hunger. Your sister has chosen the best dish of all— listening to me—and it will not be taken away from her."

Bethany

Bethany was a small village about 5 miles east of Jerusalem, toward Jericho. Jesus seems to have stayed here quite often and was very close to Mary, Martha, and their brother Lazarus. This painting, found in a church in Bethany, shows Jesus raising Lazarus from the dead.

Tableware

Romans in the first century used elaborate plates and cups at their meal tables, whereas the Jews tended to use plainer ones. The potter was an important person in every town, because everyone needed his wares. Cups generally didn't have handles. There were no knives or forks, either—Jesus and His friends would have picked food out of dishes and eaten it with their fingers.

❖ ABOUT THE STORY ❖

Jesus is gently teaching Martha about priorities. She thinks that the most important thing is to entertain her guests, but it stopped her from learning about God through Jesus's teaching. She wasted a unique opportunity to be fed spiritually, because she was too concerned about physical food. Jesus taught that God was more important than food because life with Him lasted forever.

Lazarus is Brought Back to Life

MARTHA and Mary had a brother, Lazarus, and they all became firm friends with Jesus. But the time soon came for Him to move on once again.

Some weeks later Jesus was preaching and healing far away when a messenger came to Him with an urgent request.

"Lazarus is seriously ill," the messenger explained, "so ill that Martha and Mary fear he is dying. They beg you to come as quickly as you can to make him well again."

The disciples knew how fond Jesus was of the family and expected Him to drop everything and hurry off. To their surprise, Jesus just remarked, "This will not end in Lazarus's death. He has been struck down as a way for God to show His glory through me." And Jesus calmly stayed where He was, continuing His work.

Two days later Jesus announced that He was heading back to Bethany. But the disciples were worried.

"Master, you have many enemies there," they said. "Some people have even sworn to stone you! Surely you shouldn't go back there."

"It is not time yet for my life to end. I will be safe for the moment," Jesus replied. "Now our friend Lazarus has fallen asleep and I must go and wake him."

"Lord, if he is sleeping, he will wake up on his own," the disciples protested, not quite understanding.

"Lazarus is dead," Jesus sighed, "and I am glad that I was not there when he died. Because of this, your belief in me will grow." Jesus smiled at His bewildered followers. "Now let's forget these fears and go to him right away."

By the time Jesus arrived at Bethany, Lazarus had been dead for four days. A pale-faced Martha came out of the village to meet Him.

"If only you had been here, Lord, my brother would not have died," said Martha, her voice cracking. "But I know that God will do anything you ask."

Jesus was filled with compassion at Martha's faith.

He said to her, "I am the resurrection and the life.

❧ ABOUT THE STORY ❧

This was not only one of Jesus's greatest miracles, it was also a great teaching moment too. When He wept, Jesus showed how much sorrow death brings, and how much it grieved Him. When He spoke to Martha, He showed that He was the God who could control life and death. And when He called Lazarus out, He showed that the power of God is absolute.

Sarcophagi
This is an elaborate stone coffin. Only a few rich people in Judea were buried in them, however. Most dead bodies, including those of Lazarus and, later, Jesus, were wrapped up in bandages and placed on a ledge or in a natural cave or tomb cut out of a rocky hillside.

Sleeping
Jesus said that Lazarus was not dead, only sleeping, an image often used in the Bible. Jesus uses this image to teach His disciples that physical death is not the end, but leads to a new spiritual life.

Anyone who believes in me and dies will live again, and anyone who believes in me and lives will never die." He held Martha's gaze. "Do you believe this?" He asked.

"Yes, Lord," Martha whispered in awe. "I believe that you are the Christ, the Son of God." And she ran back to the house to fetch her sister.

As Jesus watched Mary and her grief-stricken friends, a shadow clouded His face. Mary fell at Jesus's feet and sobbed as if her heart were breaking.

Jesus asked her gently, "Where have you buried him?"

And as Jesus was shown the way to Lazarus's tomb, He too broke down and wept for His dear friend.

Lazarus had been laid in a cave, with a large rock rolled across the entrance to keep out wild beasts or bandits.

Jesus's voice was low and firm.

"Take away the stone," He ordered.

Martha gave a little gasp. "Lord, he has been dead for four days now. His corpse will smell."

"Didn't I promise you that if you only believe, you will see the glory of God?" Jesus replied. "Roll away the stone."

As Martha and Mary's friends began to heave the huge rock, Jesus began to pray.

"Father, I thank you for hearing my voice," he said. "I know that you always hear me. But I want everyone here to know and believe that it is you who sent me."

The friends heaved one last time and the rock moved aside. Jesus took a step forward and shouted into the gloomy interior.

"Lazarus!" His voice echoed. "Come out!"

No one moved a muscle.

All was perfectly still and silent.

And then they heard the sound of muffled footsteps coming toward them from the depths of the cave, and the dead man came slowly walking out into the sunlight, all wrapped up in a shroud. He stopped in front of Jesus.

> " *The dead man came out, his face wrapped with a cloth.* "

"Unbind him," Jesus ordered, "and let him go."
And the overjoyed Martha and Mary did just that.

CHRISTIANS STILL USE JESUS'S WORDS "I AM THE RESURRECTION AND THE LIFE" AT FUNERALS. IT REMINDS THEM OF THEIR BELIEF THAT THEY WILL RISE FROM THE DEAD WHEN JESUS RETURNS TO EARTH.

Tomb of Lazarus
Many years after New Testament times, people built this monument to Lazarus at the place in Bethany where they think his tomb was.

The Unmerciful Servant

MOST of the astonished men and women who had seen Lazarus walking out of his tomb believed they had witnessed a miracle. However, a few troublemakers thought it was a trick. They hurried to the chief priests and Pharisees, calling an emergency council meeting at once.

"What on earth are we going to do?" they grumbled. "It doesn't really matter whether He's genuine or not. If we let Him keep on like this, soon everyone in Judea will believe in Him. The Romans will think that there's a serious threat, crush the whole nation, and destroy our religion."

The high priest, Caiaphas, had a different opinion.

"This Jesus will die for the good of us all," he prophesied. The chief priests and Pharisees wouldn't listen. From that moment on, they made up their minds that it was more important than ever to find a way to have Jesus put to death.

Jesus was well aware that He wasn't liked by everybody, but He always preached that people should forgive their enemies—such as the time when Peter came to him with an important question.

"Lord, how many times should I forgive someone who does me wrong?" Peter asked. "Up to seven times?"

Jesus replied, "Not just seven, but seventy times seven—forgive them every single time." And He told a story to explain why.

"There was once a generous king who had kindly lent money to several of his servants. The time came for the servants to repay their debts, and the king called them in, one by one. One servant in particular had borrowed a vast

sum of money—ten thousand talents, in total. And when it was this servant's turn, he stood in front of the king ashen-faced, his knees knocking. He had failed to make enough money to pay back what he owed.

"The king followed the terms of the contract and ordered that the loan should be made good by selling the servant, his wife, and his children into slavery, and auctioning all of his possessions. The devastated man fell on his knees, sobbing and begging forgiveness.

"'My lord!' he cried. 'Have mercy on me! Bear with me a little while longer and I promise I will find every last penny that I owe you.'

"The good king took pity on the poor man and agreed to give him some more time to pay. Trembling with relief at his narrow escape, the servant rushed from the throne room. As he left the palace, he came across one of his

Prisoners go to work
This ancient stone relief shows prisoners handcuffed to each other and escorted by guards. They may be going to work. Most prisoners in ancient times worked in labor camps instead of being kept in jails.

Restraint
When prisoners were kept in a jail, they were usually shackled in some way. Having their feet locked in a kind of "stocks" was the most common form of restraint. Sometimes prisoners were chained to their guard to stop them from escaping.

work colleagues, a man who owed him the rather small amount of one hundred denarii. The servant was desperate. Grabbing his frightened friend around the throat, he pushed the man up against the wall and threatened him. 'Give me my money!' the servant demanded. 'I need it now—or else!' Just as the servant had done, the man broke down and begged for more time to pay. The servant was ruthless. He had the man immediately flung into prison until he found a way to come up with the money.

"When the other palace employees heard about the servant's behavior, they went to tell the king. Soon, the cruel man found himself back in the throne room. This time, the king wasn't smiling, he was frowning angrily.

"'You wicked servant!' the king roared. 'You begged me to be merciful, to not sell your belongings and put you in prison, and I gave you more time to repay your debt. Don't you think you should have shown similar forgiveness to your friend?' And the king had the hard-hearted servant thrown into jail at once."

> 'Should not you have had mercy on your fellow servant, as I had mercy on you?'

Jesus explained what the parable meant. "The king is like my heavenly Father," He said. "And if you don't find it in your heart to forgive people, your punishment will be the same as the unmerciful servant's."

THE UNFORGIVING SERVANT WAS SELFISH. HE GRABBED HIS OWN FREEDOM BUT DENIED SOMEONE ELSE THEIRS. JESUS USED THIS AS AN EXAMPLE TO SHOW THAT PEOPLE SHOULD BE KIND TO EACH OTHER.

Forgiveness
This painting of Jesus offering forgiveness and a welcome into heaven reminds people that any sin is a sin against God. The New Testament teaches that forgiveness is offered freely by God as an act of grace.

ABOUT THE STORY

In this story Jesus wants His listeners to see how great God's forgiveness is and to learn to treat each other as God treats them. It is hypocritical to accept His forgiveness yet not offer it to others, because people who love God are called to imitate His ways in their lives. Indeed, if people did not forgive each other, Jesus warned, they would be unable to appreciate what God had done for them.

Zacchaeus is Forgiven

ZACCHAEUS was a fat little man. A fat little man whom nobody liked very much. For Zacchaeus was Jericho's chief tax collector. And by collecting his countrymen's hard-earned money for the hated Romans—and taking extra for himself—he had made himself very rich.

"Here comes that traitor, Zacchaeus," people would say as they saw him walking down the road, and they'd cross over to the other side of the street.

"Here comes that crook, Zacchaeus," people would sneer as they saw him out shopping, and they'd shut up their market stalls to avoid serving him.

"Here comes that liar, Zacchaeus," people would whisper as they saw him entering the synagogue to pray, and they'd turn their backs as he went past.

All Zacchaeus's ill-gotten wealth couldn't make up for the hatred people felt toward him and for the loneliness of his life.

Just like all the other citizens of Jericho, for many months now Zacchaeus had heard stories of an amazing holy man named Jesus of Nazareth, who preached the most inspiring sermons and performed miracles of healing. And when Zacchaeus heard people gossiping outside his window of how Jesus would be passing through Jericho that very day, Zacchaeus was determined not to miss the opportunity to see Him. He locked up the tax office at once and went out into the street. It wasn't difficult to work out where Jesus was going to be. He could already hear a buzz of excitement coming from the other side of the city. Zacchaeus hurried off at once, as fast as his short legs would carry him.

By the time Zacchaeus reached the route that Jesus was expected to take, crowds of people had already lined the streets—10 or 12 people thick in places. Zacchaeus jumped up and down, trying to see over their shoulders, but he was too small. All he could see was row

upon row of the back of people's heads. So Zacchaeus tried pushing. He set his shoulder to the jostling wall of bodies in front of him and heaved, trying to squeeze through. All he got was his toes stamped on and an elbow in the eye. He was just as shut out of the ranks as before.

Then Zacchaeus had an idea. Huffing and puffing in the hot noonday sun, he set off again running—right down the road behind all the crowds. Hurry, hurry, he thought to himself. Hurry or you might miss him. Zacchaeus didn't quite know why he wanted to see Jesus so much, but he knew he did. He realized with surprise that nothing else would have gotten him running so fast through the streets of Jericho.

> ❝ *And he sought to see who Jesus was, but could not because he was small of stature.* ❞

Just when Zacchaeus thought that his legs were going to give way and his heart was going to burst inside his chest, he reached what he was looking for—a tall, thick sycamore tree that he used to climb as a boy. Come on, Zacchaeus, the panting chief tax collector thought to himself, you can still do it if you put your mind to it. And he reached up on tiptoe into its branches.

How everyone would have laughed if they had seen the fat man scrambling up the tree trunk in a most undignified way. No one was paying any attention. They were far too intent on peering into the distance to catch the first glimpse of Jesus coming down the road.

As Zacchaeus balanced himself uncomfortably among the branches, the crowd began to cheer and jump up and down. Way above their heads, Zacchaeus could see everything. Making their way slowly through the clamoring, grabbing people was a group of very simply dressed men. And in the middle of them was a man with the kindest face he had ever seen.

Zacchaeus knew he had to be Jesus of Nazareth. The way Jesus smiled so gently at the noisy rabble all around Him made Zacchaeus feel truly ashamed of the swindling he had done in the past, and he longed to jump straight down from the tree and join him.

Jesus was drawing nearer and nearer, until He was right underneath Zacchaeus's sycamore tree. And the chief tax collector nearly fell off his perch with shock, for Jesus suddenly stopped, peered up through the leaves right at him and said his name.

"Zacchaeus, hurry up and come down," Jesus said. "I'm on my way to stay with you."

The crowd fell silent. They weren't just amazed to see Zacchaeus, the chief tax collector, nesting in a tree; they were also stunned that the holy man had even lowered Himself to speak to him—let alone say that He wanted to visit his house.

"What about us?" they began to murmur. "Why does the preacher want to go and stay with a nasty man like that?"

The delighted Zacchaeus didn't give them a chance to persuade Jesus to change His mind. The little man leaped out of the tree and bowed down before Jesus.

"Lord," Zacchaeus said, "you know that I am a sinner. However I stand before you today a changed man. I intend to give half of everything I own to the poor. And I'm going to look back through my records and give anyone that I've ever cheated four times as much as I owe them."

Jesus smiled and laid His hand on Zacchaeus's arm. "I have come to find people just like you," He said.

With that, Zacchaeus eagerly escorted Jesus to his house.

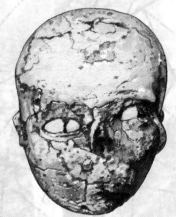

Jericho
Zaccheus lived in Jericho, believed to be the oldest walled town in the world. This plaster-covered skull dates from about 7000 B.C. It was made when the people of Jericho prayed to their ancestors.

✦ ABOUT THE STORY ✦

Zacchaeus responded to Jesus with great generosity because he appreciated his forgiveness. The Jewish law said that a thief should pay back twice what he had taken, but Zacchaeus paid back four times as much. This is an example of "repentance": showing our sorrow by what we do. It was a sign that Zacchaeus had changed.

The Workers in the Vineyard

WHEN people came to see Jesus, and he was able to forgive them their sins, they had the chance to start again with a clean slate. One of Jesus's parables gave people a life-changing sense of freedom and hope. "There was once a land-owner who went out early one morning to the marketplace to hire workers," Jesus began. "He saw that there were many laborers waiting to be hired, and he offered them the usual fee of one denarius per day. The men agreed and got down to work picking the grapes.

"Three hours later, the landowner went out again to the marketplace. Just as he had expected, several latecomers were hanging around hopefully.

"'If you're looking for work, go to my vineyard. I'll pay you a fair rate at the end of the day,' the landowner said.

"The pleased men hurried off right away.

"At midday, the landowner went again to the marketplace and found workers who were delighted to be hired. And he went once more in the middle of the afternoon and picked up yet more grateful laborers.

"When there was only about one hour left before the

Treading grapes
In order to make wine, grapes need to be pressed to get the juice out. This was done by putting them into large vats and treading on them, as shown in this Byzantine mosaic from Beth-shan.

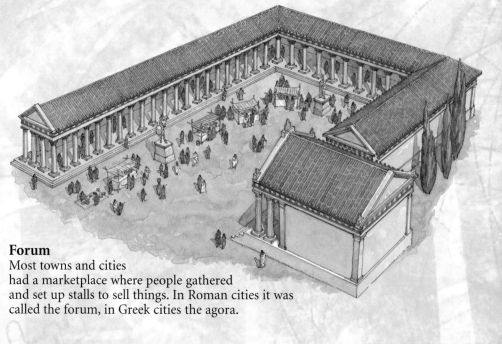

Forum
Most towns and cities had a marketplace where people gathered and set up stalls to sell things. In Roman cities it was called the forum, in Greek cities the agora.

laborers were due to stop work, the landowner hurried to the marketplace one last time, and soon there were even more workers in his vineyard. He didn't want them to feel unwanted and go home without any wages.

"As the sun set, the landowner told his steward to hand out the wages. The hot, exhausted men who had been working in the vineyard all day long were surprised when the landowner said, 'Pay the last shift of workers first.'

"'Evening shift—one denarius!' the steward announced, pressing a shiny coin into each of the worker's hands. The men were startled and delighted. A whole day's pay for less than an hour's work. How generous the landowner was!

"The mid-afternoon shift stepped forward. If those who had done less work than they had been paid one whole denarius, they wondered, how much would they get?

"'Mid-afternoon shift—one denarius!' the steward cried.

"At first, the laborers were disappointed. But they soon cheered up. We've still got a whole day's wages for less than a day's work, they thought.

"'Midday shift—one denarius!'

"This time the workers weren't at all pleased. Is this a joke? they wondered. We could have turned up at the very last minute and still have been paid the same!

> " 'Now when the first came, they thought they would receive more.' "

"And then the steward called out for a final time. 'Early-morning shift—one denarius!'

"There was nearly a riot. 'What do you mean by all this?' demanded the men. 'You've paid these shirkers the same as us, yet we've toiled in the scorching heat all day long!'

"The landowner was calm and kind. 'Friends,' he said. 'I'm not cheating you. Didn't we agree that you'd be paid one denarius? It's my choice to give these latecomers the same wages as you. Can't I spend my money as I like?'"

When Jesus explained the parable, his audience's hearts leaped. "The kingdom of heaven is like the landowner and his vineyard," Jesus said. "Even if you only find your way to God at the last minute, you'll still be as welcome as those who have been with God a long time."

Grape picking
Vineyards, places where people grow grape vines, were important in Israel. Vines grew well in the sunny climate, so grape production was an important part of the economy. They were eaten as fruit, and pressed to make wine. They were also dried to make cakes of raisins. This Egyptian wall painting shows grape pickers harvesting the crop.

❖ **ABOUT THE STORY** ❖

Jesus intended this parable to be applied in two ways. First, it applied to the newcomers to the faith, who were despised by the "old guard." Secondly, it applied to those who would come to trust Jesus later from outside the Jewish religion. In heaven, He was saying, all are equal. This is not to encourage people to delay believing in Him, but to reassure those who realize at the last minute.

Blind Bartimaeus

EVERYBODY in Jericho knew Bartimaeus the beggar. He had been blind from birth and lived rough on the streets. Clutching his rags around him, he'd lift his dull eyes whenever he sensed people approaching and would hold out his begging bowl in hope. Occasionally, someone would take pity on him and drop a denarius into it. Bartimaeus was such a familiar figure that the people of Jericho had stopped thinking about his sad plight a long time ago.

One day used to seem very much like another for Bartimaeus. Every day he'd wake in darkness, sit by the roadside in darkness, and then go to sleep in darkness.

But one morning, Bartimaeus got up to find that things were different. The road he sat beside was much busier than usual, and there were excited crowds hanging about all around him.

"What's going on?" Bartimaeus cried, as hordes of people swept past him in both directions. "Who are you waiting for?"

"Jesus of Nazareth is going to pass by here on His way out of Jericho," said a voice.

Bartimaeus's pulse began to race. He had heard people talking about Jesus of Nazareth before. Bartimaeus thought that the man sounded amazing. People said that you had only to hear Him talk and your spirits would be lifted. They said that He healed lepers, cured paralytics, and even raised dead people back to life! Bartimaeus had longed to encounter the preacher for himself. He was sure that if the great man could do all these wonderful things, He'd be able to make him see, too. But he had never dared to dream that he might actually get the chance to meet the holy man.

Now, hope suddenly flooded into the blind beggar.

"Son of David!" he began to shout, forgetting everyone around him in his desperation. "Have pity on me!"

From somewhere, Bartimaeus found a strength he never knew he had. He raised his voice louder, determined that Jesus should hear him. As he did so, the noise of the crowd grew more excited all around him, and Bartimaeus knew that the holy man was nearby.

"Jesus of Nazareth, please have mercy on me!" he yelled, his cries ringing out above the hubbub.

"Shut up, Bartimaeus!" came voices from all around.

❧ ABOUT THE STORY ❧

When Bartimaeus used the term "son of David," he was recognizing that Jesus was not just a remarkable man but also the Messiah. It was this "faith" that Jesus commended. The blind man's prayer, too, was one of faith and dependence. He asked first and foremost for mercy. He knew that before God, everyone was a spiritual beggar, whether they were rich or poor.

Hebrew calendar
Bartimaeus didn't live by the calendar because every day was the same to him. This is a fragment of a Hebrew calendar. It is divided into 12 months, but they are different from ours.

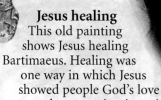

Jesus healing
This old painting shows Jesus healing Bartimaeus. Healing was one way in which Jesus showed people God's love and compassion in action.

"We can't hear what he's saying."

But Bartimaeus just shouted louder than ever. "Jesus, son of David, take pity on me!"

"Bartimaeus, be quiet!" the voices came again—but this time they were filled with surprise. "Be quiet and listen! Jesus is calling for you. Quickly! Go to him."

In his hurry to get up, Bartimaeus got in a terrible tangle in his tattered cape. He ripped it from around him and threw it away, groping his way forward. All of a sudden, he sensed that Jesus was there, right in front of him. "Bartimaeus, what do you want from me?"

"Oh Lord," the beggar gasped, "please let me see." Bartimaeus felt gentle fingertips on his eyelids and immediately the gloom began to lift into a thick fog that swirled and cleared into a world of bright colors, the beauty of which he had never been able to imagine.

> ❝ *He said, 'Lord, let me receive my sight.'* ❞

"Go in peace," Jesus said, "your faith has made you well." There was no way that the grateful beggar was going to leave the man who had given him such a precious gift. Joining on behind Jesus's disciples, Bartimaeus danced down the road, weeping aloud with joy and praising God.

FAITH IS BELIEVING THAT GOD CAN DO WHATEVER HE WISHES, AND TRUSTING HIM TO DO WHAT WILL BRING HONOR TO HIM AND BE BEST FOR US. FAITH LETS GOD DECIDE WHAT THOSE THINGS ARE. ❧

Begging

Beggars were sadly a common sight in Bible times. They were often treated like vermin by some religious people, who believed that God had cursed them. Jesus went out of His way to help and heal poor people.

The Wedding Feast

JESUS once said, "Many that are first will be last, and the last first." By this, He meant that some of the most important and distinguished people on earth will eventually be considered worthless by God; and many people who are looked down on and despised on earth will be precious in God's sight. If you were someone who always seemed to be down on your luck, Jesus's words were very comforting. If you fell into the "important and distinguished" category though, like the Pharisees, His words were deeply disturbing—not just a criticism, but a warning, too.

One night when Jesus had been invited to eat at the house of a Pharisee, He told a story that He hoped would help His host to reach heaven.

"Once upon a time there lived a king who had a dearly beloved son. The prince was about to get married, and the king gave orders for a fantastic wedding banquet to be thrown. Only the very best would do for his son! Menus were discussed, recipes were tasted, wine was ordered, entertainment was booked, invitations were sent out, seating plans were drawn up, the silver was polished, flowers were arranged. And after months of preparation, all was finally ready. The delighted king sent out his servants to summon the guests to the celebrations.

"But they all returned alone. Trembling, they ventured before the king one by one and gave the guests' pathetic excuses. One guest said that he'd just bought a field and he really had to go out and plow it right away. Another said that he'd just bought a herd of oxen to do some urgent work on his farm. A third said he couldn't come because he'd only just gotten married himself, and he couldn't leave his wife! And so it went on . . .

"The king was deeply offended and disappointed by the rudeness of his friends and relatives.

"'Go and invite them again!' he roared, and sent the servants scurrying off once more.

"But yet again, not a single soul would come.

"'That's it! I've had enough of that ungrateful lot!' the king shouted. 'They don't deserve to come and enjoy themselves here anyway.'

"He called for his servants one more time.

"'Go out into the streets and lanes of my kingdom,' he told them, 'and bring me all the homeless people you can find. The poor, the lame, the blind—invite them all! I'm going to give them the party of their lives! And give everyone a special robe to wear in honor of the occasion.'

"The banqueting hall was soon filled with the joyous sounds of feasting. And at the head table, the king was the happiest of all. He sat and watched the total strangers with the utmost pleasure. They seemed to be enjoying his hospitality far more than his friends and relatives had ever done, and they were certainly more grateful.

"Suddenly, among the rows of guests, with their richly decorated and brightly colored clothes, the king's eyes fell on a man dressed in rags. His plate was piled high with food and he was tucking in, oblivious to everything and everyone around him. The king sprang angrily to his feet and marched down the rows of guests to where the man was seated.

"'Where is your robe?' the king demanded. 'Everyone invited by my servants was given a robe as a gift. Get out of here! You're an impostor!'

"While the man mumbled and spluttered, searching in vain for an excuse, the furious king called for his guards.

"'Tie him up and sling him outside into the darkness!' the king ordered. Then he gave the signal for the party to carry on . . .

> ❝ *'For many are called, but few are chosen.'* ❞

"Remember," Jesus told the alarmed Pharisee who had invited Him to dinner, "many receive a special invitation to join God's kingdom, but only those who whole-heartedly want to be a part of it will be allowed to enter."

Wedding entertainment
Weddings in every culture often include singing and dancing. In Judea people sang and danced to the music of pipes and lyres. These are Egyptian musicians.

Hammurabi
Hammurabi was a king in Babylon about 1,800 years before Christ. He is pictured at the top left of this 8-foot obelisk, receiving laws from the god Shamash. Engraved on this obelisk are 280 laws relating to such things as marriage, the subject of this story, and murder. Some, but not all, of them are like the laws that God gave to Moses.

◆ **ABOUT THE STORY** ◆

The picture of the kingdom of God as a wedding party shows that heaven is a joyful place, where people are united with God and can celebrate his love. They also need to be "clothed" in this life with his love, too, and not be wrongly "dressed" in bad ways of behaving, like the man in the story. Jesus said people couldn't expect to get to heaven if they just pleased themselves.

The Wise and Foolish Bridesmaids

IT was only natural that after listening to Jesus preach about the coming of the kingdom of heaven, people should ask, "Lord, when will this happen?"

Most of Jesus's disciples assumed that judgment day would be in the next few years, and certainly within their lifetimes. But Jesus explained to them in parables that only God knew when the end of the world would be.

"Picture ten bridesmaids at a wedding reception, waiting for the bride's new husband to arrive," Jesus told His disciples. "Darkness is falling, and the bridesmaids are standing outside with lamps to welcome the bridegroom in. But five of the bridesmaids have been foolish. They haven't thought to take flasks of spare oil with them.

"Unfortunately, there's no sign of the bridegroom. He's taking such a long time that the bridesmaids' legs begin to ache from standing up for so long, and they all sink to the floor for a short rest. One by one, their lamps grow short of oil and flicker out. In the quiet darkness, the weary bridesmaids all drift off to sleep.

"Suddenly they're being woken by a shout. 'The bridegroom is on his way! The bridegroom is on his way!'

"They spring to their feet. The wise bridesmaids refill their lamps with the oil they've brought and light them up. The foolish bridesmaids are left looking rather silly.

❧ ABOUT THE STORY ❧

Jesus said that when He returned to earth, the world as we know it would end. Evil would be punished, justice would be seen to be done, and God's people would be united with Him for ever. Before that, He said, there would be many troubles that His people would need to be ready for. This story tells Christians to keep alert so they are ready for whatever God wants to them do.

A modern wedding
Marriage is a sign that a couple are leaving their old family and setting up a new family or household together. They pledge their faith to each other and also to God. This is a modern Jewish wedding, similar to the one Jesus's story is about.

IT WAS DIFFICULT FOR THE DISCIPLES TO UNDERSTAND THAT ONLY GOD KNEW WHEN JUDGMENT DAY WOULD BE. JESUS SAID WE COULD BE JUDGED BY GOD AT ANY TIME, SO WE MUST ALWAYS BE READY. ❧

"'Please lend us some of your oil,' they ask their friends, somewhat sheepishly.

"The five sensible girls refuse. 'We're sorry, but we can't,' they explain. 'The bridegroom may still be a little way off yet, and if we share our oil with you, none of our lamps will last long enough. Why don't you hurry off and buy some more oil?'

66 *'And while they went to buy, the bridegroom came.'* 99

"The bridesmaids do as their more thoughtful friends suggest, and it just so happens that while they're gone, the bridegroom arrives. The guests all come out of the house to meet him, and amid much joyous singing and dancing,

the five remaining bridesmaids hold their lamps high to light the way. Everyone bustles the laughing bridegroom into the house and when the last guest is inside, the door is closed behind them.

"When the five foolish bridesmaids return, their lamps lit once again, they are dismayed to find that they're locked out of the party. They bang on the door.

"'I'm sorry,' calls a voice, 'but I don't know you. I can't be sure who you are.'

"And the girls are left outside in the cold darkness.

"Don't be foolish like the five forgetful bridesmaids," Jesus warned His disciples urgently. "Make sure you're always prepared for God's coming, because you can never have any idea when it will be."

Oil lamps
Oil lamps provided the main form of lighting in Bible times. The shallow bowl was filled with olive oil, and a wick was draped over the lip and lit. In the house they were placed on ledges.

Torchlight procession
At Jewish weddings in Biblical times, the groom usually went to the bride's house, then took her to his house for the party, accompanied by an ever-growing procession of friends and relatives. Sometimes the party was held at the bride's house. Often the procession was at night—hence the need for the lamps, as there were no streetlights.

The Parable of the Talents

DESPITE all Jesus's teachings, as he drew nearer and nearer to Jerusalem some of His disciples became more and more convinced that the kingdom of God was about to appear. They still expected Jesus to lead a revolution in Jerusalem to overthrow the Romans. Jesus knew, as He'd already told His disciples, that far from gaining political power, He was going to be arrested, tried, and eventually put to death.

"While you wait for the coming of the kingdom of God," Jesus said, "make the most of everything God has given you." Then Jesus told them this parable.

"A prince had to travel far away to claim a kingdom that was his rightful inheritance. Because he would be away for some time, he called his trusted servants to him.

"'Will you look after things for me while I am gone?' he asked them; and he gave them his bags of money for safekeeping—five bags to one servant, two bags to another servant, and one bag to a third servant. Each bag held one "talent", which was a large sum of money. Then the prince departed, leaving the men with their borrowed fortunes.

"Year followed year, and the servants heard no word from their prince. Just as they began to wonder if they would ever see him again, he returned home, now a king, with a kingdom and all the fine trappings that went with it! After weeks of

celebrations, he called his three trusted servants to him to ask about his money.

"'Now, tell me what you did with my savings,' the king said, excitedly. 'Did you put them to good use?'

"The first servant hauled in ten sacks of coins.

"'Your highness,' he said. 'I decided to trade with your five bags of money. I worked hard at it and I have made you another five bags on top.'

"The king was overjoyed. His servant had repaid his trust better than he could ever have imagined. 'Oh well done!' he cried. 'I shall reward you by making you governor over ten of my new cities.'

"Then the second servant came forward, heaving four bags of coins before the king. 'Your highness,' he said. 'I traded with your money, too, and have also doubled the sum. Here are four bags of coins.'

"The grateful king clapped his hands in delight. 'My thanks and congratulations to you, too!' he said. 'How would you like to be governor over five of my new cities?'

> 66 'For to every one who has, more will be given.' 99

"Then the third servant stepped forward, with only one, quite grubby, sack of money. He looked down at his feet and mumbled, 'Your highness, I didn't do anything with your money. I've seen how ruthless you can sometimes be and I was afraid. So I just hid the coins safely in the ground.' And the servant handed back the single bag of money with which he had been entrusted.

"The king was hurt and annoyed. 'You mean to tell me that you have done nothing with my gift?' he exclaimed. 'How can you have been so idle? Even if you didn't feel able to trade with it yourself, you should have taken it to my bankers. They could have invested the money, so it was still being of some use.'

"The king swung around to his guards.

"'Take the money off this servant and give it to the man who made ten bags of money,' he commanded, 'then kick the worthless servant out. For those who are deserving and have worked hard for their reward will receive more. Those who haven't bothered to try, will have what little they possess taken away from them.'"

Banking
The Romans had a banking system, part of which was licensed by the state. The Jewish bankers tended to be moneylenders rather than savings bankers. This stone relief shows a Roman banker at his desk, perhaps in a marketplace.

Burying money
There were no banks for Jews to use at this time, no safe places to deposit metal ingots, coins, or jewelry. People who wanted to hide their wealth buried it in the ground.

❧ ABOUT THE STORY ❧

The talents referred to in this parable were units of weight for precious metals. This measurement was used in ancient Greece, Rome, and the Middle East. Because we use the word "talent" to mean "what you are good at," it is an encouragement to use everything we have (not just money) to honor and serve God.

Judgment Day

"AT the end of the world, the Son of Man will come in all His glory, surrounded by angels," Jesus promised His disciples. "He will sit on his magnificent throne and all the peoples of the world will gather before Him. Every last soul who has ever walked the earth will be there; every single man, woman, and child God has created since the very start of time; all human beings from all nations.

"The Son of Man will call each person forward one by one—there will be no hiding from Him. 'Go to the right,' he will say to one. 'Go to the left,' to another. And everyone will find they have no choice but to obey. So the Son of Man will separate out the vast crowd of souls into the righteous and the wicked, just as a shepherd separates out the sheep and the goats among his flock.

> ❝ *'He will separate them one from another as a shepherd separates the sheep from the goats.'* ❞

"When every last soul has been accounted for, the good people will all be gathered at the Son of Man's right hand. He will smile at them and throw His arms open wide, saying, 'Come with me! You have been blessed by my Father. It's now time for you to enter the kingdom that has been being prepared for you since the beginning of the world. For when I was hungry, you gave me food; when I

Jesus the shepherd
Pictures of the shepherd and his sheep are found in churches, because Jesus called Himself "the good shepherd" who looked after His people. Hence, in the parable, people who love in the way He wants are called "sheep," as opposed to the goats who did not serve Him.

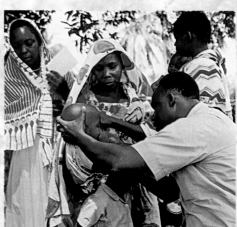

Christian charity
This aid worker is helping sick people in Africa. Christians believe that it is essential to do something practical to help people as an expression of their faith.

was thirsty, you gave me drink; when I was a stranger, you befriended me; when I had no clothes, you bought me new ones; when I was ill, you came and held my hand; even when I was in prison, you came faithfully to visit me.'

"The righteous will turn to each other in bewilderment.

"'Lord,' they will say, 'when did we do all these things for you?'

"And the Son of Man will explain, "Whenever you said a kind word or did a generous deed for any one of your fellow men and women—no matter who they were—it was just as if you were doing it for me.'

"Then the Son of Man will turn to the evil souls on His left. They will cower away before His gaze and tremble in terror at the sound of His voice.

"'Be gone from my presence,' He will command. 'For when I was hungry, you let me starve; when I was thirsty, you let me choke; when I was alone and needed a friend, you made no effort to get to know me; when I shivered in rags, you let me freeze; when I was sick, you let me suffer; when I was locked up, you abandoned me.'

"The appalled souls will cry out in despair, 'But Lord, when did we come across you being hungry or thirsty or a stranger or naked or sick or cast into a dungeon? When did we ignore you?'

"'Whenever you walked past someone who needed your help,' the Son of Man will reply, 'it was just as if you were doing it to me.'

"And they will be driven into hell, where they will be punished for ever. But the good people will be carried straight to heaven, where they will live in happiness for ever more."

Church door
The angel at the top of this church door is to protect people who enter, and the mythical animals down the sides keep evil at bay. These also symbolize entering God's kingdom.

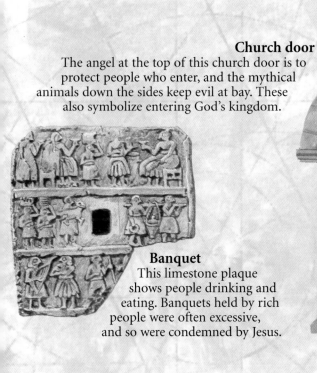

Banquet
This limestone plaque shows people drinking and eating. Banquets held by rich people were often excessive, and so were condemned by Jesus.

❖ ABOUT THE STORY ❖

On a previous occasion, Jesus had said, "By their fruits you shall know them." He meant that people who claimed to follow Him but acted selfishly were betraying their Lord. This parable stresses that point. In the book of James it says that faith without action is dead. However, Jesus is not saying that kindness alone, without any faith, will get someone to heaven.

Teachings of Jesus

PEOPLE have always admired the teaching of Jesus in the Gospels. Some of His sayings have become part of everyday life: "Turn the other cheek"; "Go the extra mile"; "Do to others as you would have them do to you." Jesus taught a lot of other things besides how to get on with our (sometimes difficult) neighbors. In fact, He taught mostly about God—what He is like and how we can get to know Him.

His key teaching was about the kingdom of God, which He said had arrived when He started His ministry. This wasn't a physical place; rather, it was anywhere that God's rule was obeyed. He said it was growing from small beginnings as a big plant grows from a tiny seed, and that it grew alongside the kingdoms and values of this world like wheat growing among weeds. God's people—those who truly belonged to His kingdom—would be separated out from the rest on the day of judgment and spend eternity in heaven with God.

In order to enter the kingdom, people had to believe in Jesus. "Faith," to Jesus, was about trusting God. So He taught that God was like a loving parent who really did care for a child. Some people at the time thought God was a bit of an ogre. Not so, said Jesus in the Sermon on the Mount. If you know to give your child some bread to feed him when he's hungry, and not a stone to choke him, surely God will give us His loving gifts too.

Jesus taught His disciples to pray, asking God for all the things they needed and trusting Him to supply them. But

He also warned them that they couldn't have everything they wanted. The Christian way, He said, was "a narrow way." It meant self-sacrifice—saying no to our desires in order to serve God and others first.

Part of that self-sacrifice was to be kind and loving to our neighbor, and in His parable of the good Samaritan, Jesus defined our neighbor as "anyone in need." He also said that a rich person should go and sell all his possessions and give the money to the poor. Jesus did not say that to every rich person, but in this case (as in others) the man's wealth was more important to him than God's kingdom. Jesus constantly challenged people to get their priorities right. Who was in charge of their life—them or God? What drove them—the desire to be rich and famous or the desire to honor God?

That was the point of the most famous collection of Jesus's teaching, in what is known as the Sermon on the Mount. Some of it is repeated in the Sermon on the Plain in Luke 6, and both sermons are unlikely to have been taught at any one time. The Gospel authors have collected together some of Jesus's sayings into one place—He probably repeated them on many occasions.

The Sermon on the Mount begins with a reversal of normal human values and goes on to remind Christians that their role in the world is to be like salt, preserving it from going bad and being God's "flavor" or influence within it. Their "light"—their faith, applied in life—is to be seen, not hidden. Christianity, He is saying, is a public religion not a private philosophy.

In order to be salt and light in the world, Jesus's followers are to obey God completely and to aim for perfection, which is God's standard. People that are perfect in this way do not harbor anger against others, even if they have wronged them. They respect others, not treating them as objects who exist only to satisfy their desires.

Sermon on the Mount
The sermon that, according to the gospel of Matthew, Jesus gave "on the mountain" has been described by some people as the first text on what it means to be a Christian and how one can lead a life following Jesus. It is as part of the Sermon on the Mount that Jesus teaches the people "The Lord's Prayer," and tells them that they can address God as the "heavenly Father."

Jesus and the apostles
Within His large group of followers Jesus chose a special few to whom He gave extra teaching. These men are normally called "apostles". The apostles were not always able to work out exactly what Jesus meant in His parables, so Jesus would explain to them what He meant.

~THE LORD'S PRAYER~

OUR FATHER WHO ART IN HEAVEN,
HALLOWED BE THY NAME.
THY KINGDOM COME,
THY WILL BE DONE
ON EARTH AS IT IS IN HEAVEN.
GIVE US THIS DAY OUR DAILY BREAD;
AND FORGIVE US OUR TRESPASSES,
AS WE FORGIVE THOSE WHO
TRESPASS AGAINST US;
AND LEAD US NOT INTO TEMPTATION,
BUT DELIVER US FROM EVIL.
FOR THINE IS THE KINGDOM AND THE POWER
AND THE GLORY, FOR EVER.
AMEN.

Throughout the Bible, God is shown to keep His promises absolutely and to forgive sinners willingly. The person who follows Him is to be faithful and true as well, willing to help others and not to seek revenge or to stand in unfair judgment of others. They will then become generous to others, and their religious practice will be sincere, coming before all personal ambitions. Such an attitude is likely to experience real answers to prayer.

Jesus taught that if God really is in charge of your life, and you are seeking Him and His love above all else, then you'll discover the one thing everyone seeks: happiness. You won't have to worry, because you'll know that God is in charge and that He will provide all you need, even if He doesn't give you all you want.

You can also be assured that He'll help you at all times, even at the hardest times, when you think you cannot carry on. Toward the end of His short life, Jesus told the disciples to expect to receive the power and help of God the Holy Spirit. He would help them to understand what Jesus had taught and would reassure them of God's loving presence at all times. He would also go ahead of them in their ministry, making people aware of their need for God.

In other words, being a follower of Jesus affected every part and every moment of a person's life. Jesus sometimes pictured the kingdom of God like buried treasure found in a field. The finder went and sold all he had in order to buy the field—and get the treasure. It was that valuable, and that important.

✦ THE BEATITUDES ✦

This well-known series of short sayings starts off Jesus's Sermon on the Mount. They are a guide for the people who wish to enter the kingdom of God. They start with the word "Blessed," which some versions of the Bible translate as "How happy." It means, "If you do what follows, you will receive God's kindness and blessing." Each is then followed by a promise. Probably the most famous of these is "Blessed are the meek, for they shall inherit the earth."

Beatitude	Means: If you are...	Then you will...
Poor in spirit	aware of your deep need of God	enter God's kingdom
Mourning	really sorry for your sins and the world's sin	know God's forgiveness and comfort
Meek, gentle	obedient to God in all ways	receive God's good gifts
Hungry for uprightness	longing to know God and do His will	be spiritually satisfied for ever
Merciful	sorry for others and helping them in their need	experience God's kindness
Pure in heart	sincere in every way	stay in touch with God
Peacemaker	helping enemies to become friends	be doing God's most important work
Persecuted	suffering for God's cause	receive a hero's welcome into heaven

Women in the New Testament

THE Gospels deal with women in very different ways from how people would have expected at the time. The first announcement of the expected birth of Jesus was to a woman (His mother); the first announcement of the birth was to shepherds. And the first appearance of Jesus after His resurrection was to women. Yet women and shepherds were regarded as inferior citizens. Their word was not trusted in a Jewish court. In a demonstration of the "good news of the kingdom," the Gospels show that Jesus came especially to show God's love to people who were despised by others.

During His lifetime, Jesus demonstrated that same concern and compassion. Although He did not break with His culture to the extent of having any women among His closest disciples, in all His dealings with them He treated women with dignity, respect, and love. Indeed, without a large group of mostly anonymous women who provided food and shelter, the disciples would have had a much harder time. Some women, however, play a more prominent part in the Gospels.

Mary Magdalene

This Mary had a troubled past, but we are not told the details. Jesus had cast seven demons out of her, and she was devoted to Him with gratitude for the new life He had given her. She was at the cross when He died, and was the first to see Him alive three days later, although she at first thought He was the gardener.

Martha and Mary of Bethany

With their brother Lazarus, these two women were especially close to Jesus. They were probably unmarried (or possibly widowed) and invited Jesus to make their home a base when He was in the south of Judea.

One day Martha scurried around getting supper for Jesus and His disciples, annoyed that Mary, her (probably younger) sister, didn't help, but instead sat with the men listening to Jesus. Mary, Jesus said, had chosen the better option, taking advantage of a unique opportunity to learn about God. Her knowledge would remain forever, but food could wait.

However, later at the tomb of Lazarus, Martha made a statement of faith in Jesus which is equal to that of Peter: "You are the Christ, the Son of the living God."

Salome

Salome is believed to have been the wife of Zebedee and mother of James and John, two of Jesus's closest disciples. She may also have been the sister of the Virgin Mary, and hence Jesus's aunt. She too was at the cross and witnessed the resurrection of Jesus.

TIMELINE

• Jesus performs the miracle of feeding five thousand people.

A.D. 30

JESUS FEEDING THE FIVE THOUSAND

LAVER BOWL

• Jesus walks over the Sea of Galilee toward the disciples' boat. Peter walks on water also, but loses his faith in Jesus and sinks.

JESUS AND PETER

• Jesus calls Peter "the Rock" on which He will build His church.

• The disciples Peter, James, and John, witness Jesus transfigured into a heavenly being with Moses and Elijah.

THE TRANSFIGURATION

Unnamed women Jesus helped

The "sinner" who anointed Jesus's feet while He ate supper in a Pharisee's house is not named in the Bible, but her devotion was commended and her faith brought her wholeness and healing.

So too did the woman caught in adultery (John 8:1–11). Here was an example of the double standards of the time. She was sentenced to death, but the man she had been with was not. Jesus simply said, "Whoever is without sin can cast the first stone," upholding the law but making it impossible for anyone to execute its sentence. Then, forgiving her, He said, "Go and sin no more." She had a new start.

The Virgin Mary, mother of Jesus

Pre-eminent among the saints, she conceived Jesus while a virgin as a unique sign that her child was the "Son of God" and also fully human at the same time. She was probably quite young at the time and was a woman of clear and trusting faith. During Jesus's childhood, when strange things happened (as when He remained for three days in the temple when He was twelve), Luke tells us that she "treasured these things in her heart" (Luke 2:51).

She was present at the cross, grieving at His death, and Jesus showed His great love and compassion for her by asking John to take Mary and look after her. She was also one of the first witnesses of His resurrection. However, she is not mentioned in the rest of the New Testament.

❖ WORSHIPING MARY ❖

Later in church history Mary was declared to have been taken bodily into heaven (without dying). Many people pray to her today as one of the saints.

Shrine
This is a traditional shrine to Mary which has been built at the side of the road.

JESUS AND THE SINNING WOMAN

• Pharisees send soldiers to arrest Jesus, but they return without Him.

• Jesus teaches the people about the power of prayer.

• Jesus tells the stories of the prodigal son and the good Samaritan.

• Jesus cures ten lepers, but only one man, a Samaritan, comes to thank Him.

JESUS AND THE LEPERS

• Jesus forgives the corrupt tax collector Zacchaeus in the city of Jericho.

JESUS AND MARY

LAZARUS RAISED FROM THE DEAD

• Jesus visits His friends Mary and Martha in Bethany and raises Lazarus from the dead.

A.D.33

DEATH AND RESURRECTION

The final days of Jesus's life on Earth, His resurrection from death and His triumphant ascension into heaven

Death and Resurrection

HERE you can read about Jesus's last days on earth, from His arrival in Jerusalem to His betrayal by Judas, which led to His arrest, trial, and death. It ends with the story of His miraculous resurrection and His ascension to heaven, where He was reunited with God His Father.

Via Dolorosa
This carving shows Jesus on the way to Golgotha, just outside Jerusalem. It is situated on the Via Dolorosa, the "Way of Sorrow," in Jerusalem, along the route Jesus would have taken. It shows Simon of Cyrene helping Jesus with His cross.

The story begins with Jesus's last visit to Jerusalem. Jesus Himself was already aware that His entry into the city would lead to a final confrontation with the authorities, finishing with His own death. He told His disciples exactly what would happen, but they found it hard to believe His words. The visit took place during Passover time, so the streets were crowded with thousands of pilgrims. Instead of slipping in unnoticed, Jesus made a dramatic entry, riding on a donkey. This was interpreted as a fulfillment of the prophecy that the Messiah would enter Jerusalem on a donkey.

On His arrival in the city, Jesus immediately threw out of the temple the traders who were making money out of the pilgrims and increasing the profits of the corrupt temple officials. During the days that followed, Jesus preached in the temple area, while the religious leaders did their best to trick Him into incriminating Himself with statements of blasphemy—that is, speaking against God. As the conflict escalated, the Jewish elders grew more determined to remove this troublemaker once and for all.

At the end of Passover week, Jesus held a farewell meal for His disciples. During this Last Supper, He gave some final instructions to His closest followers and also revealed that He knew there was a traitor in their midst. After the meal, Jesus went to pray in the Garden of Gethsemane. He begged God to spare Him from His suffering, and God sent an angel to give Him strength. Shortly after this, Jesus was arrested. The disciple Judas had betrayed Him to the Jewish elders and had led them to the garden, showing them who Jesus was with a kiss.

Immediately after His arrest, Jesus was tried by the Jewish court, the Sanhedrin, and found guilty of blasphemy. Under Jewish law, blasphemy was punishable by death. At this time, though, only the Roman governor could pass the death sentence. Under Roman law,

Mount of Olives
In the hours before Jesus was arrested, He went to the Mount of Olives, shown here. He often went to the Garden of Gethsemane, which was on the Mount, to find peace from the bustle of Jerusalem itself.

the charge of blasphemy was not even recognized. Because the Jewish leaders wanted Jesus dead, they brought Him before the Roman governor, Pontius Pilate, on a charge of treason. Although Pilate could find no case against Jesus, he bowed to public pressure and condemned Him to death by crucifixion.

Before the crucifixion took place, Jesus was savagely beaten and cruelly mocked by the Roman guards. The crucifixion itself involved a slow and very painful death. Throughout His ordeal, Jesus prayed to God to give Him the strength to bear the pain. One of the two thieves crucified alongside Jesus was impressed by His words of forgiveness and concern for others, even during His dreadful suffering. When Jesus died with a final cry of "It is finished," His body was taken down from the cross and buried in a nearby tomb.

According to the Bible, Jesus's tomb was found to be empty on the Sunday morning after His crucifixion. It was a group of women who made the discovery, and shortly afterward, one of them, Mary Magdalene, saw Christ alive again. For some weeks after this, Jesus made several appearances to His disciples, both in Galilee and in Jerusalem. When He had convinced them that He had overcome death and assured them that He would continue to help them even when He was no longer physically present, He departed, leaving them to carry on His work. The disciples watched in amazement as their master ascended to heaven, to return to His Father.

Throughout these stories we can see Jesus's suffering and His strength in the face of that suffering. Jesus accepted His death and never denied God. Christians believe that when Jesus died, He took upon Himself the sins of everyone, so that anyone could be forgiven by God and live with Him forever. They believe that Jesus accepted the pain of death in order to show, by His resurrection, that God and His love are not defeated by death. Christians try to follow Jesus's example, living their lives according to God's purpose of saving the world through love.

The other important aspect is Jesus's miraculous resurrection. The Christian idea of resurrection was different from the beliefs of other religions at the time. Christians thought of the body as being resurrected, and of its being transformed so that it was suitable for the eternal life to follow. The Greeks were different. They thought of the body as a hindrance to true life and believed that after death, the soul would leave the body behind entirely. Their concept of life after death was in terms of a soul that never died. The Jews believed in resurrection, but thought it would be with the same body.

The resurrection has been of central importance to the Christian faith since the earliest preaching began. Right from the start, Christians believed that Jesus had risen from the dead, and that they too would rise after death to be with God eternally. Jesus said, "I am the resurrection and the life; he who believes in me, though he die, yet shall he live."

❖ DEATH AND RESURRECTION ❖

Here you can read of Jesus's last days, His crucifixion, resurrection, and final ascent to heaven.

JESUS TEACHING IN GALILEE
Matthew, Ch. 20; Mark, Ch. 10; Luke, Ch. 7 & 18; John, Ch. 12.
JESUS IN JERUSALEM
Matthew, Ch. 21, 22, 24, and 26, Mark, Ch. 11–14; Luke, Ch. 19–22, John, Ch. 2, 11–14
JESUS ARRESTED AND CRUCIFIED
Matthew, Ch. 26 & 27; Mark, Ch. 14 & 15; Luke, Ch. 22 & 23; John, Ch. 17 to 19.
JESUS'S RESURRECTION
Matthew, Ch. 28; Mark, Ch. 16; Luke, Ch. 23 & 24; John, Ch. 20 & 21; Acts Ch. 1.

Jesus taken from the cross
After He died, Jesus was taken down from the cross by Joseph of Arimathea, seen here with Mary Magdalene and Mary, mother of James and John. Joseph was a member of the Sanhedrin, the ruling Jewish council who wanted Jesus dead, although he had voted against Jesus's death. The Bible tells us that Joseph was a secret disciple of Jesus. Joseph was wealthy, so he was able to provide rich linen in which to wrap Jesus's body. He also had his own tomb carved out of the rock, and it was in this tomb that Jesus was buried.

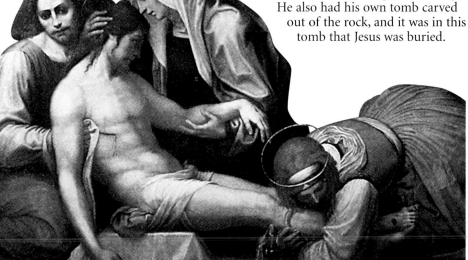

Jesus in Jerusalem

THE CITY OF JERUSALEM, where Jesus was tried and crucified, was, even at this time, a very important city. Its history can be traced back to at least 3,000 years before the birth of Jesus, and today it is considered sacred not only to Christians but also to followers of Judaism and Islam. The first part of its name means "foundation." The second part, *salem*, probably originally referred to Shalem, a Canaanite god or goddess. The Canaanites were the race of people that lived in this area before the Israelites arrived. So the original meaning of the name was probably "foundation of Shalem." Over the years, though, the second part of the name probably came to be associated, in the minds of the Jewish people living there, with the Jewish word *salom*, meaning peace.

Since the start of His ministry, Jesus had known that He would meet His death in Jerusalem. He had told His disciples many times that this would be the case, but they had never entirely believed him. Jesus wanted to make sure that as many people as possible heard and understood His message, so His last days in Jerusalem are full of symbols that the people could have picked up on, and that would give them clues as to His mission.

Jesus deliberately made His final trip to Jerusalem at the time of the Jewish festival of Passover. During this feast the Jews remember the events that took place when their ancestors were slaves in Egypt. Before the Egyptian pharaoh would release the Israelites from slavery, God, through Moses, had inflicted nine plagues upon the pharaoh and his country. In the tenth and final plague God killed all the first-born children and animals in Egypt. However, He "passed-over" the houses of the Israelites, who had followed special instructions for the first Passover meal given to them by God through Moses.

When Jesus enters Jerusalem during Passover week, not only is the city more crowded than usual because of all the pilgrims who have come to the holy city to celebrate, but these people are already thinking about death and being saved by God, as it is the reason that many of them are in Jerusalem.

Jesus made a highly symbolic entry into the holy city. The Old Testament tells how a Messiah would come and save the Jewish people. This Messiah, the Bible says, would enter Jerusalem on a donkey. Jesus knew exactly what message He was giving the people. Throughout His ministry, Jesus had told only His disciples that He was the Messiah, and He had told them not to tell anyone. At this stage, though, He is arriving in Jerusalem to fulfill the role on earth that God gave Him and He can tell everyone that He is the Messiah.

Soon after entering Jerusalem, Jesus went to the temple and again fulfilled Old Testament prophecies by clearing the traders from it, as He had done once before. By making His anger and displeasure publicly very clear, Jesus was making known His anger at the religious authorities of the time, the Sadducees and the Pharisees, for allowing, and sometimes encouraging, the traders and the money-changers into the grounds of the temple.

Jesus's time in Jerusalem is traced on this map. The Bible tells us that He was staying in Bethany and came every morning of Passover week to the temple to teach the people. You can see the site of the Passover meal that Jesus took with His disciples, the Last Supper, before the group followed Jesus out to the Garden of Gethsemane for Jesus to pray. In the Garden, Jesus was betrayed to the authorities, as He knew He would be, by Judas. Jesus was arrested and taken for an unofficial trial at the house of Annas, the former High Priest. Jesus was then taken to the house of Caiaphas, the high priest, where He was tried for blasphemy, speaking against God, by the whole Sanhedrin, the Jewish council. The punishment under Jewish law for this crime was death, but the Jewish authorities could not order Jesus's execution; only the Roman governor could do that. The elders had a problem, though. They knew that Pontius Pilate, the Roman governor, would not recognize a charge of blasphemy, as he was not concerned with the Jewish religion. In order to get Jesus executed, they changed the charge: they told Pilate that Jesus was trying to stir people up to fight against the Romans. The elders hoped that the governor would not be able to ignore a charge of this kind. Even though Pilate could find no charge on which he could find Jesus guilty, the elders had done such a good job of stirring up hate among the people of Jerusalem that Pilate eventually bowed under the pressure from the public and allowed Jesus to be led away. Jesus was taken to Golgotha, outside the city walls, where the Romans crucified Him.

Death of Christ
The death and the resurrection of Jesus are the most important events in the Christian faith. Christ's suffering is sometimes used symbolically, such as in this image of a peasant praying before Christ. The peasant, dressed as he is, could not have been present for the real crucifixion. He is praying to the forgiving spirit of Jesus.

GOLGOTHA

Antonia fortress

Temple

To Bethany

GARDEN OF
GETHSEMANE

UPPER CITY

Palace of
Herod Antipas

Herod's
Palace

ESSENE QUARTER

LOWER CITY

Last Supper

Return
from Bethany

Jesus Prepares for Jerusalem

THE twelve disciples had been traveling around Judea for three years. Every day they had walked for hours, relying on the goodness of strangers to feed and shelter them. Every day, they had dealt with the masses of pushing, shouting people who had come to see Jesus. The disciples had listened to hundreds of people pour out their problems. They had given the downcast men and women new hope by preaching Jesus's message of God's kingdom. They had seen people with terrible illnesses and diseases, taking many to Jesus for healing and healing others themselves. They had stood up against the anger of the religious authorities, who insisted that Jesus was a wicked hoaxer

leading the people into sin. They had faced the violent mobs who came to stop Jesus and His disciples by force. In private, the disciples had struggled to understand as Jesus explained His teachings. Each one of them had carried in his heart the great secret Jesus had told them: that He was the Messiah, God's chosen one, the one the prophets said long ago would be sent to save the world from its sins.

It was hard work, and one night's sleep was never enough. However, the disciples were dedicated. They believed wholeheartedly in Jesus and were determined to follow Him, no matter how difficult it was.

One morning, Jesus was already up and saying His prayers. The disciples hurried to join Him. Then they sat back and waited for Jesus's instructions. Jesus's words were strange and worrying.

"It is time for me to go to Jerusalem," He announced.

Jesus looked around and saw both excitement and worry in the disciples' faces. He had told His twelve

❧ ABOUT THE STORY ❧

Jesus had probably been to Jerusalem several times during His three-year ministry. He knew that this time would be different. The opposition had grown to fever pitch. He must have been afraid, because He knew it would be painful. He also knew that this was why He had come into the world. So Jesus set out to do God's will, because He knew that God's will was the best for Him and for everyone.

The Messiah
In the Old Testament, it is prophesied that the Messiah will come to save the Jewish people. In the New Testament, Jesus is described as the Messiah, come to save mankind. The word "messiah" comes from the Hebrew word meaning "anointed one." The Greek word for anointing, "christos," is the origin of Jesus's title, "Christ."

helpers long ago that they were working their way toward Jerusalem, and the disciples were well aware of the dangers that lay ahead there. Although the Romans were governing Judea, the elders in Jerusalem had great power, and they wanted Jesus out of the way. Once Jesus was in the capital city, it would be much easier for the priests, scribes, and Pharisees to get their hands on Him.

Jesus looked at His anxious friends and smiled sadly.

"I've already told you what will happen to me there," He said, "but I know that none of you have been able to believe it. Yet my words are true. In Jerusalem, everything that the ancient prophets said would happen to the Son of Man will finally come to pass. I will be handed over to the chief priests and scribes. They will condemn me to death and give me to my enemies to be mocked and tortured. Finally, I will be put to death by crucifixion, and three days later, I will be raised up to life again."

The disciples all began to speak at once, clamoring and questioning and protesting. Jesus held up His hand for silence. As the twelve men brooded, their eyes downcast and their minds troubled, the mother of James and John came hurrying up and knelt before Jesus.

> ❝ *'Grant us to sit, one at your right hand and one at your left, in your glory.'* ❞

"Lord," she said. "Please let my two sons sit beside you in your kingdom—one at your right hand, the other at your left."

Jesus's voice was low and firm.

"Only my Father can grant that," He replied. "However, I can tell you that anyone who would be great in my Father's kingdom must be a humble servant to others here on earth. I myself came here to serve others—not to have others serve me—and to give up my own life to save the lives of many."

Brooch
The Romans wore many types of jewelry including brooches like this one. Brooches were often ornate and were worn by both men and women. They had safety pins on the back and were used to fasten clothes, such as cloaks, at the shoulder.

Jesus's journey to Jerusalem
During His ministry in Galilee, Jesus visited Jerusalem several times. The journey that He made from Capernaum to Jerusalem was a long one, nearly 100 miles on foot.

Christian symbol
The cross is a sign of Christianity because it represents the cross on which Jesus was crucified. Some Christians wear a cross, usually around the neck, as a sign of their commitment to Jesus.

Jesus is Anointed

ON His way to Jerusalem, Jesus stopped at the little town of Bethany to stay with His close friends Mary, Martha, and Lazarus.

The two sisters and their brother were overjoyed to see Jesus. They had every faith in His teachings and loved Him dearly, not least because Lazarus owed his life to Jesus. Once, after a sudden illness, Mary and Martha's brother had died. Four days later, Jesus had arrived and brought Lazarus walking out of his tomb, alive and well.

Now the little family welcomed Jesus with open arms, each providing the best hospitality they could. Martha rushed around in the kitchen, preparing a delicious meal. Lazarus was the perfect host, keeping all his guests entertained and happy while they sat waiting at the table. Mary saw how weary the travelers were from their journeying and slipped away to fetch something to soothe and refresh Jesus. She decided on a tiny bottle of scent she had been saving—the most rare and expensive perfume that money could buy. Mary didn't give Jesus just a few dabs of it. Instead, she cracked open the precious alabaster flask and let every last drop of the cool, beautiful perfume trickle over His hot, tired skin.

Several of the disciples leaped to their feet in shock at the very extravagant gesture.

"What are you doing, woman?" cried Judas Iscariot, totally appalled. "You would have been better off selling that perfume and giving all the money to the poor!"

"Leave Mary alone," Jesus scolded. "You will always have poor people to show generosity to, but you will not always have me. By anointing me with this beautiful perfume, Mary has in fact prepared my body for burial."

> " *In pouring this ointment on my body she has prepared me for burial.* "

The disciples looked at each other in puzzlement and began to whisper about what Jesus could mean by speaking of burials and of not always being with them. Jesus Himself stayed silent, wrapped up in memories of another time, not too long before, when a woman had shown Him a similar kindness.

Once, when He had been dining at a Pharisee's house, a woman He had never met before had hurried to see Him. The woman had been a terrible sinner all her life, but she had heard Jesus speak of love and repentance, and she had felt something inside her change. From then on, all she had truly wanted was to be forgiven and to be able to make a new start.

The woman had sat behind Jesus and cried. Her tears had fallen on His feet, dusty from the road, and had washed them clean. She had dried Jesus's wet feet with her hair and tenderly kissed them. She opened up an expensive bottle of perfume that she had brought with her especially, and scented His skin.

Jesus had been very touched by the woman's kindness, which was quite the opposite of His host's. The Pharisee hadn't gone to any trouble at all to make Jesus feel welcome. When he had seen that Jesus was allowing the sinning woman to touch Him, the Pharisee had practically turned up his nose and shifted his seat farther away in disgust.

At this, Jesus had told His host a story. "Two men owed money to a moneylender," He had said. "One owed a large amount and the other owed a small amount. Neither man was able to repay what he had borrowed, and the moneylender let them both off their debts. Which man would feel more grateful?"

"The one who owed more money," the Pharisee had replied.

"Exactly," Jesus had agreed. "Compare yourself with this sinning woman. You gave me no water to wash with, but this woman has washed my feet with her tears. You gave me no towel to dry them, but she has dried them with her hair. You gave me no kiss of greeting, but she has covered my feet with kisses. You gave me no scent to freshen up with, but this woman

has brought me expensive perfume. I can tell you that all her sins are forgiven, and so she shows me much love."

The other guests had murmured angrily, "Who does this man think He is, to say that He can forgive sins?"

But Jesus hadn't paid any attention to the offended guests' remarks. Instead, He had simply turned to the young woman and smiled. "Your faith has saved you," He had said, gently. "Go in peace."

Alabaster
The perfume bottle in the story is made from a translucent stone called alabaster. Alabaster is very soft and easy to carve; this Turkish relief is made of alabaster. Only expensive perfumes would have been kept in alabaster bottles. Everyday perfumes were kept in pottery jars.

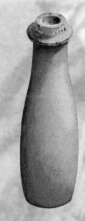

Precious perfume
Perfumes were made from many kinds of plants, herbs, and spices and were imported into Palestine from countries such as India and Egypt. When Mary anoints Jesus with her best perfume, she is honoring Him as a special guest and showing her devotion to Him.

❖ ABOUT THE STORY ❖
The Pharisees thought that by keeping all their religious ceremonies they would be good enough to please God. They forgot that sometimes there was anger, hatred, and greed in their hearts. That was a sin against God. This woman knew she had sinned and said she was sorry. She could be forgiven. People who did not think they had done wrong could not please God. They had to say sorry for their sins, too.

The First Palm Sunday

IT was the week before the great feast of the Passover. Jews from all over Judea were hurrying to Jerusalem for the celebrations, and the authorities were desperate to know whether Jesus would dare visit the temple with all the other worshipers. The chief priests and scribes and Pharisees had given out strict orders that if anyone knew where the "troublemaking" preacher was, they should let them know immediately, so they could arrest Him.

Jesus and His disciples were at Bethany with Mary, Martha, and Lazarus. By the time the authorities heard, hundreds of people had left Jerusalem to see Jesus.

The Jewish elders were furious. They couldn't possibly seize Him in the middle of His supporters. Instead, the chief priests and scribes and Pharisees gathered their spies to them once again.

"We'll have to wait and see if Jesus comes to Jerusalem for Passover," they hissed. "Keep a sharp eye out. He'll probably try to mingle unnoticed among the crowds."

They needn't have gone to such trouble. The Sunday before Passover, Jesus and His disciples set off quite openly for Jerusalem, surrounded by a cheering crowd. The disciples sang Jesus's praises aloud as they accompanied their master to Beth-page, which lay close to the capital city on the Mount of Olives.

"Go into the village," Jesus instructed two of His disciples. "There you will find a donkey tethered to a doorway. Untie it and bring it to me. If anyone asks what you're doing, just say that the Lord needs it."

The men hurried off, and, sure enough, they found the donkey, just as Jesus had said. As soon as the owners found out who it was that wanted to borrow the animal, they threw their robes on its back for a saddle and gladly brought it to Jesus themselves.

"Be careful though," the owners told Jesus. "He might be quite wild. No one has sat on him before."

When Jesus mounted the donkey, it stood still and calm and obedient. It was on the gentle, gray animal's back that Jesus set off again, heading for the holy city.

At this, a new wave of excitement rippled through the crowd accompanying Jesus. The ancient prophets had foretold that the Messiah would one day enter Jerusalem on a donkey! This must be Him, they thought.

Hundreds of men, women, and children came running out to greet Jesus, cheering excitedly. Some took off their robes and spread them out over the road, while others paved the way with broad palm leaves and flowers.

"Hosanna!" they shouted. "Blessed is He who comes in the name of the Lord! Hosanna in the highest!"

All the way to Jerusalem, people poured out to welcome Jesus. When Jesus saw the city itself, He began to weep.

> **"** *So they took branches of palm trees and went out to meet Him.* **"**

"Oh Jerusalem!" He murmured. "Though you greet me now, you will fail to believe that God has come to you. Because of that, you will be utterly destroyed."

Everyone was far too excited to notice Jesus's sorrow, as the joyful procession wound its way around the city.

JESUS ENTERED JERUSALEM LIKE A VICTORIOUS KING. BUT THE VICTORY STILL HAD TO BE WON. HE WOULD DEFEAT SIN AND HIS DEATH ON THE CROSS WHEN HE ROSE FROM THE DEAD. ❧

Palm Sunday
Here is Jesus on the donkey, making His way to Jerusalem. The people lining the route are laying palm leaves on the ground in front of Him. Many churches celebrate Palm Sunday today with processions in which branches of palms are carried.

"Hosanna to the son of David!" they cried. "Blessed is the King who comes in the name of the Lord! Hosanna in the highest!"

"This is outrageous!" the purple-faced Pharisees yelled at Jesus. "These people think that you're the Messiah! Tell them to stop at once!"

"Even if they were silent," Jesus replied, "the very stones would cry out."

Passover meal
Jesus entered Jerusalem in the week before the great Jewish feast of the Passover. People now date the Christian Easter celebration in the same way the Jews decide the date of Passover, based on the Jewish cycle of the moon.

The graceful palm
A palm is a tall tree with a straight, narrow trunk and a cluster of huge feathery leaves at the top. Palm leaves were a symbol of grace and victory. They were laid down in front of Jesus as a mark of respect.

❧ ABOUT THE STORY ❧
King David and his family had ridden on donkeys (or mules) in Old Testament times. There was an Old Testament prophecy that said the Messiah would enter Jerusalem like this. So Jesus was showing that He had come to fulfill the prophecies and that He claimed to be David's successor. It was a powerful visual message. Some people, though, like the Sadducees, did not believe the fulfillment of the prophecy before their eyes.

Jesus in the Temple

JESUS was horrified to find that the great temple of Jerusalem was being used as a marketplace. Money changers were converting foreign coins into Jewish shekels and making handsome profits for themselves. Stallholders were selling sacrificial animals to the pilgrims at ridiculously high prices. Instead of the reverential silence Jesus expected, the buzz of bartering, the lowing of livestock, and the shouting and gossiping of friends assaulted His ears.

Jesus had seen the temple dishonored in this way a couple of years before. With a furious cry of, "Take these things away! You will not make my Father's house into a business place!" Jesus had driven all the traders out by force. It had not taken them long to return.

Now Jesus exploded with even greater anger.

"The temple should be a house of prayer for all the nations of the world!" He roared. "You have made it into a den of thieves!"

Jesus went through the courtyards like a whirlwind. He pushed over the money changers' tables, sending coins spilling onto the floor and cascading down the steps. He smashed open the birdcages, releasing doves into the air. He flung the livestock traders into the dusty streets, sending their cattle and sheep stampeding after them.

Finally, the temple was cleared. It didn't stay empty for long, though. Crowds of people soon flooded back in to see Jesus, packing the courtyard.

"Tell us about God's kingdom!" came the shouts. "What must we do to have our sins forgiven?"

Other voices cried out for healing.

As soon as Jesus began to speak, the temple fell silent as everyone concentrated on His every word.

Each evening through Passover week, Jesus would return to Bethany. Then, every morning, He would go straight back to the temple in Jerusalem. He would stand until nearly dusk, preaching His message of hope and salvation and laying His hands on whoever was in need, making them well again.

When the Jewish elders saw the wonderful things Jesus did and heard the excited children crying out, "Hosanna to the Son of David!" they couldn't stand it. They came stomping right into the middle of the crowds and shook their staffs in Jesus's face.

"By whose permission are you teaching here?" the Jewish dignitaries raged. "Who has given you the authority to stir up the people like this?"

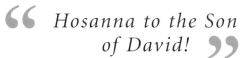

❝ *Hosanna to the Son of David!* **❞**

"Let me ask you a question, and if you can answer it, then I'll tell you," Jesus replied calmly. "Now, who gave my cousin John the right to baptize? Did God want him to do it or was it just the people?"

The Jewish elders scratched their heads.

"If we say God, Jesus will ask us why we didn't believe John's teachings," they argued. "However, if we say the people, the crowds here will probably stone us. For they believe that John was a true prophet from God."

"We don't know!" they spat, their faces like thunder.

USUALLY, PEOPLE GET ANGRY WHEN THEY HAVE BEEN HURT PERSONALLY. JESUS'S ACTION SHOWS THAT GOD FEELS ANGRY AND HURT WHEN PEOPLE DO NOT TAKE HIM AND HIS WORSHIP SERIOUSLY. ∾

Temple traders
Roman traders in the temple are selling doves to be used as sacrifices to God. Jesus is angry when He sees this going on, as this kind of behavior is wrong in a place of worship. To make matters worse, the traders are taking advantage of the pilgrims' faith by charging high prices for the birds.

They knew that they could not give either answer.

"Well, if you can't tell me that," replied Jesus, "then I can't tell you by what authority I say and do these things."

Once again, Jesus had managed to keep the hostile Jewish authorities at bay. However, they weren't about to give up and leave Him alone. For the chief priests, scribes, and Pharisees, plotting Jesus's death had become their number-one concern.

Pilgrims
People who travel to a holy place for religious reasons are called pilgrims. Many of Jesus's followers traveled long distances to see Him and listen to His teachings. These pilgrims are in Jerusalem during Passover week.

Weighing their wares
This bronze steelyard was hung by its upper hook and used by traders for weighing their goods. The object to be weighed was attached to the lower hook, and the acorn-shaped weight was moved along the long arm until it balanced in a straight line.

The Wicked Tenants

BY Tuesday of Passover Week, everyone in Jerusalem knew that Jesus was speaking out against the authorities.

"Once upon a time," Jesus preached, "a man planted a vineyard. When all the work was done, he had to leave for another country. So he brought in tenants to look after the vineyard.

"Time passed, and the owner sent a servant to bring back some of the first crop of grapes for him to sample. The servant returned empty-handed and covered in bruises. The tenants had refused to hand over any crops and had beaten up the servant. The vineyard owner tried again. However, the second servant came back more severely wounded than the first. The third time the vineyard owner sent a servant, he didn't return at all. The tenants killed him.

"Still the vineyard owner didn't give up. He kept on sending servants. The tenants beat up some and murdered others, until there was only one man left: his own son, whom he loved dearly. "Surely they will respect him," the vineyard owner thought. To his great sorrow and regret, the tenants butchered his son just like the others.

> ❝ *'I will send my beloved son.'* ❞

"Now, I will tell you what the vineyard owner will do next," Jesus announced to the crowds in the temple. "He will come and destroy the wicked tenants and give the vineyard to others who deserve it."

Everyone knew that Jesus meant the tenants were the Jewish elders and the vineyard was the kingdom of God. The elders seethed to hear it.

❧ ABOUT THE STORY ❧

Jesus is not just telling this story against the religious leaders of His day. It includes their ancestors, too. It is a sad story that sums up how people had treated God's servants for many centuries. The tenants are the leaders in every age. The servants are prophets whom God sent to call people back to Himself. So often, these servants were ignored or gotten rid of. Soon, this generation of leaders will kill God's Son, Jesus.

Grapes and wine
This glass flask, made to look like a bunch of grapes, would have been used to hold wine. Grapes were very important in Roman times. Grown in vineyards, they were eaten as fresh fruit and dried as raisins. They were also pressed to make juice and wine. The Romans drank a great deal of wine, and wine-making was a well-established business during these times.

Jesus as the son
In this story, Jesus is using the death of the vineyard owner's son to symbolize His own death, as the son of God, at the hands of the Sadducees and Pharisees.

The Barren Fig Tree

ONE morning when Jesus was hurrying from Bethany to Jerusalem, His stomach began to rumble. He had left so early to get to the great temple to begin preaching and healing that He and His disciples had had no time for breakfast. So when Jesus caught sight of a fig tree growing by the roadside, He called a halt for a few seconds and went over to pick some of its juicy fruit for Himself and His companions to eat.

However, when Jesus drew closer to the tall, leafy tree, He was dismayed to find that there wasn't a single fig among the branches.

"May you never grow any fruit ever again!" He cried.

The disciples stood and watched open-mouthed as, all at once, its leaves faded to yellow, then crinkled to brown, then fluttered from the branches to the ground. The tree that had been alive and green just a few moments ago now stood bare and dry and withered.

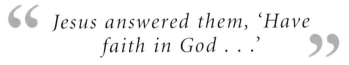

> *Jesus answered them, 'Have faith in God . . .'*

The twelve men gasped. Even though they had witnessed Jesus perform many dramatic miracles, they had never seen Him use His powers except to help people in some way. In fact, whenever anyone had challenged Jesus to prove Himself by performing a miracle "just for show," He had always refused. Now all of a sudden He had destroyed a harmless tree.

"Why?" the stunned disciples spluttered.

"To show that if you only have faith in God, you will find that you can make anything happen," Jesus replied. "I tell you that when you pray, if you truly believe that God has heard you and will answer you, you will surely receive whatever you prayed for. Remember, always forgive others who do you wrong. For then, in turn, your Father in heaven will be able to forgive the things that you yourself do wrong."

Deep in thought, the disciples continued with Jesus on their way. . .

FAITH IS NOT LIKE KNOWLEDGE. IT CANNOT BE TESTED IN AN EXAM TO SEE HOW MUCH WE HAVE GOT. EITHER WE HAVE IT OR WE DO NOT, BECAUSE FAITH IS SIMPLY TRUSTING GOD.

Picking figs
This picture shows a man picking ripe figs from a tree. Along with grapes and olives, figs were an important fruit. The common fig is mentioned more than fifty times in the Bible, and the Hebrew language has four different words for "fig." Figs were eaten as fruit, pressed into fig cakes, and also used in medicine.

❧ ABOUT THE STORY ❧
This is a strange thing for Jesus to do—He did not usually destroy things. It was even harder to understand because it was not the right time of year for figs! Jesus is acting out a parable. God's people are meant to bear fruit—that is, to do what God wants. He is saying that the fig tree stands for God's people who have rejected Him and that they will wither away like the tree. Sure enough, in A.D. 70, the Romans destroyed Judea.

Jesus is Put to the Test

THE Jewish authorities were desperate. "There must be something we can do to stop this Jesus of Nazareth!" the highest Jewish officials discussed in secret. "We can't get rid of Him by force because He's always surrounded by adoring crowds. If we went to arrest Him and they turned on us, we'd be totally outnumbered.

"We've warned everyone that Jesus isn't even a prophet, let alone the Messiah, and we've told the people that He's turning them away from our true religion. They're so bewitched by Jesus that they're not paying any attention.

"We can stand in the middle of the temple and shout and yell and stamp our feet as much as we like. It doesn't seem to have the slightest effect on Jesus."

After a lot of scheming, the chief priests and scribes decided to try a different tack. They ordered their spies to go and mingle with Jesus's

supporters in the temple. They were told to try to lead Him into saying something that would break the law. The Jewish elders rubbed their hands with glee at the thought of finally catching Jesus out. Their enemy would soon be hauled in front of the Roman provincial governor for judgment and punishment—and the harsher the better!

"Teacher," the spies wheedled from among the temple crowds. "We know that you truly teach the way of God. He is the only leader you respect, and the law of heaven is the only law you follow. So what should we do about earthly leaders and earthly laws? For instance, the Roman Emperor Caesar demands that we give him taxes. Should we pay this tribute or not?"

"Why are you putting me to the test?" Jesus said. He wasn't fooled for one second.

> " *Knowing their hypocrisy, He said to them, 'Why put me to the test?'* "

"Look at this coin," Jesus instructed, showing a piece of Roman money to the spies. "Whose head and inscription does it have on it?"

"Caesar's," the spies mumbled.

"Exactly," replied Jesus, flipping the coin at them. "So give to Caesar the things that belong to Caesar, and give to God the things that belong to God."

With his answer, Jesus had dashed the plans of the Jewish elders yet again. Despite their bitter frustration and disappointment, even they couldn't help but be awed by the wisdom of the carpenter's son from Nazareth.

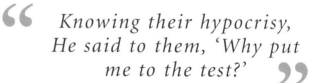

∾ ABOUT THE STORY ∾

One of the big debates among the Jews of the 1st century A.D. was how they should regard the Romans who occupied their country. Some wanted to rebel and fight the Romans. Others accepted the invaders in order to make life easy. So this was a clever question. If Jesus sided with the Romans, He was a traitor to the Jews. If He sided with the Jews, He was a traitor to the Romans. He still got out of it!

The Roman battlefield
The taxes that Caesar demanded were used to run the empire. This included paying for the hated Roman army, pictured here in a battle with barbarians.

Roman standard
The Roman standard was the ceremonial emblem, carried on a pole, by soldiers in the army. The Roman army was the most efficient in the world, and the standard was a symbol of power and strength.

Jewish Elders Try a Trick

THE Sadducees tried to trip Jesus up and expose Him as a fraud. They thought up the trickiest question they could imagine and strode confidently to the temple to put it to Jesus.

"If a woman has been widowed seven times," the smug Sadducees asked Jesus, "which of the seven men she married will be her husband in the life after death?"

The Sadducees didn't know the answer to questions like these, so they had come to the conclusion that life after death couldn't exist. They still thought they were cleverer than everyone else for having come up with the questions at all.

Yet Jesus wasn't at all foxed.

"You know nothing of the scriptures or the power of God," He replied bluntly. "When people are raised from the dead, they are not married. They are like angels in heaven. As for life after death, haven't you read in the scriptures that God said, 'I am the God of Abraham and Isaac and Jacob'? As you know, He's not the God of the dead, He's the God of the living!"

After that, the stunned Sadducees didn't dare ask Jesus any more questions. The Pharisees did.

"What is the greatest of all of God's commandments?" they asked Jesus.

"To love God with all your heart and mind and soul," Jesus replied at once. "Second most important is to love your neighbor as you love yourself. All the other commandments rest on these two."

The Pharisees were dumbstruck. Jesus didn't just know the scriptures better than anyone else, he understood them better, too.

"Now let me ask you a question of my own," Jesus said. "If the Christ is the son of King David, how come in the scriptures David calls the Christ 'Lord'?"

Of course, the Pharisees didn't know the answer. And, as they stood gaping open-mouthed, they heard titters of laughter ripple through the temple crowds.

"This man is making us look like fools!" the chief priests, scribes, Sadducees, and Pharisees raged in private. "We have to get rid of Him if it's the last thing we do!"

Jesus and the saints
This stone carving shows Jesus surrounded by symbolic representations of the saints Matthew, Mark, Luke, and John. These saints wrote the four Gospels, the books in the Bible that tell us about Jesus's life and teaching.

> ❧ **ABOUT THE STORY** ❧
> *The Sadducees accepted only the first five books of the Old Testament, and they would not believe anything that was elsewhere in the Bible. They were very unpopular and acted in a very superior way. They loved intellectual arguments, which were of no help to people who wanted to know God better. They were not open to what God might say; they just wanted to prove that Jesus was not one of them.*

The Great Denunciation

THE trouble between Jesus and the Jewish authorities had reached boiling point. It was as if the temple itself were split into a battlefield, with the chief priests and scribes mustering their forces on one side, while Jesus roused His loyal troops on the other.

"The scribes and Pharisees follow in the footsteps of Moses," Jesus preached, in a loud, clear voice. "So do as they say." He paused for a second, to make sure He had everyone's full attention. "However, make sure you don't do as they do, for they are hypocrites!"

The hundreds of listeners gasped as if with one voice.

Jesus's eyes sparkled with anger. His hair bristled with outrage. "Everything they do is for show!" He roared. "They recite long, elaborate prayers many times a day, but they stand in full view of everyone to do it, to make sure that they are seen and admired by all. They wear long, fancy robes to make sure that everyone notices them. They make sure they sit up front at feasts and at the synagogue, so that everyone knows they are there. They tell you to address them as 'Rabbi,' so they can feel that they're superior to you all."

Both murmurs of agreement and gasps of shock came from the crowd.

"Well," Jesus went on, "I tell you to call no one 'Rabbi.' You have one master, who is the Christ. You have one teacher. You have one father—our Father in Heaven—and you are all brothers and sisters. I can assure you that whoever sets themselves up as superior to others will one day find themselves the lowest of the low. Whoever does their best to serve others will one day find themselves honored with greatness."

Jesus shook His head sadly. "Yes, I feel sorry for the scribes and Pharisees," He cried, "for they will never see heaven themselves. Worst of all, these blind fools are leading you, the general public, astray, so they're shutting the gates of the kingdom not just against themselves but against others, too."

The crowd erupted into a clamor of outrage.

"Let me give you an example," Jesus said. "They tell you that an oath on the temple is meaningless, but an oath on the sacred temple gold is binding. This is ridiculous! For which is greater: the gold or the temple which made the gold sacred? Similarly, they tell you that to swear by the altar means nothing, yet to swear by a holy altar sacrifice is to make a solemn vow! Nonsense, again! For which is greater: the sacrifice itself or the altar which makes the sacrifice holy?"

The listening men and women looked at each other. It was hard to argue with that type of logic. . . .

Jesus continued, "So I tell you that anyone who swears by the temple swears by it and by He whose house it is!"

Ripples of applause broke out among the stunned crowd. The temple was full, and everyone was listening intently to Jesus's words.

"Furthermore," Jesus went on, "the scribes and Pharisees tell you that the hundreds of tiny rules they follow are vitally important. By doing so, they put a heavy burden on the shoulders of anyone who wants to follow God. Moreover, their preoccupation with minor matters causes them to neglect the weightier matters of the law, such as justice and mercy and faith! I tell you that the scribes and Pharisees are like whitewashed tombs, which from the outside appear beautiful, but on the inside are full of dead men's bones. They are the sons of those men who, through history, were so blinded by their own self-righteousness that they refused to listen to the prophets. Even today, they are persecuting, driving out, and killing the very people sent by God to help and warn them. O Jerusalem! How many times have I tried to show you the way to salvation? Yet your house is tumbling into ruins! You will not see me again until you say, 'Blessed is He who comes in the name of the Lord.'"

Jesus looked around at the hundreds of faces in the crowd. Angry discussions were breaking out between those who agreed with His criticism of the elders and those who thought He had gone too far. Jesus could see that many of the men and women hadn't really grasped what He meant.

His eyes fell on a tiny, bent-over old woman, hobbling to the temple collection box on crooked legs. Younger, richer people were sweeping past her, nearly knocking her over. One by one, they dropped in their handful of silver or gold with a smile of self-satisfaction and stalked away, head held high. Eventually, the poor widow reached the collection box for her turn. She shoved a shaky hand into her tattered pocket and brought out two coppers—the only money she had left in all the world. She dropped the coins into the box without a moment's hesitation and stood for a while, saying a silent prayer, before hobbling away.

Jesus smiled, and pointed the poor and feeble woman out to everyone in the crowd that had gathered around Him.

> **'Truly, I tell you, this poor widow has put in more than all of them.'**

"That widow has done more good than all the scribes and Pharisees put together," He told the hushed throng. "For they donate only as much as they reckon they can afford, making sure they still have riches left over. This woman has very little, yet she has given it all for the love of God."

Synagogues
A synagogue is the Jewish place of worship. It also serves as a center for the Jewish community. There are religious services three times a day, with readings and prayers. The religious teacher at the synagogue is called the rabbi. Synagogues may date back to the exile in Babylon in the 500s B.C., when the people were far from Jerusalem and had no temple. By the time of Jesus, most Jews outside Jerusalem came together on the sabbath at their local synagogue.

❧ ABOUT THE STORY ❧

Many people think that pleasing God is a matter of keeping certain rules. That is quite natural. Rules give us a structure for daily life. Jesus never said we should ignore God's rules; He encouraged people to keep them. The rules the Pharisees kept had been made up by them. They were customs. The main rules that God and Jesus want us to keep are to love God from our hearts and to love others as we do ourselves.

The End of the World

JESUS headed back to Bethany for the night. His footsteps were heavy as He trudged wearily along the road, His mind full of the troubles that He knew were close at hand. Jesus began to silently pray to His Father in heaven, asking for guidance and courage. Suddenly His thoughts were disturbed by gasps of awe from His disciples behind Him.

"Look, Master!" came their voices. "How wonderful!"

Jesus spun round to see what His disciples were marveling at—a fantastic view of the whole of Jerusalem, glowing in the setting sun. The huddles of whitewashed houses nestling in the hills were shimmering pink and orange. The gardens that overflowed down the slopes were flooded with rosy light. Towering over everything, the holy temple itself was ablaze against the skyline, golden fire rippling across its pillars.

"The house of God is truly magnificent!" the disciples cried. "Absolutely breathtaking!"

Jesus nodded His head sadly.

"Take a good look," He said, "and remember. For I tell you that the day will come when not a single stone of all this will remain standing."

With that, Jesus turned back on His way, leaving His disciples puzzled, murmuring among themselves.

"Whatever can He mean?" they wondered, hurrying to catch up. "How would the temple be destroyed? When? Who would dare to pull it down?"

Later, Peter, James, John, and Andrew drew Jesus to one side and spoke with Him in private.

"Lord, can you tell us when the end will be?" they asked Jesus. "What signs will there be to show us that it's about to happen?"

Jesus sat quietly for a while, His all-seeing eyes gazing far off into the distance. Then He looked at His friends and sighed.

"The end will not come," He said, "until nation has risen against nation, and kingdom against kingdom. There will be wars and earthquakes and famines, and this will still only be the beginning. Before the time draws near, my gospel must be preached throughout the world to all peoples. You who follow me and who spread my teachings will be persecuted for my sake—even by those whom you most love. You will suffer being beaten and put on trial and even executed. You must have courage to be my witness in spite of it all. The Holy Spirit will tell you what to

say and will give you the strength to endure through everything that is sent to test you. In the end, whoever has stood firm will be saved.

"Be very careful that no one leads you astray. There will be many who come in my name, saying, 'I am the Christ,' but you must not listen to these false prophets. They will

work wonders and show you great signs and warn you that the end is about to come—all to get you to abandon me and follow them. Do not believe them. Remember that I told you all this would happen, and take heart.

"When the end of time finally draws near, the sun will darken, and the moon will no longer give out light. The stars will fall from the skies, and the seas will rise up against the earth. People everywhere will tremble with fear and faint with terror at what is happening, for the very powers of the heavens will be shaken. But my faithful followers should not be afraid. It is then that you should raise your heads and look up with glad hearts. For your salvation will then arrive. The Son of Man will come riding on the clouds in all His glory with all the angels. He will send them out on the winds to all four corners of the earth, and He will gather every single good person to Him.

> 66 *'Take heed, watch; for you do not know when the time will come.'* 99

"When exactly this will happen, I cannot tell you. No one knows—not the angels in heaven, not the Son of Man —only the Father Himself. Be ever watchful. You do not want God to come suddenly and find you sleeping. For if the Lord comes on a day you do not expect, and you have left it too late to prepare yourself, there will be no hope for you. You will be cast out into hell, where souls suffer eternal punishment, and you will be left to weep and wail for ever in the darkness of utter despair."

❧ ABOUT THE STORY ❧

Jesus taught a lot about the future, but He never gave people enough detail to enable them to work out exactly what would happen when. In fact, "the end of time" in the Bible is really the whole period between Jesus's resurrection and His return or "second coming." He says people are not to waste time trying to work out what the future will be, but to use their time wisely so that they are ready for anything.

Destroying the temple
As Jesus predicted, the temple in Jerusalem was destroyed by the Romans, in A.D. 70. This stone relief shows them plundering the temple and stealing its treasures.

The end of the world
This is the explosion of a nuclear bomb. In the story, Jesus warns His disciples that the world will come to an end and tells them to be prepared for this. Today, many people see the image of a nuclear explosion as a symbol of the end of the world brought about by humankind.

Judas Plots Betrayal

THE chief priests and scribes, Pharisees and Sadducees, were at their wits' end. They had tried to trick Jesus and it hadn't worked. The crafty Nazarene troublemaker had foiled every trap they had laid. No, cunning was no good. The Jewish elders would have to go back to their first option—force. They still had the same old problem—Jesus's crowds of supporters felt so passionately about their teacher that they'd fight tooth and nail to defend Him. Even though the authorities desperately wanted Jesus out of the way, they didn't want to risk their own lives in doing it.

Secretly, the Jewish elders gathered together in the palace of the high priest, Caiaphas. They brainstormed and schemed and argued long into the night, and came up with just one possibility. Sooner or later, they decided, Jesus would be on His own, without the support of His disciples. They would have to seize the moment with both hands. They would approach Jesus by surprise, backed up with troops, and arrest Him swiftly and without any fuss. The elders were determined that nothing would go wrong this time. The opportunity would be rare and they might only get one chance.

One big hurdle still remained. Even with their spies in the crowds, the Jewish dignitaries couldn't watch Jesus every minute of every day and night. After all, He was closely flanked by His twelve disciples at all times, and they disappeared off together now and again in private. However were the elders going to be able to find out where and when to make their move?

Who knows, the Jewish authorities might never have gotten the chance at all if it hadn't been for a traitor inside the camp. Months before, Jesus had warned the disciples that one of them would turn to evil. The shocked men hadn't been able to believe it and had instantly laughed it off. Even so, the thought had haunted them for a while. Which one of them was Jesus talking about? What kind of evil could they possibly turn to? As time had passed, each one of the twelve had pushed the ridiculous thought farther and farther to the back of their minds until they had all totally forgotten it.

Roman atrium
Wealthy people, such as Caiaphas would have received guests in a large hall, called an atrium, inside the front door. This picture of an atrium in Pompeii shows that the roof was open to the sky, to let in light. An atrium often contained a pool, which helped to keep it cool, as well as plants and statues.

Caiaphas's house
This picture shows the stone steps that lead up to Caiaphas's house. Caiaphas was the Jewish high priest and, as such, was the head of the Sanhedrin (the Jewish high court). Meetings such as the one described in this story may have been held in Caiaphas's house in order to keep them secret.

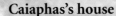

Yet Satan hadn't forgotten. He had been niggling away at the heart of Judas Iscariot for some time now, playing on his weaknesses, eating away at his doubts, filling him up with the poison of jealousy. On the fateful night that the elders sat plotting in Caiaphas's palace, Judas found that a wicked idea popped into his head as if from nowhere.

> ## *Then Satan entered into Judas called Iscariot, who was of the number of the twelve.*

The chief priests and scribes, Pharisees and Sadducees, never found out what made Judas Iscariot do what he did. In any case, they didn't care. In the end, they were just glad that he came knocking on their door, although at first they glowered at him with suspicion.

"Everyone knows that you're after Jesus of Nazareth," Judas swaggered. "Well, I'm one of His most trusted friends."

"Y-e-s," the high priest uttered in a low voice. "Go on . . ."

Under Caiaphas's stony gaze, beads of sweat began to break out on Judas's forehead. His dull eyes blinked shiftily.

"Surely I'm exactly what you need. Someone who can get closer to Jesus than you ever could," he blustered, "if the price is right, of course."

An excited murmur went around the table, and eager smiles lit up the elders' wrinkled faces. They could hardly believe their good fortune! Urgently, the corrupt officials huddled together and conferred for a while.

It seemed like a lifetime to Judas, all alone in the middle of Caiaphas's great hall, with his heart pounding inside his chest. Finally, the Jewish elders settled themselves back into their chairs and arranged their robes around them.

"We will pay you thirty pieces of silver for delivering Jesus of Nazareth into our hands," they announced haughtily. "No more and no less."

Judas swallowed hard.

"Done," he said.

After a quick drink with his new friends to seal the matter, he hurried off into the night. There wasn't a moment to lose if he was going to claim that reward.

Love of money
The Jewish priests hand over the money to Judas. Judas is prepared to betray Jesus to satisfy his own greed. The Bible states that you cannot serve both God and money, and that money should be valued for what can be done with it, not in its own right.

❧ ABOUT THE STORY ❧

No one knows exactly why Judas betrayed Jesus. He seems to have been a loyal member of the disciples up until then. He was probably motivated by several reasons, money being the least of them. He may have been very mixed up about who Jesus was and what He had come to do. Maybe he thought this action would help. His action, though, warns readers that even those closest to Jesus can turn from Him, or even against Him.

Jesus Faces His Betrayer

JESUS knew that time was running out. He would very soon be leaving the troubles and wickedness of this world and would return to His Father in heaven. He was filled with great sadness at the thought of leaving behind all those He loved on earth. He and His twelve closest friends would be able to share just one more evening together—the Passover supper. Yet in order to enjoy each other's company for the last time, they had to keep the arrangements secret, so Jesus's enemies couldn't find Him.

"Go into Jerusalem and watch for a man carrying a pitcher of water to pass by," Jesus instructed two of His disciples. "Follow him and he will lead you to a certain house. Ask the owner of the house to show you where your teacher is to celebrate the Passover. You will then be taken to a large upstairs room where you'll find all you need to make everything ready."

Later that evening, the disciples made their way cautiously to the appointed meeting place. Their mood was serious. It certainly wasn't going to be the joyful Passover supper of previous years. This time, everyone was deeply worried. Only two days before, Jesus had warned His friends once again that He was soon to fall into the hands of His opponents and that they would put Him to death. Even though the disciples still couldn't bring themselves to believe it, they were all very on edge. It was an extremely somber group of men who sat down to eat that night.

The disciples were stirred from their grim thoughts when Jesus suddenly stood up, took off His outer robes, tied a towel around His waist and filled a bowl with water. They realized with shock that He was preparing Himself to wash the dust from their feet—a job usually done by the lowliest servants.

Then Jesus came and knelt down beside Peter, who was horrified.

"Master, I can't allow you to do that for me!" Peter cried, laying hold of Jesus's hands.

"You don't understand now what I'm doing," Jesus replied, "but trust me—later you will." Peter was adamant and swung his legs out of reach.

"I'll never let you wash my feet, Lord," he said, firmly.

"Then I can't call you my friend," Jesus said to him with a sad smile.

"Well, in that case, wash my head and hands too!" Peter urged his friend and master.

"No," said Jesus, gently wetting Peter's feet. "Anyone who bathes needs only to have their feet washed to take away the dust from the road."

Jesus busied Himself with the towel.

"All of you are clean—except for one," He said to

Jesus the servant
Jesus took on the role of a servant and washed His disciples' feet. He taught His followers to serve each other as equals.

Foot washing
Most people wore open sandals, so their feet quickly became dirty. It was therefore customary for guests to have their feet washed on arrival at a house. A servant would usually carry out this task, using a water bowl like the one shown here.

Himself. He moved around the group of friends, attending to them in turn, and returned to His place at the table.

"You call me 'teacher' and 'Lord,'" He said to the twelve companions, "and that's what I am. Just as I have stooped to wash your feet, so you should humble yourselves before others. Remember that a servant is not greater than his master, and always show other people the kindness, care, and respect that I have shown you today."

Jesus paused for a moment and sighed a heavy sigh. His brow grew furrowed and His face darkened.

> ## For He knew who was to betray Him.

"One of you will betray me," He said in a low voice.

Hurt cries of protest went up from all around the table, and Jesus held up His hand for quiet. He refused to say anything more and motioned for everyone to return to their meal.

As the disciples went back to their eating and chatting, Peter found he had suddenly lost his appetite. He signaled to John, who was sitting nearest to Jesus.

"Please ask Jesus to tell us who He means," Peter whispered.

John leaned over for a moment and murmured to His master, and the hushed answer came back, "The one to whom I will give this bread."

Peter watched as, slowly and deliberately, Jesus tore off a piece of His bread, dipped it into the dish in front of Him and offered it to Judas Iscariot.

"Do what you have to do," Jesus said quietly, "but do it quickly."

Without a word, Judas got up from the table and left the room.

The disciples who noticed him go thought that Jesus was sending him on some kind of errand—perhaps to buy some more wine, or to go to distribute some food to the poor. They didn't give him more than a sideways glance.

Yet Jesus had looked deep into Judas's eyes. He had seen that they were cold and hard.

E SOMETIMES PREFER TO BOSS PEOPLE AROUND RATHER THAN BE KIND. JESUS'S EXAMPLE SHOWS PRESENT-DAY DISCIPLES THAT NO JOB IS BENEATH THEM IF IT HELPS OTHERS. IT TAKES COURAGE TO HELP PEOPLE.

Teachers and pupils

Much of Jesus's teaching took place in the temple, which was officially used as a school for Jewish children. Many Roman children, though, did not go to school since they had to work. Richer children went to an elementary school between the ages of six and eleven. After this, some boys went to a secondary school.

The Last Supper

JESUS motioned for His eleven friends around the table to fall quiet. Soon, all attention was fixed firmly on Him.

Jesus reached out for a hunk of bread. He shut His eyes and lifted the bread up heavenward. Loud and clear, He said a blessing over it, giving thanks to God. Then Jesus broke the bread into pieces and handed it around to each of the disciples.

"Take it . . . eat it, . . ." He said, pressing the bits of bread into His friends' hands. "This is my body, which will be given up for you."

The wide-eyed men did as their master instructed.

Next, Jesus poured some wine. He reverently lifted the goblet up and blessed it, praising God aloud. Then Jesus held the brimming cup out to His friends. "Take this, all of you, and drink from it," He said. "This is my blood, the seal of a new and everlasting promise from God. My blood will be spilled for you and for all people so that your sins may be forgiven."

> " *'This is my body which is given for you. Do this in remembrance of me.'* "

One by one, the disciples took the goblet to their lips and drank.

"I am giving you a new commandment," Jesus told them. "To love each other as I have loved you. Then everyone will know that you are my followers. May my peace always be with you. Don't let your hearts be troubled, and don't be afraid. Just follow everything that I have told you and be joyful. For you will know that I am alive in the Father, that you are alive in me, and that I am alive in you. If you keep my commandments, you will show that you truly love me. My Father in turn will love you."

Jesus rose to His feet. "Now come," He said, opening His arms and smiling at His friends. "Accompany me to the Mount of Olives. I should like to pray for a while in the Garden of Gethsemane."

As they walked through the moonlight, Jesus continued to talk. He had many things still to tell the disciples and only a little time left in which to say them.

"I want you to do the things I've done tonight as a way of remembering me," Jesus told the disciples. "For I will be with you only a short while longer and then I must go away. Where I am going, you cannot follow."

The disciples turned to each other in disbelief.

"Lord, where are you going?" Peter cried.

"I will not leave you forever," Jesus consoled them. "I am going to prepare a place for you in my Father's house. I will return for a while, and then I will have to go away again. Even though you won't be able to see me anymore, I'll always be with you—inside your hearts. Later on, when the time comes, you will follow me and we will all be together again."

Peter couldn't bear the thought of Jesus leaving them. "No!" he insisted, stopping in his tracks. "Why can't we follow you now?"

Jesus looked at His companions sadly. "By the end of the night, you will all have deserted me," He said.

Site of the supper
Jesus's last meal with His disciples is traditionally believed to have been held in the building shown above. It is called the Coenaculum and is situated on Mount Zion in Jerusalem.

The Holy Grail
In medieval legend, the Holy Grail is the cup used by Jesus at the Last Supper, or the dish that was on the table during the meal. The medieval knights of the Round Table went on quests to find the Grail which are described in the stories of King Arthur, written from the 1200s onward. The word "grail" comes from the Old French word "greal," meaning a kind of dish. The image of the Grail is also used to represent the human body containing the Holy Spirit.

CHRISTIANS HAVE DIFFERENT VIEWS ABOUT THE WAY THEY SHOULD CELEBRATE THIS LAST SUPPER. SOME CALL IT MASS, OTHERS EUCHARIST OR HOLY COMMUNION, SOME THE LORD'S SUPPER OR BREAKING OF BREAD. FOR ALL THEIR DIFFERENCES, THEY AGREE THAT THIS IS THE CENTER OF WORSHIP. IN SHARING BREAD AND WINE, THEY SHOW THEY DEPEND ON GOD AND WANT TO DRAW ON HIS GRACE FOR THEIR LIVES. ❧

"Not me!" Peter cried. "I will never desert you! I would lay down my life for you!"

There was a chorus of agreement from the other disciples, who were just as shocked.

"Would you, Peter?" Jesus said softly. "My friend, before you hear the cock crow to greet the dawn, you will have denied three times that you know me."

Peter almost wept.

"I will never deny that I know you," he gulped, "even if it means that I have to die with you."

Remembering Jesus
This is a picture of the Last Supper by the Italian artist Leonardo da Vinci. Christians today commemorate Jesus's last meal with His disciples by eating and drinking holy bread and wine. The bread and wine are referred to as the body and the blood of Christ.

In the Garden of Gethsemane

In the Garden of Gethsemane, the disciples yawned wearily. "Stay here and rest," Jesus said kindly to the disciples.

As the grateful men began to collapse to the ground, Jesus stopped Peter, James, and John.

"My friends, I know you are tired, too," He said, "but would you keep me company?"

The three disciples saw that Jesus's face was creased with sorrow and His eyes sparkled oddly. They accompanied Him farther on. They had never seen Jesus so sad and troubled before. "I must be on my own to talk to my Father," He said. "My heart is so heavy, I fear it is breaking. Will you watch over me while I pray?"

Peter, James, and John looked on helplessly as Jesus sank to His knees, clutching His head in His hands.

"Oh my Father!" Jesus cried out from His soul.

He felt the sins of all the world pressing in on Him from all sides, and He knew the horror of what lay ahead. "Father, nothing is impossible for you. I beg you, please take away the suffering that I have to face."

Jesus prayed for a long while and Peter, James, and John were overcome by sleep. "Couldn't you have stayed awake just one more hour for me?" Jesus whispered to them. "Be careful of temptation," He said, softly. "Your spirits are willing, but your flesh is weak."

Again He prayed, "If this torment must come, then I will endure it. Your will, not mine, should be done."

Eventually Jesus arose and went back to His friends.

"I beg you, wake up!" He whispered urgently.

The three exhausted men stirred, but didn't wake.

Trembling, Jesus returned to His lonely prayers.

"Father, I know the hour has come," He groaned. "Give me the strength to die gloriously. Holy Father, look after these people so they may reach you safely. I pray also for those whom I haven't met, but who believe because they hear about me through others."

> ❝ *'Judas, would you betray the Son of Man with a kiss?'* ❞

Jesus returned one last time to Peter, James, and John.

"Are you still sleeping?" He murmured. "No matter. It's time. Look, my betrayer is here."

Suddenly, flaming torches came flashing through the dark. Shadows loomed forward from all around.

The disciples woke and dashed to Jesus's side. They faced a band of armed men—hirelings of the elders.

We don't often think of Jesus's needing us, only of our needing Him. However, on this occasion, when He needed His friends to encourage and help Him, they failed. Today, Jesus needs people to be His hands and His voice in the world. Each time He is let down, His tears flow again. ∾

Jesus's retreat
The Garden of Gethsemane was situated to the east of Jerusalem, near the Mount of Olives. In Hebrew, "Gethsemane" means "oil press," and this is where the mountain olives were brought to be pressed into oil.

Kneeling to pray
Jesus and his disciples often went to pray in the Garden of Gethsemane. The way Jesus went down on his knees to pray gave rise to the Christian custom of kneeling to pray.

"Who are you looking for?" Jesus asked.

"Jesus of Nazareth!" the men shouted angrily.

"I am He," announced Jesus.

There was something so powerful in His voice and manner that the thugs shrank back nervously.

Then a face the disciples knew well came forward.

"Master!" said Judas Iscariot, greeting Jesus with his usual embrace.

"Oh Judas," Jesus sighed sadly, "must you betray me with a kiss?"

It was the sign the thugs had been waiting for, and they leaped forward to seize their enemy.

Jesus didn't resist, but the disciples flung themselves at the soldiers. Peter had brought a sword, but his wild slashes only cut off the right ear of the high priest's servant.

"Enough!" roared Jesus. "Put away your sword, Peter, for those who use violence die by violence. If my Father meant for me to be protected, armies of angels would speed to my rescue."

Jesus touched the wound. At once, the ear was healed. Then Jesus turned to the mob.

"Am I a criminal, that you come to take me like this?" He demanded. "Every day I was there in the temple. Yet this fulfills the prophecies. It is evil's greatest hour."

With that, Jesus was marched away. Panic broke out among his followers, and as the remaining guards turned on the yelling crowd, the disciples fled for their lives.

Betrayed with a kiss
When Judas kisses Jesus, he is giving a signal to the soldiers. Jesus is sad that His disciple has betrayed Him with a kiss, which was normally given as a sign of affection or respect.

Christ's passion
Jesus expressed His anguish at His fate in a prayer to God. He knew that His mental pain would be even worse than the physical punishment He was to endure.

❧ ABOUT THE STORY ❧
Jesus knew, and He had always known, that He would be crucified in Jerusalem. He had foretold it often enough to his apostles, but knowing it did not make it any easier. Crucifixion was a horrible, painful way to die. The human side of Jesus almost opted out of His divine calling. Despite His struggle with His natural human fears, He knew that God's eternal will was more important than His short-term suffering.

Peter's Denial

MARCHING along to the soldiers' rhythm, Jesus saw the mighty city of Jerusalem rearing up in front of Him. Guards held Him tight on either side, and lowered spears were aimed at the ready at His back. Without slowing the pace, the soldiers tramped straight through the city gates and along the streets to the grand house of Caiaphas, the high priest. All the time, following behind them was Peter, cloaked by the night. He made sure he kept at a safe distance, but he didn't let Jesus out of his sight for a single instant. Peter even followed the soldiers right into Caiaphas's courtyard. Then he could go no farther. Jesus was taken through Caiaphas's huge front doors, and they slammed shut. Peter's friend had disappeared from view and he himself was shut out in the cold.

Peter turned and found himself looking into the curious faces of strangers. The high priest's servants and maids had built themselves a fire in the middle of the courtyard, and they were huddled around it to keep warm. Trying not to draw any more attention to himself, Peter drew his robe farther over his face and lowered his head. He edged nearer the circle of people to join them and did his best to enter into the general conversation.

Even though Peter was now standing near the blazing fire, nothing could take away the cold fear that grasped his heart. Ice seemed to be running through his veins, and it was as if an empty blackness were eating away at his stomach. Peter shuddered, and a serving maid peered at him through the flickering flames. A look of recognition crossed her face, and she pointed her finger at him.

"You're one of the prisoner's followers, aren't you?" she blurted out.

Peter's heart began to race. Here he was, all alone in the midst of his enemies.

"Of course not!" he muttered. "I don't know what you mean."

Very gradually, Peter shifted into the shadows a little.

As he sat alone and shivered, footsteps drew near.

"You are," said another serving maid, looking hard into Peter's face.

She raised her voice to her co-workers around the fire. "This man was with Jesus of Nazareth," she cried.

"No I wasn't," Peter insisted frantically. "I don't know anyone of that name."

He gathered his robes more tightly around him and hoped desperately that no one would notice that he was breaking out into a cold sweat.

"You must be one of Jesus's followers," said a servant, coming right up close. "You speak with a Galilean accent."

The crowing of the cock
Many people kept poultry, and the sound of a cock crowing at dawn would have been a familiar one. It was a signal that the night was over and the next day was beginning.

Peter
Peter's denying that he knows Jesus is an example of human weakness. Even the most dedicated followers of Jesus are vulnerable when their loyalty is tested. This reminds us that only God can provide us with the strength to avoid temptation.

Galilee
The area in northern Israel where Jesus and Peter grew up is called Galilee. It is mostly hilly, with a large lake known as the Sea of Galilee. Galilee was a much wealthier region than Judea, having made the most of the Roman occupation, and its people were not popular in Jerusalem. The people who accused Peter recognized his strong Galilean accent.

"Yes," said another, moving in toward them. "Didn't I see you in the garden with Him?"

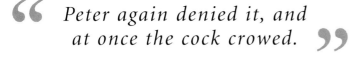

> *Peter again denied it, and at once the cock crowed.*

Peter sprang to his feet in terror. His voice was high and shrill. "I've told you!" he cried. "I don't know the man!"

As the servants nervously backed away, a raucous noise ripped through the air—the sound of a rooster. Peter's heart began to pound in his chest as he remembered Jesus's words: "My friend, before you hear the cock crow to greet the dawn, you will have denied three times that you know me." Then the tears began to pour uncontrollably from Peter's eyes, and filled with utter misery and sadness, he stole away to be by himself with his shame.

Peter's weakness
Peter denies that he knows Jesus. When Jesus had predicted this, Peter had been adamant that he would die before denying Him. However, concern for his own safety took precedence, and Peter was not strong enough to stand by his master and friend. Jesus had known this would happen.

Armed with spears
The soldiers who arrested Jesus would have carried spears similar to the ones shown here. Earlier spears had now been replaced by the heavy javelin (called a *pilum*), which had a sharp, narrow point. The javelin was thrown through the air, and its point could pierce the shield and even the armor of an enemy.

❖ ABOUT THE STORY ❖
While he was with Jesus and the other disciples, Peter was brave and determined. Once he was on his own, his courage melted away. He was confused and frightened. This story shows the human side of one of Jesus's greatest followers. It shows that even the best can fail, even when they expect to succeed. Peter's mistake was to stop trusting God just when he needed that trust most. The good news was that later Peter was forgiven.

Trial Before the Sanhedrin

CAIAPHAS'S palace was filled with a sinister silence. Jesus's footsteps echoed as he was marched down the long corridors, then through a big, heavy door. Jesus found himself in an important-looking chamber. Annas, the former high priest, was standing at the window. "So this is the famous Jesus of Nazareth," he said.

He looked Jesus straight in the eye.

"I've heard so much about you," he said, with a stony smile, "but I'd rather hear it from your own lips."

Then the questioning started. What did Jesus think about the scriptures? What miracles did He claim to have worked? Who did He think He was? Throughout it all, Jesus remained quiet and calm. He didn't say a word, even when Annas peered closely into His face. Finally, the former high priest lost his temper.

"Answer me!" he spat. "Or I'll have you thrown into prison until you find your tongue!"

"I have always spoken openly," Jesus replied softly. "I have preached in public. I have never taught in secret, so why ask me about my work? Why don't you ask any of the people who came to hear me?"

SMACK! A guard's hand stung Jesus's cheek. "Is that how you talk to your betters?" the soldier raged.

"If I have said anything wrong, explain to me what it is," Jesus said. "If not, why have you hit me?"

Annas had had enough. He was getting nowhere.

"Take him away!" he barked.

Jesus was marched off to Caiaphas, the high priest, and the council of Jewish elders, the Sanhedrin. The officials

Money changers
The priests in the story are described as corrupt because they took advantage of their positions to increase their own wealth. They insisted that only one currency be used to pay taxes at the temple and to buy sacrificial animals. Money changers exchanged currency for the worshipers at the temple, charging them for this service. The priests claimed part of the proceeds for themselves, and this was one of the things for which Jesus condemned them.

Public meetings
Jesus used to preach a great deal in public places. He often used open spaces in the countryside so all the people could hear Him. Open-air theatres, like this one, were built throughout the Roman Empire and could accommodate large crowds.

began to fire false accusations at Jesus. They even brought out false witnesses whom they'd bribed with money. Yet no two witnesses could be found to agree on a story.

Eventually, a couple of men came forward.

"We both heard this man say that He could destroy the temple of God and rebuild it in three days," they agreed.

Jesus had said this, but He had been referring to His own body. He was foretelling that He would be raised up to life three days after His death. The men, like most people, had misunderstood.

> ❝ *I have said nothing secretly.* ❞

"Have you nothing to say to that?" Caiaphas raged. Still Jesus didn't move a muscle.

"Right!" Caiaphas yelled, losing all patience. "I order you to tell us, under solemn oath, whether you think you're the Son of God!"

When Jesus spoke, there was majesty in His voice.

"I am," he said, "and one day you will see the Son of Man seated at the right hand of the Father in Heaven."

"Blasphemy!" Caiaphas bellowed, purple with fury. "He has insulted God! What shall we do with Him?"

"Put Him to death!" the elders roared.

At long last, they had Jesus where they wanted. They blindfolded Him and spat on Him, and punched and kicked Him, saying, "Let's hear you prophesy, now, Christ! Tell us who it was that struck you!" Their laughter rang through the night.

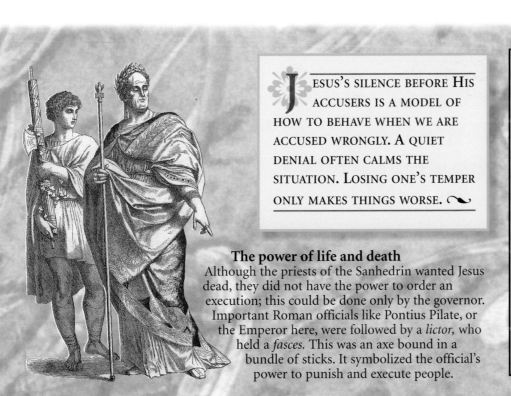

J ESUS'S SILENCE BEFORE HIS ACCUSERS IS A MODEL OF HOW TO BEHAVE WHEN WE ARE ACCUSED WRONGLY. A QUIET DENIAL OFTEN CALMS THE SITUATION. LOSING ONE'S TEMPER ONLY MAKES THINGS WORSE. ❧

The power of life and death
Although the priests of the Sanhedrin wanted Jesus dead, they did not have the power to order an execution; this could be done only by the governor. Important Roman officials like Pontius Pilate, or the Emperor here, were followed by a *lictor,* who held a *fasces.* This was an axe bound in a bundle of sticks. It symbolized the official's power to punish and execute people.

❖ **ABOUT THE STORY** ❖

When Jesus first mentioned to His apostles that He was the Son of God, He made it clear to them that they were not to tell anyone. He did this because people were expecting the Messiah to be an earthly soldier and leader who would fight the Romans and force them to leave Judea. However, now Jesus knows that the time for Him to reveal the truth has arrived. He can tell the truth, and the prophecies will be fulfilled by Him.

Pontius Pilate

EVEN though the chief priests and scribes had passed sentence, one more hurdle lay in front of them: an execution could be ordered only by the Roman governor, Pontius Pilate. They didn't have a moment to waste . . .

The whole of Jerusalem awoke that morning to the news that the elders had condemned Jesus of Nazareth to death. When the gossip reached the ears of Judas Iscariot, he was appalled at what he had done. Filled with shame and remorse, he ran to the temple as fast as he could to try to put things right.

"I have committed a terrible sin!" he cried to the chief priests. "Jesus is innocent, and I have betrayed Him!"

The Jewish officials just stared at Judas coldly.

"That's not our problem," they said. "It's yours."

Despair flooded over Judas. He threw his thirty pieces of silver onto the temple floor and ran out into the city streets. Later, Judas Iscariot's body was found hanging. He was too disgusted with himself to go on living.

Meanwhile, in another part of the city, Jesus was standing in Pontius Pilate's judgment hall. The Roman governor looked at the weary, bruised man and then said, "So, are you the King of the Jews?"

"Are you asking me this for yourself," Jesus replied softly to the governor, "or because you've heard other people say it about me?"

Pilate looked away from Jesus's steady gaze. "Look," he said seriously, "your own people and priests have handed you over to me. Tell me what you've done."

"My kingship is not of this world," Jesus said. "If it were, my servants would have fought to prevent my being handed over to the Jews."

"So you are a king?" the intrigued Pilate challenged.

"Yes," said Jesus. "I was born for this and I came into the world to bear witness to the truth."

Pilate paused for a while, deep in thought.

"The Jewish elders tell me that you've been plotting against the Roman government," he said.

Jesus said nothing.

"They say that you're rousing up the Jews against us," Pilate continued, "that you're encouraging them not to pay Caesar's taxes, and setting yourself up as their leader."

Again, Jesus remained silent.

Roman Robur
When Jesus was beaten by the Roman soldiers, He was probably taken to a robur like this one. It was a pit, deep underground, for beating prisoners.

Pilate's judgment
This picture shows Jesus standing in front of the Roman governor, Pontius Pilate. Only Pilate had the authority to sentence him to death. Under Roman law, blasphemy was not a crime. So, in order to persuade Pilate to pass the death penalty, the Sanhedrin told him that Jesus was guilty of treason against Rome.

"Hmmmm," said Pilate. He strode out, leaving Jesus with the guards.

"I find that this man has done nothing wrong," Pilate announced to the elders.

> ❝ *For he knew that it was out of envy that they had delivered him up.* ❞

"He's a troublemaker!" they insisted. "He's been stirring up people all the way from His home in Galilee to Judea!"

"Galilee!" Pilate suddenly spotted a way out of this situation. "Well, if He's from Galilee, then it's Herod who should deal with Him."

Herod happened to be in Jerusalem that week, so Pilate hurriedly had Jesus marched over to see him. Jesus was soon back in Pilate's palace, though. Herod was unable to find Jesus guilty of any crime either. On top of everything, Pilate's wife said, "Last night, I had a dream about Jesus of Nazareth. He is innocent of everything that the Jews have accused Him of. Have nothing to do with Him."

"That settles it," Pilate thought. The Jewish elders have delivered this man up out of envy. He strode out and found that a huge crowd had gathered outside.

"This man has done nothing to deserve death," Pilate announced to the Jewish elders and the people. "I shall have Him flogged and let Him go!"

With that, Pilate's guards dragged Jesus away to be soundly whipped.

The praetorium
The military headquarters and palace where a Roman provincial governor, such as Pontius Pilate, lived was called the praetorium. It had a large tower at each corner, as in the picture. Two of these towers overlooked the main temple. Pilate's soldiers brought Jesus to the palace's private judgment hall, where he was tried.

❖ **ABOUT THE STORY** ❖
The Sanhedrin have to send Jesus for trial to the Roman governor, as they do not have the power to order His execution themselves. However, they realize that Pilate will not listen to their complaints about Jesus's religious claims, so they tell Pilate that Jesus has been plotting against the Roman government, thinking he will be more likely to convict Jesus. The governor realizes that the charges are unfounded, and releases Him.

Condemned to Die

THE Jewish authorities had done their work well. They had mingled with the crowds, persuading them that Jesus was a blasphemer and a liar. As Pilate turned to walk away into his judgment hall, the citizens of Jerusalem cried out in protest. "No!" the hundreds of men and women cried out to Pilate. "Kill him! Kill Jesus of Nazareth!"

Pilate was totally taken aback.

"Why?" he said. "Whatever has he done?"

The Roman governor felt sure that Jesus was innocent. All at once, he had an idea that would help him get Jesus off the hook. Pilate had remembered that it was the custom at Passover to release a prisoner of the people's choice. He knew that there was a murderer in the cells by the name of Barabbas. Pilate felt sure that the people of Jerusalem would much rather

have Jesus walking among them in the streets than a bloodthirsty killer.

"Whom would you rather have me release?" Pilate asked the crowds. "The King of the Jews or Barabbas?"

"Not Jesus of Nazareth!" the shouts came back. "We want Barabbas released! Give us Barabbas!"

Meanwhile, the Roman governor's soldiers were taking great delight in punishing their Jewish prisoner. They had gathered the whole battalion to come and join in the fun. Armed with cruel barbed whips, they rained down blow after blow, lashing Him with all their strength. Each soldier stopped only when he was out of breath and the sweat was dripping off his forehead; then another immediately stepped forward to take his turn. Every time Jesus was forced to His knees by the constant pain, the guards hauled Him up roughly to withstand more. Their leather thongs ate into Jesus's flesh. The blood streamed off His body and ran along the floor. Even then, the

---

❧ ABOUT THE STORY ❧

The charge that Jesus was the Son of God made Pilate afraid. Like many Romans, he was superstitious. He believed that there were many gods and that it was a good idea not to get on the wrong side of any of them. However, He was more concerned about getting a bad report from the Jews, which could stop him from getting promotion. (Judea was not a very important posting.) So he sacrificed Jesus for himself.

Punishment before death
Jesus is flogged by the Roman soldiers. The punishment of flogging was often used before putting someone to death.

Crown of thorns
In Roman times, a crown was a symbol of royalty and kingship, just as it is today. Crowns were usually made of gold or other precious metals, but the Roman soldiers made a crown by weaving together the stems of a thorny plant. By putting this on Jesus's head, they were making fun of the idea of Him as a king.

soldiers hadn't had enough. They braided a crown of thorns, pressed it into Jesus's scalp, and threw a regal purple cloak around His shoulders. The Roman guards gave Jesus a reed to hold for a royal scepter, and propped Him up in the midst of them.

"Hail, King of the Jews!" they mocked, knocking Jesus to the floor and spitting on Him.

Suddenly, Pilate himself strode in.

"Help the man to stand and bring Him out here with me," he ordered. "Immediately!"

So Jesus was brought bleeding in His crown and cloak before the jeering crowds.

"Look!" shouted Pilate. "Look at this man! I have not found Him guilty of anything!"

The chief priests and elders began to cry, "Crucify Him!"; and the crowds quickly picked up the chant.

> **" The chief priests answered, 'We have no king but Caesar.' "**

"Take Him yourself and crucify Him!" Pilate roared, knowing that under Roman law they couldn't. "In my eyes, He's done nothing wrong!"

"By Jewish law He should die!" the Jewish officials shouted back. "He says He's the Son of God."

At that, a look of terror came over Pilate's face. Right away, he had Jesus marched inside again so he could speak to Him in private one last time.

"Who are you?" he urged, lifting up Jesus's drooping head. "Where have you come from?"

Jesus didn't answer.

"Why won't you speak to me?" Pilate moaned. "Don't you know that I hold in my hands the power to have you either put to death or set free?"

Jesus raised His eyes.

"You would have no power at all over me if it hadn't been given to you from above," He said quietly. Pilate made up his mind.

"I shall release this man!" he announced to the crowds.

A deafening roar of disapproval went up all around the Roman governor.

"Then you will be no friend of Caesar's," warned the chief priests. "Anyone who says he's a king is flaunting their defiance of Rome!"

The last thing Pilate wanted was to get into deep water with the emperor himself. Trembling with nerves, he called for a bowl of water and a towel. As the Roman governor washed his hands in front of everyone, the clamoring crowds fell into an expectant hush.

"I cleanse myself of this man's blood," Pilate declared.

This time, the noise that went up from the crowd was that of cheering.

Minutes later, Barabbas the murderer was released, and Jesus was led out to be crucified.

Washing away the guilt
Pilate washes his hands before Jesus's crucifixion. By doing this, he was telling the crowd that he did not want to be held responsible for Jesus's death.

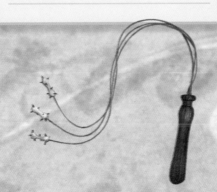

POLITICIANS TODAY VALUE PUBLIC OPINION. THEY OFTEN MAKE POLICIES TO WIN THEM VOTES. THE BIBLE REMINDS US THAT PLEASING GOD IS MORE IMPORTANT THAN PLEASING PEOPLE.

Tortured and mocked
This Roman whip is similar to the one that would have been used to flog Jesus. It consists of three leather cords attached to a handle. After Jesus had been flogged, the soldiers mocked Him by dressing Him in a purple tunic. This color was normally worn by royalty.

Crucifixion

THE slumped figure was hardly recognizable as Jesus. The crown of thorns cut into His head. Blood ran down His battered face. His robes were stained from His wounds. Yet Jesus's kind eyes still shone with compassion. His tormentors had not broken His spirit.

The guards heaved in a solid wooden cross, twice the size of Jesus, and laid it on His back. Slowly, Jesus dragged it off through the packed streets of Jerusalem. Each step took every bit of His strength and will. Eventually, He stumbled and collapsed into the dirt, the cross crashing down on top of Him. The soldiers hauled Jesus to His feet and heaved the cross onto His back. Jesus's knees buckled and He sank to the floor, unable to move any farther.

The infuriated soldiers turned toward the crowd of onlookers and dragged out a broad-shouldered man, named Simon of Cyrene. He had no choice but to carry the hateful cross on his back. Jesus staggered along behind him with two condemned thieves.

People lined the roads to see the criminals. They yelled insults and spat. Running desperately among the crowds were Jesus's friends. Many women wept bitterly, unable to turn their eyes away from Jesus's suffering, even though they could do nothing to help.

"Don't weep for me," Jesus told them, "but for yourselves and your children for the destruction that is to come."

Eventually they reached Golgotha. A soldier offered Jesus wine and painkilling herbs, but He refused. Then came the agonizing hammering—one long nail through each hand and one piercing both feet.

"Father, forgive them," cried Jesus, "for they don't know what they are doing!"

A placard was fixed above Jesus's head, reading: "Jesus of Nazareth, King of the Jews" in three languages.

"It shouldn't say that!" the elders shouted in protest. "It should say, 'This man said, "I am King of the Jews."'"

Pontius Pilate silenced them with a glare, and they turned their attention to taunting Jesus instead.

"If you're the Son of God, come down from the cross!" the chief priests mocked.

"He said He saved others, now He can't save himself," scoffed the Pharisees.

"You said you could destroy the temple and rebuild it in three days," yelled the elders, "so why can't you get free?"

> ❝ *'Father, forgive them; for they know not what they do.'* ❞

While the officials yelled their jibes, two other crosses were raised, one to either side of Jesus's twisted body.

"You said you were the Christ," sneered one of the thieves. "So save yourself and us too!"

"How dare you!" gasped the other thief. "We deserve our punishment, but this man is innocent! Lord, remember me when you reach your kingdom."

"I promise you," Jesus whispered, "today you will be with me in paradise."

Suddenly darkness fell over the whole land. A cold wind screeched, drowning out the soldiers at the foot of the cross who were casting lots for Jesus's clothes.

All those who loved Jesus clung together in grief, as close to the cross as they dared. Among them were Jesus's mother, Mary, the disciple John, and Jesus's friends Mary Magdalene and Salome.

"Mother," came Jesus's voice, "look after John as your son. John, take care of my mother as your own."

For three long hours, the weeping friends watched Jesus's silent agony. Then suddenly His voice rang out: "My God, my God! Why have you abandoned me?"

One of the mourners rushed to lift a stick with a sponge full of wine on the end for Jesus to drink.

"Father, I give up my spirit into your hands," He cried loudly. "It is finished!" His head drooped

At that moment, a great storm broke. The ground shook and rocks split open. The veil that hung in the temple ripped in two. Some people later swore that they saw graves open and spirits rise out of them.

The Roman centurion at the foot of the cross gasped, "This man truly was the Son of God."

And terror struck the hearts of everyone at Golgotha.

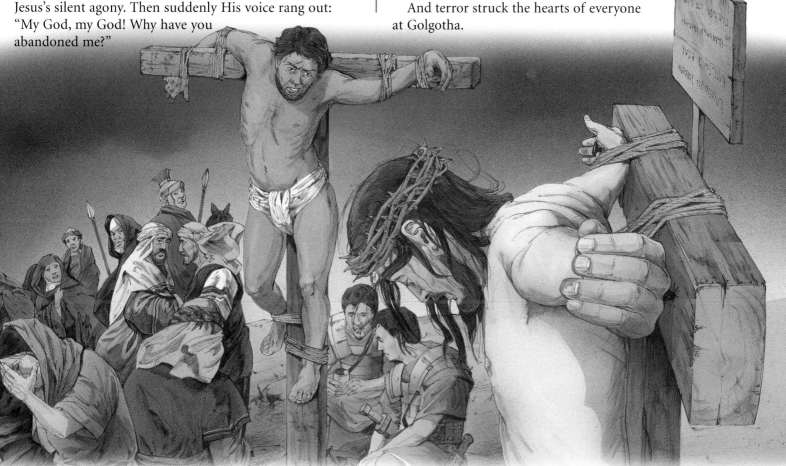

❖ ABOUT THE STORY ❖

This story is packed with symbolism. Jesus refuses the wine to dull the pain, because He has to carry the weight of sin without help. Darkness falls as a sign that Jesus has been cut off from God. Pilate is more accurate with his placard than the religious leaders realized.

Golgotha
It is not known exactly where Golgotha was, but it is often thought to be this hill outside Jerusalem.

Simon of Cyrene
The man who carried the cross for Jesus, Simon of Cyrene, was probably a pilgrim visiting Jerusalem for the Passover. Cyrene was a city in North Africa, with a large Jewish population.

Jesus is Buried

THE dead body of Jesus hung on the cross until evening was drawing near. Then the Jewish elders began to grow rather agitated. Sunset would mark the start of the Sabbath, and the holy day would be made unclean if the men weren't taken down from their crosses, and the thieves that had been crucified with Jesus were still alive.

The Roman soldiers didn't need much encouraging. Glad to speed things up, they marched over to the thieves and broke their legs with a couple of savage blows. The robbers sank down under their own weight, which made it impossible for them to breathe. Within minutes, they had suffocated to death.

The soldiers didn't bother doing the same to Jesus—everyone knew that He was already dead. As the Romans walked away, one soldier spitefully thrust his spear as deep as he could into Jesus's side, just for good measure. Jesus's watching friends saw blood and water gush from the wound. They shuddered and turned away in horror.

As dusk began to fall on the city of Jerusalem, Pontius Pilate sat alone, brooding on the death of Jesus of Nazareth. A servant disturbed the Roman governor from his troubled thoughts to tell him that a wealthy member of the Sanhedrin was begging to see Pilate at once.

When the visitor was ushered in, Pilate was mightily relieved to find it was Joseph of Arimathea, a Jewish official widely held to be good and just and fair.

Joseph bowed low. "Sir," he began, "I come to confess a secret. I myself am one of the followers of Jesus of

Roman burial urn
Jesus's body was buried, but some Romans at this time had their bodies cremated and the remains put into urns. This marble burial urn contains the ashes of a woman named Bovia Procula. The inscription on the urn describes her as a "most unfortunate mother." This may mean that she died during childbirth, as many women did at this time.

Jesus and Nicodemus
This bronze carving shows Jesus talking to Nicodemus, a Pharisee who came to Him for secret teaching. Not much is known about Nicodemus, but he was probably a member of the Sanhedrin.

Harrowing of Hell
This Greek Orthodox icon shows Jesus going down to Hell after His death. In medieval times, this episode was called the "Harrowing of Hell."

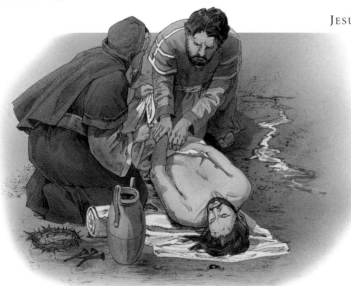

Joseph had prepared for his own burial—and they laid Jesus inside. Then Joseph and Nicodemus rolled a heavy stone in front of the tomb to close it up. There was nothing more that could be done, and at last everyone went their own sad way into the night.

Meanwhile, an extremely annoyed Pilate was busy giving an audience to yet more callers from the Sanhedrin.

"Sir, when that imposter was alive, He said He'd rise up to life again after three days," the officials said. "Therefore, order a guard to be set around the tomb until the third day, so His friends can't come and steal the body and trick everyone into thinking His words have come true."

"You have your guard!" snapped Pilate.

By the time darkness had fallen, armed guards were the only living things in the garden of graves where Jesus lay.

Nazareth," Joseph continued, "although I did not tell my colleagues, who, as you well know, envied and hated Him. I was one of the few on the Sanhedrin who voted against this innocent man's death. Now I have come to ask a favor. Please allow me to take Jesus's body down from the cross and bury it."

> ❝ *Joseph took the body and laid it in his own new tomb.* ❞

Pilate didn't have to think twice. "Very well," he said.

So it was that, in the dim evening light, a member of the very Council that had bayed for Jesus's blood tenderly recovered His body from the cross. A friend named Nicodemus had brought burial spices of myrrh and aloes, and he and Joseph hurriedly wrapped Jesus in a linen shroud. Together, the two men carried Jesus's body to a nearby garden cemetery, and the women who had been friends of Jesus followed close behind, wailing aloud. A small cave-like tomb had been carved out—the tomb that

Myrrh and aloes
In the story, Nicodemus provides expensive spices for Jesus's burial. Myrrh is a sweet-smelling gum from the bark of a tree. Aloes is the bitter juice of the aloe plant. Before burial, the body was washed and wrapped in a linen cloth, and the head was wrapped in a linen square. The spices would have been put between the folds of linen.

Joseph of Arimathea
Joseph of Arimathea carries two flasks containing Jesus's sweat and blood. With Nicodemus, Joseph prepared Jesus's body for burial.

❧ **ABOUT THE STORY** ❧
There was no doubt that Jesus died. Roman soldiers had seen many dead bodies; they knew all the signs. The blood and water is a sign for later readers, however. It showed that the red and white cells of Jesus's blood had begun to separate around the heart, which happens after death. There was no trickery or mistake which caused Jesus to live on. Furthermore, the Gospel writers saw Jesus's death as a fulfillment of Old Testament prophecy.

Jesus Disappears

THE torches of the Sanhedrin's guard flickered outside Jesus's tomb all night of that first Good Friday. Sitting in the cemetery among the dead, the soldiers were very glad when they saw the light of Saturday finally dawning. They kept watch all that next long day, through the evening, and into Saturday night. As it grew closer to the dawn of the third day after Jesus's death, the soldiers became increasingly jumpy. The Sanhedrin had assured them that they had to fear only the living, not the dead. They were on the lookout only for Jesus's friends coming to steal the body, not for ghosts. No, those haughty Jewish officials certainly didn't believe that a dead man was going to come walking out among them—but then they weren't sitting in front of the tomb, were they?

> " *Tell people, 'His disciples came by night and stole Him away while we were asleep.'* "

When the first light of the sun crept over the horizon on Sunday morning, the soldiers kept their eyes open, brandishing their spears and swords at the slightest rustle of the birds among the bushes.

Suddenly, the earth began to tremble under the soldiers' feet. It began to shake so violently that the guards were flung headlong onto the ground. A searing white light blazed out of the sky and descended over the tomb, dazzling the soldiers where they lay. They peered through

their fingers and saw with astonishment that a man as luminous as lightning, as white as snow, was rolling away the massive stone from the entrance of the tomb. Nearly paralyzed with fear, the cowering soldiers managed to scramble to their feet and flee for their lives.

At the same time, a group of sorrowing women were making their way to the tomb, among them Jesus's devoted friends Mary Magdalene, Mary the mother of James and John, Salome, and Joanna. They had seen how hurriedly Joseph and Nicodemus had had to prepare Jesus's body before sundown brought the Sabbath, and the kind women meant to attend to the body properly, anointing it and wrapping it with all the customary care and attention. As the grieving friends walked along through the earliest rays of the morning sun, they worried that they might not be strong enough to move away the huge stone. When they drew close to the spot, their pulses began to race. They could see that someone had already

Easter parade
Here you can see an Easter day procession in Jerusalem. Christians are gathering to reenact Christ's walk to Golgotha with the cross.

Ossuary
In Roman times, there were two stages to a Jewish burial. First the body was wrapped, anointed, and placed in a tomb. Later, when the flesh had decayed, the family gathered up the bones and put them in a stone box called an ossuary.

Meanwhile, the terrified guards had taken their amazing story straight to the chief priests, and an emergency meeting of the Sanhedrin was called. There was much shouting and arguing, thumping of tables and blaming of each other. In the end, a desperate decision was reached.

"Take this for your troubles," the elders said, soothingly, pushing bags of coins into the sweating hands of the pale soldiers. "When people ask you what happened, tell them that you all fell asleep on duty in the night, and that Jesus's disciples crept up on you and stole the body. If Pilate himself somehow gets to hear of this mess, we'll buy his silence too. Don't worry, just say what we've told you and we'll make sure you don't get into trouble."

That was the story that was soon spread around the Jews of Jerusalem.

done it. Hearts pounding, the women raced to the tomb. Wherever were the soldiers who had been set to guard the body? Which wicked people had gotten there before them? What terrible things were they doing to their beloved Jesus's body, even at that very moment?

When the first two women reached the tomb and squeezed inside, they screamed. Jesus's body was gone, and sitting where His body should have lain there were two shining men in radiant clothes.

"Why are you looking for the living among the dead?" came the men's voices. "Don't you remember that the Son of Man said He'd rise on the third day?"

The startled women nearly fell over each other in their hurry to get out of the tomb. Pushing their friends before them and sobbing an explanation, they ran away as fast as their legs could carry them.

JESUS HAD TOLD THE DISCIPLES THAT HE WOULD RISE FROM THE DEAD, BUT THEY HAD NEVER UNDERSTOOD OR BELIEVED HIM. REAL FAITH TAKES GOD AT HIS WORD, AND EXPECTS HIM TO FULFILL IT. ∿

Mary Magdalene
When she first met Jesus, Mary Magdalene was possessed by evil spirits. When Jesus cured her of this "illness," she became a devout follower of His. It is not clear from the Bible whether her illness was physical, mental, or moral, or some combination of the three.

❖ **ABOUT THE STORY** ❖
The Bible writers do not tell us what happened to Jesus between His death and resurrection. There is one hint in Peter's second letter which suggests Jesus told the good news of His victory over sin and death to the people who had died before and were waiting in "Hades," or Hell. The Bible writers focus instead on the supernatural elements of the resurrection. This action, they are saying, is a miracle of God.

The Women Meet Jesus

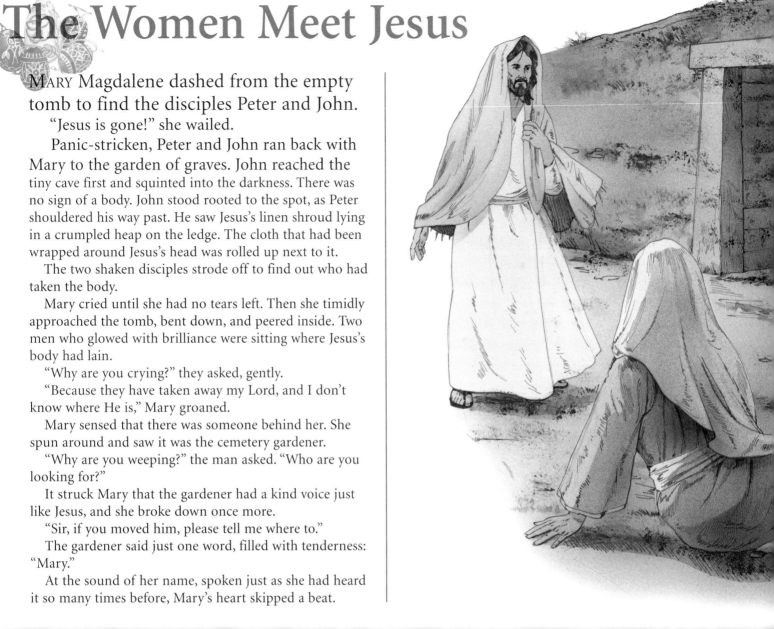

MARY Magdalene dashed from the empty tomb to find the disciples Peter and John.

"Jesus is gone!" she wailed.

Panic-stricken, Peter and John ran back with Mary to the garden of graves. John reached the tiny cave first and squinted into the darkness. There was no sign of a body. John stood rooted to the spot, as Peter shouldered his way past. He saw Jesus's linen shroud lying in a crumpled heap on the ledge. The cloth that had been wrapped around Jesus's head was rolled up next to it.

The two shaken disciples strode off to find out who had taken the body.

Mary cried until she had no tears left. Then she timidly approached the tomb, bent down, and peered inside. Two men who glowed with brilliance were sitting where Jesus's body had lain.

"Why are you crying?" they asked, gently.

"Because they have taken away my Lord, and I don't know where He is," Mary groaned.

Mary sensed that there was someone behind her. She spun around and saw it was the cemetery gardener.

"Why are you weeping?" the man asked. "Who are you looking for?"

It struck Mary that the gardener had a kind voice just like Jesus, and she broke down once more.

"Sir, if you moved him, please tell me where to."

The gardener said just one word, filled with tenderness: "Mary."

At the sound of her name, spoken just as she had heard it so many times before, Mary's heart skipped a beat.

The Garden Tomb
It is not known exactly where Jesus's tomb was situated. The Bible tells us only that it was in a garden near where the crucifixion took place. Christians believe its most likely location is here, a place called the Garden Tomb, in Jerusalem.

Easter eggs
In many European countries, people celebrate Easter by decorating eggs and giving them as gifts. Eggs and flowers are a symbol of new life.

"Teacher," she cried and sank to her knees, gazing up adoringly at the man she loved above all others.

"Go now," Jesus said, smiling. "Find my disciples and tell them that I will soon be returning to my Father."

Meanwhile, the other women who had seen the stone rolled aside were still scurrying home together in fear. All at once, they saw the dim form of a man appear in front of them in their path, and they sprang back in alarm.

"Good morning," said the figure.

The women couldn't believe their ears at the familiar voice. They fell to the ground with amazement.

"It can't be!" they whispered. "Jesus, is it really you?"

"Don't be afraid," Jesus smiled, holding His arms out toward His friends. "Go and tell my disciples to travel to Galilee, and I will meet them there soon."

> **Mary Magdalene went and said to the disciples, 'I have seen the Lord!'**

The vision disappeared as suddenly as it had arrived.

A little later, Mary Magdalene burst into the room where the disciples sat together in grief, red-eyed and miserable. Her face was flushed with excitement.

"I have seen the Lord !" she cried, and in a joyful rush of words, she told them everything that had happened.

The disciples shook their heads sadly. They wanted to believe Mary, but they had seen Jesus hanging on the cross with their own eyes. There was nothing anyone could say to change that.

❖ ABOUT THE STORY ❖

Many attempts have been made to "prove" that Jesus did not truly rise from the dead, and that this was a "spiritual" experience like a vision. The Gospel writers include little details that have a ring of truth. The grave clothes are lying as if the body has passed through them; Jesus did not just take them off. Grave robbers are not so careful. Mary failed to recognize Jesus because she was upset, not in a spiritual state of hope.

Jesus appears to Mary Magdalene
This painted wooden statue, dating from the 1600s, shows Mary Magdalene meeting Jesus, after He has risen from the dead. Mary Magdalene was the first person to see Jesus after the resurrection. She set off for the tomb with a group of women, but apparently ran ahead of them and arrived before them. When she discovered that the tomb was empty, she immediately went to find Peter and John. After they had gone to search for the body, Mary remained alone at the tomb, weeping. It was then that she saw two angels, followed by Jesus Himself, risen from the dead.

On the Road to Emmaus

LATER on that morning of the third day, two of Jesus's disciples began walking out of Jerusalem on their way to Emmaus, a little village about seven miles away. The subdued companions trudged along with heavy hearts, going over and over Jesus's sudden capture, unfair trial, and terrible death. As they walked, a stranger caught up with them on the road and asked to walk with them.

"Of course, friend," replied one of the disciples, Cleopas, and then carried on with the conversation as before.

The stranger seemed puzzled.

"Can I ask what you're talking about?" He said.

Cleopas stared at the man, stunned.

"You must be the only person in the whole of Jerusalem who hasn't heard about the events of the past few days," the disciple remarked.

The stranger shrugged His shoulders innocently.

"What events?" He asked.

"The things that have happened to Jesus of Nazareth, the greatest prophet who ever lived," replied Cleopas, reverently. "You must have heard of how our chief priests and elders seized Him, persuaded the Roman governor to condemn Him to death, and then had Him crucified?"

The stranger shook His head.

"All our hope was in Jesus of Nazareth," Cleopas went on. "We had believed that He was the one sent to save us."

He paused and swallowed hard.

"Besides all of that," Cleopas continued, waving his disappointment aside, "it is now the third day since His death. Earlier, some of the women in Jesus's company of friends brought us an amazing story about having found His tomb empty and having seen a vision of angels, who said that He was alive!"

The stranger's eyes grew wide with surprise.

"Of course," Cleopas explained, "some of us dashed straight there to see for ourselves. All we saw was that the body had indeed gone—nothing else."

The disciples hung their heads gloomily.

Suddenly the stranger seemed to know more than He

❧ ABOUT THE STORY ❧

Once again, two disciples fail to recognize Jesus. Luke brings out two important points. One is that Jesus was recognized in the breaking of bread. Christians today claim that they "meet" Jesus in a special way when they "break bread" in communion. Secondly, Jesus was known for His "burning" teaching: it gave them hope and challenged them. Today, Christians meet to hear His teaching read and explained, and to "hear" Him through it.

The resurrection

"Resurrection" means to bring a dead person back to life. "Resuscitation" can mean this too, but a resuscitated person will die eventually. Christians believe that when someone is resurrected, their soul enters a new body, in which they will spend eternity.

had previously let on.

"Don't you understand what the prophets had foretold?" the man rebuked the disciples gently. "It was necessary for Christ to suffer, in order for Him to be glorified."

The stranger went on to explain the mysteries of the scriptures as the disciples had heard only Jesus explain them before. Cleopas and his companion were so fascinated by the stranger's knowledge that when they reached Emmaus and the stranger started to bid them goodbye, they begged Him not to travel on down the road but to stop with them for the evening.

So it was that the two disciples came to be having supper with the stranger. When the man took some bread and blessed it, broke it into pieces, and gave it to them, the disciples at last realized who He really was.

"Jesus!" they gasped, pushing back their chairs and springing to their feet.

The stranger vanished before their very eyes.

"We should have known!" the disciples scolded each other as they hurried straight back to Jerusalem through the darkness. "Didn't your heart burn strangely within your chest as He explained everything to us?"

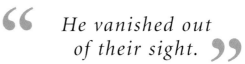

> ## He vanished out of their sight.

When the disciples reached the city, they found the disciples in a buzz of excitement. Before Cleopas and his friend could even get a word out, the disciples cried, "Peter has seen the Lord!" and dragged them into the room to tell them how Jesus had appeared to Peter and chatted with him. When the two disciples finally managed to explain how they, too, had met with Jesus, the room erupted in a riot of cheering and praying and weeping for joy. It seemed that Mary Magdalene's story was true, after all!

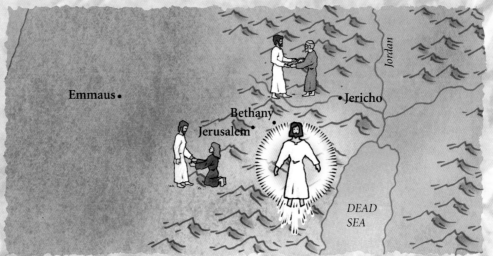

Emmaus
It is not known exactly where the village of Emmaus was situated, but some people believe it was here, at the village of Amwas, about 7 miles west of Jerusalem.

Jesus's last days
The Bible tells us that Jesus was resurrected on the third day. He appeared to Peter and to all the disciples, including Cleopas and his companion as they walked to Emmaus. Jesus used this time to visit His disciples, to reinforce their faith, and to prove to them all that He was resurrected, that His prophecies had come true.

Doubting Thomas

JESUS's followers were jubilant, and everyone in the room wanted to talk to Peter and Cleopas and his friend at once. The disciples crowded around the three men, firing questions and praising God, begging to hear them tell again and again exactly what Jesus looked like and each word of what He said.

All at once, the hubbub died away into silence. Everyone stood stock-still, staring openmouthed at the newcomer among them. No one had heard anyone knock. No one had seen anyone enter. Yet there He was. It was Jesus.

> **"** *Jesus said to them, 'Come and have breakfast.'* **"**

"Peace be with you," Jesus said, softly, greeting His friends with a familiar raise of the hand.

Everyone shrank back in fear.

"Be careful, it's a spirit!" came murmurs from the back of the room.

A frown creased Jesus's brow. "Why are you frightened?" He asked. "I am no ghost. Look here, see the wounds on my hands and feet. It's me, Jesus."

A few of the disciples began to creep nearer, cautiously.

"Yes," urged Jesus. "Don't be afraid to touch me. See, spirits don't have flesh and bones, as you can feel that I have."

As the first trembling hands touched Jesus's warm skin, the faces of Jesus's followers brightened into delight.

"Master!" they cried. "It's really you!"

Laughing at their amazement, Jesus sat down at the table in the midst of them. Together, everyone shared a meal, just as they had done so many times before.

Now there was one disciple who wasn't present to see Jesus for himself. When Thomas later heard his friends' story he found the news too hard to accept, even though he saw their gladness and joy.

"Unless I can touch the mark of the nails in His hands with my own fingers, and put my own hand into the wound in his side, I can't believe it," Thomas whispered.

No matter how hard he tried, he couldn't get rid of the doubts that nagged away inside him.

Eight days later, Jesus's followers were again gathered together in private, doors tightly locked against the prying

eyes of the Jewish council's spies. Just as before, halfway through the evening Jesus appeared silently among them. No one noticed His arrival.

> ❝ *'See my hands and my feet, that it is I myself.'* ❞

"Peace be with you," He greeted his friends and turned straight to Thomas, who had shrunk back, thunderstruck.

Jesus reached out and took the terrified disciple's hands.

"Here," Jesus said, holding Thomas's fingers against the nail wounds in His palms. "Feel the wound in my side. Don't doubt any longer. Have faith. It is true."

As Thomas's fingers sank into Jesus's flesh, he broke down and wept.

"My Lord and my God!" he cried.

"You believe now because you have seen me for yourself," Jesus said, gently. "Even more blessed are those who don't see me and yet still believe."

MOST PEOPLE HAVE DOUBTS. IN FACT, IT WOULD BE TRUE TO SAY THAT FAITH IS NOT REALLY FAITH IF THERE IS NO RISK OR DOUBT AT ALL. FAITH IS NOT THE SAME AS CERTAINTY. WE CANNOT PROVE TO OTHERS THAT GOD EXISTS OR THAT HE LOVES US. WE CAN ONLY DISCOVER GOD'S LOVE FOR OURSELVES AS WE SEE GOD AT WORK IN OUR LIVES, AND EVEN THEN ONLY WHEN WE TRUST HIM TO SHOW US. ◦◦

Doubting Thomas
Thomas was a believer but his faith was mixed with uncertainty. He could not believe Jesus was alive again unless he saw and touched the scars. The phrase "a doubting Thomas" has come to mean a person who refuses to believe something without proof.

❖ ABOUT THE STORY ❖

This story shows that even a close friend of Jesus could doubt what had actually happened. It could be said that those who believe today are in a way showing more faith than Thomas and the others. There is plenty of evidence to convince us that it did happen—the evidence of the disciples, written down for us, and the generations of Christians since.

The Appearance at Galilee

SEVERAL of the disciples gathered one evening by the Sea of Galilee. The men looked out over the water at the beauty of the setting sun. They shared fond memories of all the precious times they had been on the lake with Jesus, floating in private in Peter's little boat, far from the crowds of disciples on the shore.

Now, once again, the ex-fisherman pushed his boat into the sea and his friends jumped in—James, John, Thomas, and Nathaniel among them. They unfurled the sail and felt the wind push them into deeper waters. Under the stars, they cast their nets and sat quietly together, waiting.

All night long the men fished, but time and again they raised their nets to find them empty. There was still nothing in the nets by the time the dawn began to show itself over the glassy water.

"Have you caught anything?" came a voice, floating over the waves to the fishermen.

The disciples looked toward the shore and made out the small figure of a man on the beach.

"No! Nothing!" they hollered back.

The man cupped His hands to His mouth and called back, "Try casting your nets to the right of the boat!"

Peter and his friends decided they might as well try the stranger's advice. As they lowered the nets over the side, they felt them grow heavy with fish. In fact, it took all the disciples' combined effort to heave them back up again!

As John watched the hundreds of slippery bodies wriggling on the floor of the boat, he remembered a time when Jesus had given similar advice, and exactly the same thing had happened. "Of course!" he thought, turning to Peter and beaming broadly. "It's the Lord!" he cried.

At once, Peter's face lit up and he dived straight off the

❧ ABOUT THE STORY ❧

Just as Jesus was recognized by Cleopas by the familiar action, so John recognizes Jesus in an action that is also very symbolic. When this had happened before, Jesus had called the fishermen brothers to be His disciples. It was as if He were calling them again to go out and be "fishers of men," to draw others into His kingdom. The special words for Peter were because Peter had let Jesus down by denying Him.

Jesus the shepherd
This statue of Jesus as the Good Shepherd comes from Turkey and dates from the A.D. 300s Jesus saw Himself as a shepherd, with people as His flock. He said, "I am the good shepherd. The good shepherd lays down his life for His sheep. I know my sheep and my sheep know me."

Catching fish
In Jesus's time, people caught fish with nets, like the disciples in the story, or with a hook and line. The fish-hook shown here is made of bronze, but earlier ones were made from bone or iron. Fish were an important source of protein, for not many people ate much meat. Although fishermen often made a good living, they worked very hard. After fishing for most of the night, they then had to haul in the catch, mend the nets and sails, and dry, salt, or pickle the fish ready to be taken to markets in other towns and villages.

boat into the water. Laughing with delight, the disciples watched as Peter splashed out for the shore in his eagerness to reach Jesus. Turning the sail into the wind, they headed for the beach themselves.

Peter ran dripping up the beach to find that Jesus was busy getting a little fire going.

"Go and bring some of the fish!" Jesus called. "Then come and have some breakfast!"

The overjoyed Peter immediately ran back down the shore to where his friends were landing the boat.

"Hurry up!" he cried, practically jumping up and down with excitement.

Minutes later, together again with their master, Jesus's friends enjoyed the most delicious meal they had ever tasted, in the warmth of the early morning sun.

After they had all eaten their fill, Jesus turned to Peter and looked deep into his eyes.

"Peter," He asked, seriously, "do you love me?"

"Yes, Lord," the disciple replied, "of course I do!"

> **'Lord, you know everything, you know that I love you.'**

Jesus asked the question twice more. Each time, Peter grew more offended that Jesus felt He had to ask again. Peter didn't realize that each time he told Jesus he loved Him, his friend was forgiving him for having denied he knew Jesus on the night He was arrested.

At the third time of asking, Peter cried, "Lord, you know everything! You know very well that I love you!"

"I want you to look after my people as a shepherd looks after his flock," Jesus replied, "and follow me."

PETER'S EXPERIENCE TELLS PEOPLE TODAY THERE CAN ALWAYS BE A NEW START WITH JESUS WHEN WE LET HIM DOWN. HE DOES NOT FORSAKE US WHEN WE FAIL HIM. IT IS POSSIBLE TO WORK FOR HIM AGAIN.

Fishers of men
This picture shows Jesus speaking to the disciples as they fish from their boat. Jesus said, "Come, follow me and I will make you fishers of men." In this story, the disciples are actually fishing, but Jesus is telling them that by teaching others the ways of Christianity, they would be acting as fishermen of people.

The Ascension

FINALLY, it was time for Jesus to leave the world. He tenderly gathered His disciples together and walked with them once more to the Mount of Olives. It was there, among the groves in which the companions had walked and talked so often, that Jesus said His farewells.

"Don't leave Jerusalem yet," Jesus told His eleven friends. "For John baptized you all with water, but in a short while you will be visited by the Holy Spirit, who will baptize you again. With the powerful gifts my Father will send you, you must go and tell people about me through all nations of the world. Preach my gospel to the whole creation, to the very ends of the earth. Baptize all those who believe as my followers, in the name of the Father, and of the Son, and of the Holy Spirit, and teach them everything that I have taught you. For all those who believe and are baptized will be saved from their sins."

Jesus looked around at His friends' sad faces. He lifted up His hands and blessed them.

> " *While He blessed them, He parted from them and was taken up into heaven.* "

"Don't forget," He said, softly. "I am with you always, even until the end of time."

As Jesus spoke, He was lifted up into a dazzling cloud of glory that blazed from up above and hid Him from the disciples' view. All at once, the cloud faded to a glimmer of light, and then it disappeared. Jesus was gone, and the disciples were left gazing up into the blue emptiness of the Jerusalem sky. Their minds were filled with awe, and their

hearts were heavy with sorrow.

Voices from nearby brought the staring disciples back to earth with a bump.

"Men of Galilee," they said, "why do you stand looking up to heaven?"

The disciples shook themselves and looked around. They saw two strangers standing nearby in gleaming white robes.

"Jesus has gone from you and is now in heaven. But one day He will return, and He will be just the same as now, when you have seen Him go."

Overcome by wonder and strangely comforted, the disciples slowly made their way back to Jerusalem. In their heart of hearts, each man knew for sure that he wouldn't be seeing Jesus any more. Yet the friends also knew for certain that one day Jesus would return again in glory. After all, Jesus had proved that He never broke a promise, no matter how impossible it seemed.

Olives
In the story, Jesus walks with His disciples among the olive groves. Olives were one of the main crops of ancient Israel. Some fruit was eaten whole, but most of the crop was pressed to extract the oil. Olive oil was used in cooking, in lamps, and as a lotion to soothe the skin.

The Holy Trinity
Christians believe that there are three persons in God: the Father, the Son, or Jesus, and the Holy Spirit.

❧ **ABOUT THE STORY** ❧
This is the last resurrection appearance. The "ascension" of Jesus is an acted parable, a picture. It is supposed to make it clear to the disciples that Jesus is going where they cannot follow yet, to heaven. We use symbolic language in the same way. Heaven is not a place up in the sky. Heaven is a completely different form of existence from anything that we know or can experience on earth.

Christian Art Around the World

JESUS was crucified by the Romans, who ruled Israel at that time. He had been handed over to them by the Jewish priests, because of His refusal to submit to their authority. Although the Roman governor, Pontius Pilate, could not find Jesus guilty of any crime, he eventually bowed to pressure and sentenced Jesus to death.

The crucifixion took place outside Jerusalem, at the time of the Passover, just before the Sabbath. Jesus was 33 years old. Crucifixion was a common method of execution at that time, involving a slow, very painful, and very public death. First, the Roman guards flogged Jesus and taunted Him, forcing Him to wear a crown of thorns on His head. After this, He was too weak to carry His own cross to the place of execution, so it was carried by a pilgrim named Simon of Cyrene. When He arrived at Golgotha, Jesus was stripped and nailed to the cross, where He died after about six hours.

Three days after the crucifixion, according to the Bible, Jesus rose from the dead just as He had promised He would. A group of women went to the tomb where His body had been buried and discovered that it was empty. One of the women, Mary Magdalene, was the first person to see the risen Christ. Over a period of forty days, Jesus appeared to His disciples in Jerusalem and Galilee, and continued to teach them, just as He had done before His death. He commanded them to tell everyone the gospel, or "good news," that His death had made forgiveness and new life possible for all. Then He rose up, or "ascended," to heaven, returning to His Father.

Jesus's death is seen by Christians as the ultimate sacrifice. They believe that He gave his life to pay the price for all the sins of mankind. Because of the resurrection, Christians think of Jesus not as a dead hero, but as a living Savior who has overcome death. They believe that He helps and guides those who follow Him and that, by offering them the chance of eternal life after death, He makes it possible for them to overcome sin and death, just as He did.

During the reign of Constantine, the first Christian Roman emperor (306–337), the cross became a symbol of Christianity. At first, the cross was empty, which symbolized Christ coming back to life. More recently, the crucifix has become more important. This is a cross with Jesus still on it. As a symbol, this emphasizes how Jesus suffered for people's sins.

In the 1500s and 1600s Catholic missionaries, mainly from France, Spain, and Portugal, traveled all over the world, spreading the Gospels to people who would not otherwise come into contact with Jesus and His teachings. As a result, Christian art is today found all over the world.

Mount of Olives, Jerusalem

This is a picture of Jesus chalked on the floor near the Mount of Olives, at the very heart of Christianity. It shows a heavenly, glowing Jesus before the cross. This emphasizes Jesus's resurrection and His promise of eternal life for all who believe in Him.

Guatemala

This woman is carrying a picture of Jesus as part of an Easter procession. Processions like this one, which recreate Jesus's walk with the cross to be crucified, happen in Christian communities all over the world at Easter. This one is in Guatemala, a small country in Central America.

Far Eastern Christianity

This shrine is in Tacloban City, in the Philippines. It is made up of carved, wooden images. Christ is in the center. Around him are Matthew, Mark, Luke, and John, who wrote the Gospels.

India

This is a painting of Jesus, held by children in the city of Madurai, in India. Most of the people in India are Hindu, but the first Christian missionaries arrived in the 1500s. A missionary is a religious person who travels around the world trying to convert people in other countries to his or her religion.

Crucifixion

This is the kind of scene of the crucifixion that is most often seen in Christian art. It shows Christ on the cross and important people gathered around Him. On the left is a Roman centurion, and on the right of the picture are Mary Magdalene, Mary, mother of Jesus, and Salome.

Ethiopia

The strong history of Christianity in Ethiopia, in Africa, that is shown in this decorated altar piece, stems in part from the Bible story where the apostle Philip baptizes an Ethiopian minister. Tradition in Ethiopia claims that this minister, who was probably a royal treasurer, was the first person to spread the Gospel in Ethiopia.

Faith in Peru

Peru is a country on the western coast of South America. It has a strong Christian tradition. Most of the people are Roman Catholic. The first Catholic missionaries arrived in Peru during the 1500s.

The Gospels

THE word "gospel" literally means "good news." In the New Testament the gospel is the good news that God has fulfilled His promises to Israel by sending His Son, Jesus Christ, to save mankind. The first four books of the New Testament are known as the Gospels, but, strictly speaking, they are four different accounts of the same gospel written by four early Christians.

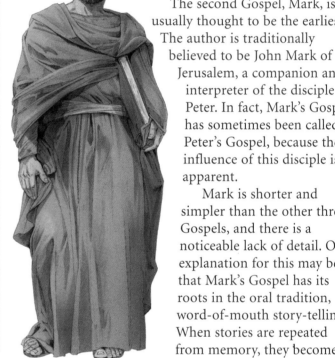

Most of the material contained in the four Gospels would have been passed around by word of mouth before it was written down. The first person to spread the gospel was Jesus Himself. After His death, the disciples carried on teaching people about His life. As those people alive during Jesus's lifetime began to grow older and die, the need was felt for a written record of events. The four books known as the Gospels were written between 50 A.D. and 100 A.D. Three of them—Matthew, Mark, and Luke—contain common material, although they present it in different ways. The fourth, John, stands apart from the others. Together the four books give a full picture of Jesus.

The first Gospel, Matthew, is presented in a very orderly way and has an emphasis on Jesus's teaching. It was traditionally believed that the author of the first Gospel was the disciple Matthew, but this view is no longer widely held.

Matthew includes most of the stories told in Mark, together with many sayings of Jesus and some other stories. He links the New Testament with the Old Testament much more closely than the other Gospels do, focusing on Jesus as the fulfillment of the prophecies about the coming of a Messiah. Matthew also describes the Christian church as "the new Israel," explaining that because Jesus was rejected by so many of the Jews, "Israel" has been expanded to include non-Jews, or Gentiles. He stresses that whereas in Judaism it was the law that was supreme, in Christianity, it is Christ Himself.

The second Gospel, Mark, is usually thought to be the earliest. The author is traditionally believed to be John Mark of Jerusalem, a companion and interpreter of the disciple Peter. In fact, Mark's Gospel has sometimes been called Peter's Gospel, because the influence of this disciple is so apparent.

Mark is shorter and simpler than the other three Gospels, and there is a noticeable lack of detail. One explanation for this may be that Mark's Gospel has its roots in the oral tradition, word-of-mouth story-telling. When stories are repeated from memory, they become

TIMELINE

JESUS, THE GOOD SHEPHERD

• Jesus turns and heads for Jerusalem.

A.D.33

JUDAS ACCEPTING HIS SILVER FOR BETRAYING JESUS

• Jesus enters Jerusalem on the back of a donkey, fulfilling the Old Testament prophecies of the Messiah.

• Jesus clears the temple of traders and money lenders.

THE LAST SUPPER

• Jesus and His disciples eat their Passover meal, the Last Supper. Jesus breaks the bread in the ceremony that becomes the Communion.

• The disciples go with Jesus to pray in the Garden of Gethsemane, on the Mount of Olives, near Jerusalem.

JESUS IS FLOGGED BY THE ROMANS

simplified. Mark's purpose in writing his Gospel was not to produce a work of literature, but to summarize the facts and communicate the truth. His Gospel is best understood as a written record of Peter's teaching.

The author of Luke, the third Gospel, was a well-educated man, with a knowledge of medicine. Through his close contact with Paul and other early Christian leaders, Luke had the opportunity to acquire firsthand knowledge about the life of Jesus and the history of the early Christian Church. Luke's Gospel, like Matthew's, includes nearly all the material contained in Mark, but it has been rewritten in a more complex and professional style. It also includes much of the teaching of Jesus that is found in Matthew, together with other information. Luke also intends his Gospel to be seen as a historical work. He does not simply tell the stories but tries also to demonstrate their reliability. More than the other Gospels, Luke focuses on the human-interest aspects, such as Jesus's concern for social outcasts. He also emphasizes Jesus's role as Savior.

It is generally believed that the fourth Gospel was written by the disciple John, or at the very least by a disciple of John's, using his memoirs as a basis. This direct link to Jesus gives the book of John a special importance. John was probably the last Gospel to be written, and the author was likely to have been aware of the contents of the other three. However, the material contained in John is quite different. Unlike the other Gospels, it focuses less on incidents that took place at Galilee and more on Jerusalem. None of the parables are included, but John includes a lot of material that does not appear in the other Gospels. One significant difference is that Jesus often speaks in long dialogues, unlike anything found in any of the other three Gospels.

John's Gospel is often seen as more of a personal interpretation of Jesus, rather than a straightforward account of His life. Instead of just telling the story of Jesus's life on earth, John brings out the meaning of it for his readers. His main purpose is to reveal the glory of Jesus as the Messiah, or Savior, and the Son of God. His aim is to convert his readers to this belief and so to bring them into eternal life.

THE
HOLY
GRAIL

• Jesus is arrested in the garden.

• Peter is accused of being a follower and colleague of Jesus. He denies knowing Jesus, and the cock crows.

• Jesus is tried by Pontius Pilate. Although Pilate cannot find Him guilty of anything, He is condemned to death.

JESUS BEFORE THE SANHEDRIN

• Jesus is crucified. Christians believe he was dying for the sins of all the world's people.

THE HARROWING
OF HELL

JESUS APPEARS AT GALILEE

• Jesus blesses the disciples and His friends and companions, and He ascends to Heaven to take His place by God.

A.D.33

SPREADING THE WORD

The adventures and travels, trials and successes of the apostles as they lay the foundations of the Christian church

Spreading the Word

WHEN Jesus died at the time of the Jewish Passover, there were many people who hoped that they would hear no more of His teaching, which had challenged so many established ideas. The apostles, Jesus's closest followers, were disillusioned and disappointed. Their hopes had been dashed.

With the news of His resurrection, hope returned to the apostles, and fear to the authorities. Yet it was scarcely believable. The apostles struggled to make sense of the resurrection. The authorities explained it away, or ridiculed it. Then something amazing happened.

It was another Jewish Festival, 50 days after Passover, the festival of Pentecost. The apostles had been told to wait for an event that they would recognize only when it happened. That day God came upon them in a way they had never known before. They felt His presence and were filled with boldness to preach the message of Jesus.

The Christian church was born. It got off to a flying start: there were 3,000 conversions in a single day. The authorities soon cracked down, though. Prison awaited the disciples when excited crowds rioted after a spectacular healing. It did not deter them or the growing numbers who recognized the real hand of God upon the apostles.

Just as the church was getting itself organized, and people were learning to share responsibility and to meet for worship regularly, Stephen, one of the strongest of the new believers, was arrested, tried, and stoned to death for blasphemy. Christians fled in all directions as, flushed with success, the authorities made one last effort to stamp out the Christian church for good. However, not even prison could stop the disciples from preaching—especially when, on a couple of occasions, the apostles were freed in what could only be described as a miracle. One disciple, Philip, fled north to Samaria

Foreign gods
This is the Temple of Apollo in modern Turkey. The apostles met great resistance from some people on their travels. All the places they visited already had gods of their own, with great temples built in honor of them, such as this one. They did not want to give up the gods they had been worshiping, sometimes for thousands of years.

Paul's base of operations
Ephesus was, at this time, the most important city in the Roman province of Asia, in what is modern Turkey. Paul's final missionary journey had Ephesus as its goal, and he stayed there for over two years. He eventually made Ephesus the base for bringing Christianity to the whole region.

and led a powerful mission in which many people turned to Christ. Others, not named, spoke about the gospel wherever they went, starting small communities of Christians across Judea, Syria, and beyond.

Leading the opposition campaign was a Pharisee named Saul. Well learned in the scriptures, he knew all the stories about God's powerful deeds in the past. Little did he expect to experience one for himself. Thrown to the ground by a thunderbolt, blinded by a heavenly light, he was confronted by the risen Christ Himself and was suddenly converted to Christianity.

The new convert to Christianity used his Roman name, Paul, from then on as a sign of his change. After a period of study and reflection, thinking about his experiences, he was found by one of the church leaders, Barnabas, and called in to help the church at Antioch in Syria. It became his base, and from there he set off on three remarkable missionary journeys.

He trekked on foot and by sea all over what is now Asia Minor and Greece, starting churches and looking after the new converts. Although a Jew himself, he became the apostle to the Gentiles, the non-Jewish people, but he was not the first to recognize their rightful place in Jesus's church. That had been Peter, the leader of the apostles since the crucifixion of Jesus.

After an eventful life, in which he was shipwrecked several times, beaten by persecutors and muggers, stoned almost to death, and afflicted by illnesses and deprivation, Paul was finally arrested and shipped to Rome for trial before the Emperor Nero. The remainder of his life is uncertain, except that he was executed some four years after his arrival in Rome.

While he traveled, he also wrote thirteen of the New Testament books. These were mostly letters to people he had met, but they included a couple of essays on religion. He was not the only one to write, however. The New Testament ends with a remarkable vision, written by John, full of powerful symbolism, about the state of the world in the period between Christ's resurrection and future return. The book captures the hope of the first Christians which caused them to face appalling hardships, persecution, and the threat of death, all for the sake of Jesus Christ.

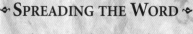

❖ SPREADING THE WORD ❖

This is the history of the early Christian Church, the acts of the apostles in the time after Jesus's death

THE EARLY CHURCH
Acts, Ch. 1–5, Ch 9–13.
PETER'S JOURNEYS
Acts, Ch. 3–5.
THE FIRST CHRISTIAN MARTYR
Acts, Ch. 6.
THE CONVERSION OF SAUL
Acts, Ch. 8 & 9.
PAUL'S MISSIONARY JOURNEYS
Acts, Ch. 11, 13–28.
THE VISION OF JOHN
Revelation

The Book of Revelation
Tradition says that the last book in the New Testament was written by the apostle John, shown here, who also wrote the fourth Gospel. The book is described as apocalyptic. This means that it says that God will eventually intervene and destroy the world to bring about his will. The book uses lots of symbolism, such as describing evil as a horned beast.

The Early Church

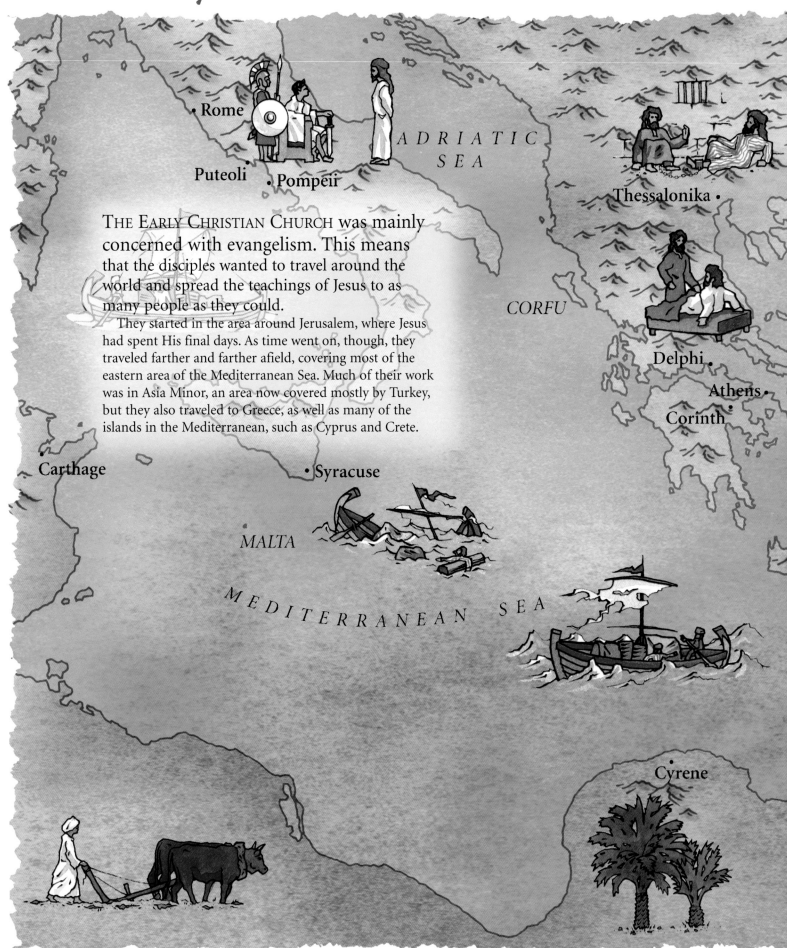

Rome

A D R I A T I C
S E A

Puteoli

Pompeii

Thessalonika

THE EARLY CHRISTIAN CHURCH was mainly concerned with evangelism. This means that the disciples wanted to travel around the world and spread the teachings of Jesus to as many people as they could.

CORFU

Much of their work was in Asia Minor, an area now covered mostly by Turkey, but they also traveled to Greece, as well as many of the islands in the Mediterranean, such as Cyprus and Crete.

Delphi

Athens

Corinth

Carthage

Syracuse

MALTA

M E D I T E R R A N E A N   S E A

Cyrene

BLACK SEA

Ancyra

Iconium

Ephesus

Miletus

Derbe

Tarsus

Antioch

Myra

Rhodes

CYPRUS

Salamis

Salmone

Paphos

Lasea   CRETE

Sidon

Damascus

MEDITERRANEAN   SEA

Caesarea

Jerusalem

Alexandria

Memphis

189

Twelve Once More

AFTER Jesus had been taken up into heaven, the disciples followed His instructions and went back to Jerusalem to wait for the Holy Spirit to come and baptize them. The friends were more than a little nervous. They had seen many extraordinary things since they had met Jesus. His miraculous return from the dead had crowned everything. Even so, the disciples couldn't imagine how the Holy Spirit would visit them, and they had no idea when it might happen. Still, the amazing events since Jesus's death had inspired new faith in the disciples. They realized that everything Jesus had ever said would happen had come to pass just as He had foretold. Even though Jesus was no longer among the disciples, their belief in Him and His teachings was unshakeable. They didn't doubt for one second that Jesus would one day come back to the world in all His glory, to establish God's kingdom on earth.

While the disciples were waiting for the Holy Spirit, they gathered together in a house in Jerusalem with Jesus's mother, Mary, the other women who had been close friends of Jesus, Jesus's brothers, and many dedicated followers—about 120 people in all. Everyone thought it best to lie low for a while. Now that the officials had succeeded in having Jesus executed, they were looking for an excuse to wipe out all His followers, too. They

Tree of Life
This engraving from the 1500s shows Jesus being crucified on the Tree of Life. The tree was said to be growing in the Garden of Eden. John sees a vision of it in Heaven, as he describes in the book of Revelation. It is a symbol of God's eternal life, a way of saying that Jesus lives forever.

The light of the world
The disciples' message was that Jesus was the only way to God. Jesus had called Himself the light of the world—that is, the one who shows people the way to God. In this painting by the English painter Holman Hunt, Jesus "the light of the world" is standing outside the door of someone's life, waiting to be invited in.

were determined to stop the spread of Jesus's teachings, which they felt sure were leading people away from the law of Moses. So Jesus's followers kept out of the way of any possible trouble and devoted themselves to praying.

There was just one thing that Peter felt had to be done.

"Jesus chose twelve of us to be His special helpers—one for each of the twelve tribes of Israel," Peter reminded the disciples one day. "Now there are only eleven of us."

The disciples hung their heads in shame and sadness as they remembered how Judas Iscariot had betrayed Jesus. Judas had waited until Jesus was in a quiet, vulnerable spot, then he had led the authorities straight to Him so they could arrest Him, all for 30 pieces of silver.

"Yes," the disciples agreed. "You are right, Peter. We feel it is what Jesus wants us to do. Whom should we pick?"

> **"** *And they cast lots for them, and the lot fell on Matthias; and he was enrolled with the eleven disciples.* **"**

The friends prayed and discussed, discussed and prayed, and finally agreed that the new disciple should be someone like them. They wanted someone who had followed Jesus right from the time when His cousin John first baptized Him and He started to teach, to the moment when He was taken up to heaven.

Out of all Jesus's followers, there were only two men who would do—Joseph and Matthias. Deciding between them was a very serious business. The disciples had to be absolutely sure that they chose the man that Jesus wanted. They prayed long and hard for guidance, and in the end Matthias was chosen. The disciples were twelve again.

Christian baptism
Baptism is a ceremony in which a person is sprinkled with, or immersed in, water. It is a sign that God forgives and cleanses people of their sins. Sometimes it includes (or is followed later by) laying-on of hands to receive the gifts of God's Spirit. This tomb from the AD 200s shows the priest laying hands on a child after baptism in Rome. The Holy Spirit is represented by the dove.

THE DISCIPLES PRAYED HARD FOR GUIDANCE. GOD LEADS HIS PEOPLE, BUT IT IS NOT ALWAYS EASY TO FIND OUT WHAT HE WANTS. PRAYER IS A WAY OF OPENING OURSELVES TO GOD AND HIS WILL.

❖ ABOUT THE STORY ❖

There was nothing magic about the number twelve, but it was an important sign to the first Christians. It showed them that God was making a new start. The Jewish race had started from the twelve sons of Jacob. The Christian Church begins with twelve disciples. The choice of the twelfth person had to be made by God, to show that the church was a spiritual fellowship, and not simply a human organization.

Tongues of Fire

THE disciples waited and prayed for a sign that the Holy Spirit was with them. Eventually, 50 days after Passover and the death of Jesus, it was time for the feast of Pentecost. This was the festival when Jews celebrated God's giving of the law to Moses. As usual, Jerusalem quickly filled with Jews from all over the known world who were coming to worship at the temple.

On the day of Pentecost itself, the disciples met together to worship. Their thoughts were suddenly disturbed by a rushing noise. They had never heard anything like it before. It was like a wind tearing through the room. They felt energy and passion blaze through them. The twelve friends turned to each other with joy, and saw that a tiny flame was hovering steadily over each man's head.

"The Holy Spirit is with us!" they cried.

To their utter astonishment, they heard each other speaking in foreign languages.

"Praise be to God!" they shouted. "We are blessed with special gifts from the Lord!"

The disciples ran out into the streets. They couldn't contain their excitement. Some disciples found themselves praising God in Greek. Others were shouting prayers in Arabic. Some heard themselves singing hymns in Latin and Persian, and other languages besides.

> "'We hear them telling in our own tongues the mighty works of God.'"

The hordes of Pentecost worshipers passing by were startled by the commotion and stopped to see what was going on. A crowd soon gathered around the disciples. Egyptians, Persians, Greeks, Romans, Libyans, Parthians, and Phrygians were all amazed to hear the disciples speaking perfectly in their own languages.

"Who are these men? They can understand and speak our language!" the foreign worshipers gasped.

Others simply scoffed at the strange sight.

"They're just talking gibberish!" some people mocked. "They must have been at the wine!"

At this, Peter called for silence.

THE HOLY SPIRIT IS GOD GIVING HIS POWER TO PEOPLE SO THAT THEY CAN SERVE HIM. THE DISCIPLES HAD TO WAIT TO RECEIVE HIM. WE CANNOT ORDER GOD TO DO WHAT WE WANT.

Church of the Holy Spirit
Pentecostal churches encourage members to use the 'gifts of the Holy Spirit'. Their worship is usually very lively.

The fire of the Spirit
The disciples saw the Spirit as tongues of flame above their heads. This medieval altar panel shows them waiting for the flames coming from the hands of God. Fire was a symbol of purity. The Spirit purified the disciples so they could work for God.

"We are not drunk!" he cried, his face lit up with exhilaration. "We are devout Jews and have been worshiping, just as we should do at Pentecost. This is the fulfillment of the prophecy of the prophet Joel."

The crowds scratched their heads as they tried to remember the Scriptures.

"Joel said that the time would come when God would pour out His Spirit over people and they would prophesy, and that in those days, anyone who turned to the Lord would be saved from punishment for their sins."

Many people in the crowd gasped and remembered.

"Israelites!" Peter continued. "We are Jews like you, yet we follow the teachings of Jesus of Nazareth. You all know that He was put to death unjustly. This was all according to God's plan. For God raised Him from the dead. We have seen Jesus alive with our own eyes! What has happened to us today is the work of the Holy Spirit flowing from Him!"

A murmur of amazement went around the crowd. It wasn't just Peter's rousing words or sudden ability to speak new languages that stirred them, it was also the disciples' happiness and passion.

"What do we have to do?" voices began to cry out.

"Be truly sorry for your sins," Peter answered. "Beg God's forgiveness in the name of Jesus Christ. Then you will receive the gift of the Holy Spirit!"

"Yes, we want to be saved through Jesus Christ!" shouted the crowd. "We want to obey Jesus's teachings!"

That very day, 3,000 people were baptized into the new Christian Church as followers of Jesus.

Judaism at the time of Christ
The first Christians were Jews or Gentiles, non-Jews who had embraced the Jewish religion. Some who were in Jerusalem on the day of Pentecost took the message of Christ to their home countries. Areas with a Jewish population are shown here in orange.

❧ ABOUT THE STORY ❧

Pentecost had originally been a celebration of the barley harvest and also of the "first fruits"—the first pickings of the fruit trees. So it was a significant day when the "first fruits" of the Holy Spirit—the people who became Christians—were "harvested." It had also become a celebration of God giving the law to Moses. Christians saw the Holy Spirit as God giving a new way of life to His people.

Peter the Healer

IN the days after Pentecost, the excitement in Jerusalem grew. Crowds came to hear the twelve preach and see them perform miracles in the name of Jesus of Nazareth. Every day more people believed that Jesus really was the Christ, the Son of God sent to save everyone from their sins, and that through Him all sinners could be saved.

One day, Peter and John were on their way into the temple to pray when a lame beggar sitting at the Beautiful Gate called out to them, "Kind sirs, do you have a few pennies you can spare?"

Peter and John stopped and stared at him.

"Look at us," Peter said kindly. "We have no silver or

gold—but what we do have, I will give you."

Peter stretched his hand toward the beggar.

"In the name of Jesus Christ of Nazareth," he said, "get up and walk."

Peter took the beggar by the hand.

As soon as the beggar touched Peter's fingertips, he felt new strength in the leg muscles and joints that had been useless for so long. His eyes lit up, and without thinking, he sprang to his feet.

He took a few steps, then a few skips, then a few jumps.

"I'm healed!" he yelled. "I'm healed!"

The beggar began to leap about and dance in delight. He followed Peter and John into the temple, praising God at the top of his voice. Worshipers hurried to see what the commotion was all about, and were astonished to see the beggar who had sat at the Beautiful Gate all his life. Before

The Beautiful Gate
Scholars are not certain where exactly Peter and John met the beggar in this story, but most think it was where the Corinthian Gate now is, on the east side of the Temple of Jerusalem. It led into the part of the temple called the Court of the Women. It would have been a good place to beg since many people passed it.

MIRACLES IN THE BIBLE ARE NOT ENDS IN THEMSELVES. THEY WILL ALWAYS POINT TO SOME TRUTH ABOUT GOD. IN THIS CASE, PETER USED THE HEALING TO PREACH ABOUT GOD'S SALVATION. ❧

A time for prayer
The Bible tells us that Peter and John were going to the temple at prayer time, 3 p.m. At this time there were set times for prayer in the temple. The morning and evening sacrifices were at 9 a.m. and 3 p.m., and there were prayer times to coincide with these. There were final prayers at sunset.

long a great crowd gathered around Peter, John, and the beggar in the temple courtyard.

"Why are you so amazed?" Peter asked the stunned onlookers. "Why do you look at us as if we're filled with strange magic powers? For it is God who has done this through us. The God of Abraham and Isaac and Jacob—and the Father of Jesus Christ—whom you put to death."

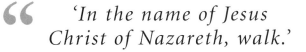

> ❝ *'In the name of Jesus Christ of Nazareth, walk.'* ❞

In a loud voice, Peter began to proclaim that God had brought Jesus of Nazareth back to life from the dead, that they had seen Him with their own eyes, and that it was their faith in Jesus Christ that had made the beggar well.

"Repent!" Peter cried to the crowds. "Turn again to God, that He may forgive your sins. Then, when Jesus Christ returns in all His glory at the end of the world, you will be blessed for ever instead of eternally damned."

The crowds suddenly fell back with fear. Temple guards armed with spears pushed through the people and marched up to the two disciples, followed by a group of angry priests and Sadducees, the religious elders.

"What are you doing?" the holy men thundered. "How dare you cause this rumpus in the temple!" They turned to the guards. "Arrest these men at once!"

Peter and John were hauled away to prison.

Statue of a sick man
This Egyptian statue dates from about 1200 B.C. In the ancient world there was little help for sick people. Many died young through disease.

Peter and John heal the beggar
This engraving shows the lame man just getting to his feet. Peter and John had been able to heal him only because God was working through them.

> ❦ **ABOUT THE STORY** ❦
>
> *Being a beggar was a miserable life. There was no social security system by which disabled or chronically sick people could get help from the government. They depended entirely on their families and the gifts of kind people. Peter and John could bring the gift of health and new life in every sense of the word—physical and spiritual. It was a sign that God was interested in every part of human life.*

Arrested

PETER and John watched the sun set through a prison window. They weren't surprised or downhearted. Jesus had warned the disciples that they would suffer opposition and danger as they tried to spread His word.

After a damp and dirty night in the cells, the two disciples were dragged before an emergency meeting of the Jewish high council, the Sanhedrin.

"Now," Caiaphas, the high priest, said, holding them in his icy stare. "Tell us by what power or in whose name you healed this lame beggar yesterday."

It was more of a challenge than a question, just as if Caiaphas were daring them to say the name "Jesus Christ."

Peter remembered that Jesus had promised that He would give His followers the words to argue against His

enemies. Peter knew he was filled with the Holy Spirit, and he had a new courage to face the high priest.

Peter said, "We healed him through Jesus of Nazareth. You tried to destroy Jesus, but God raised Him back to life. He is the only path to heaven."

The elders leaped to their feet at the disciple's boldness.

"These men are peasants!" some of the elders cried. "They are uneducated fishermen from Galilee."

> ## 'By what power or by what name did you do this?'

"Jesus of Nazareth was intelligent!" others exclaimed. "It's amazing he even spoke to these simple people. They probably can't even read or write."

"That may well be the case," others retorted, "but the

Jerusalem is central
This medieval map shows Jerusalem at the "center of the world." Jerusalem is central to the Bible story. It was where the first temple was built, where Jesus was crucified, and where the disciples first received the Holy Spirit. From Jerusalem, the message spread throughout the world.

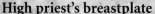

High priest's breastplate
The high priest, Caiaphas, would have worn a breastplate like this. It was studded with twelve semiprecious stones, one for each tribe of Israel. Inside the breastplate was a pocket, where high priests in Old Testament times kept the Urim and Thummim, sacred stones which may have been engraved with "yes" and "no." They were used to discover God's will.

fact remains that somehow they healed the beggar. What are we going to do about this miracle?"

The councillors argued among themselves.

"Listen!" the Jewish officials spat at last. "We order you never to mention Jesus of Nazareth again or do any type of miracles in His name. Do you understand?"

"We understand," replied Peter and John quite calmly, "but we can't do what you ask. We have to do what God wants us to do, not what you people want us to do."

At that, there was total uproar.

"How dare you defy the command of the Sanhedrin!" the enraged councillors shouted, and Peter and John were hauled away.

The elders were at their wits' end. They couldn't charge Peter and John with having broken any law, and to their immense frustration, they had no choice but to let them go with only a warning.

Back with their anxious friends, the two disciples praised God and prayed for strength and guidance.

"Lord, see how the elders have threatened us and grant us the courage to spread your gospel boldly, gracing us with the power to heal and perform miracles through Jesus Christ."

Despite the Sanhedrin's warning, the disciples carried on preaching and baptizing just as before.

Peter arrested
Peter was arrested on more than one occasion. This is an early sculpture showing him being dragged away.

Teaching the believers
Peter and John teach the early Christians. It is likely that besides formal sermons, much of the teaching was based on questions people asked.

❧ **ABOUT THE STORY** ❧

The disciples knew they were doing what God wanted. The fact that they were performing miracles, and that people were finding a new spiritual life through the power of Jesus, was proof of that. The authorities found it hard to contradict them. The problem was that Jesus's body had never been found. The disciples could be right—Jesus really had risen from the dead and was there in spirit, helping the disciples in their work.

The Early Church Community

EVERY day, the Jews who had become followers of Jesus prayed in the temple and also broke bread in their homes as Jesus had done at the Last Supper, remembering Him just as He had asked them to do. Followers old and new told everyone how they had found new happiness and peace thanks to Jesus of Nazareth and how they had received the gifts of the Holy Spirit through baptism. Their excited neighbors and friends would beg to join the new Jewish group too.

Being baptized as a follower of Jesus Christ wasn't an easy path to follow. Jesus's followers were expected to follow the disciples' leadership and live as Jesus had done. This meant giving up everything they had previously held

dear. They had to sell all their possessions and give their money to the disciples to be donated to the poor. Most followers did this willingly. They believed that it wouldn't be long before Jesus would return in glory—perhaps a matter of months, maybe a matter of years, but certainly within their lifetimes. What was the use in holding on to their possessions? Besides, they felt they had changed inside when they were baptized. They embraced the idea that they were now part of a church, a community of brothers and sisters. They were happy to share anything they needed, and found comfort and fulfillment in being kind and generous to others instead of self-centered and thoughtless.

However, others found it more difficult to give up everything they had worked so long and hard for. A man named Ananias and his wife Sapphira obediently sold everything they owned after they were baptized. Yet when Ananias went to give the money raised from the sale to the

The church goes on
The word "church" simply means a gathering. Its focus is on a group of people, not the building in which they may meet. From early times, Christians have gathered together to worship God and to learn about Him. The pattern of services may vary greatly from church to church, but they all have the same end in view, the worship of God.

Church building
Early church buildings were not unlike many of those seen today, as this mosaic from around A.D.400 shows. During New Testament times, though, there were no special church buildings. People met in the homes of Christians, outside, or in hired halls. Later the apostle Paul uses the image of a building. He says that Christians are built into a new community as stones are built into a temple.

disciples, he didn't take all of it. He and his wife decided to keep some back for a rainy day.

As Ananias laid down his sacks of money before the disciples, Peter frowned at him.

"Ananias, why has the devil filled your heart?" Peter challenged. "You are lying to the Holy Spirit and keeping back some of your money!"

Ananias and Sapphira had not breathed a word to anyone of what they had done. Ananias realized that Peter couldn't possibly have known, unless God Himself had told him! The terrified man stood openmouthed and

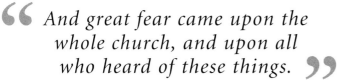

> *And great fear came upon the whole church, and upon all who heard of these things.*

spluttered. Words stuck in his throat, and he began to choke and gasp. A cold fear clutched at his heart and squeezed it with icy fingers. Then he fell down dead.

Sadly, the disciples carried him out to bury him. Three hours later, while they were still away, the unsuspecting Sapphira arrived.

"Where is my husband?" she asked, cheerfully.

Then her face fell. Sapphira saw that Peter looked grim. She felt that the atmosphere in the room was stony. Sapphira realized that something was wrong.

"First, tell me how much you have sold the land for," Peter asked her.

Sapphira swallowed hard and lied about the amount, feeling her face begin to flush with shame.

Peter's eyes flashed fire. "Why have you and your husband joined together in sin?" he demanded. "Why do you think you can deceive the Holy Spirit?"

Sapphira hung her head.

"Listen," said Peter, growing angrier by the second. "Do you hear footsteps? They are the footsteps of those who have just buried your husband. They're coming to do exactly the same to you!"

With a scream, Sapphira fainted and fell stone dead on the floor.

When the disciples came in, they found they had another body to bury. All the followers who heard of God's wrath trembled in fear. How glad they were that they had found salvation through Jesus Christ! God's punishments on sinners were terrible.

Caring for the needy
The first Christians cared for each other. They were not afraid to sell possessions and give the money to help others. They did this because Jesus had given up everything, including His life, for them. They also believed God would bless them spiritually.

❧ **ABOUT THE STORY** ❧

This story shows how important honesty and truth are. Ananias and Sapphira wanted to appear generous. They pretended they had given everything, but they hadn't. There was really nothing wrong with keeping some of the money for themselves. There was everything wrong with lying to Peter and, by doing so, lying to God. Their harsh punishment reminded the Christians that they were to respect God.

Teaching in Jesus's Name

PETER became famous as a healer. People from towns and villages all over Judea began to put sick people out in the streets, in case Peter passed by. They believed that if even his shadow fell on them, they would be healed.

The officials of the Sanhedrin were worried. Even though Jesus was dead, it was in His name that people were being stirred up. Even some of the priests had been baptized as followers.

"We must put a stop to this!" the officials exclaimed.

Once again they had Peter and John arrested and flung into the city prison with murderers, robbers, and thugs.

Peter and John weren't behind bars long. That night, an angel of the Lord came and released them.

"Go to the temple and tell everyone about salvation

through Jesus Christ," the angel told them, before he disappeared. That's exactly what Peter and John did.

Meanwhile, the Sanhedrin members were waiting for the guards to bring Peter and John before them. Caiaphas sat impatiently drumming his fingers.

Down in the dungeons, the guards were panicking. Peter and John were nowhere to be found. The baffled guards trembled with fear as they returned to Caiaphas.

"The prisoners have gone," the guards mumbled.

"What do you mean, gone?" the high priest roared.

The cowering soldiers shrugged.

"The sentries were on guard and the doors locked, but Peter and John weren't there."

Remains of Peter's house
These remains in Capernaum are believed by some scholars to be of the house where Peter lived. It was used as a church for some 300 years, and later a church was built over part of it, which suggests that the first Christians thought it special.

Leader of the disciples
Peter was the spokesman for the twelve disciples during Jesus's lifetime and afterward. He often spoke up when the others were afraid.

"Allright!" shouted Caiaphas. "That's it! You're going into the dungeons yourselves until . . ."

Luckily for the guards, a servant burst in.

"Well?" snapped the high priest.

"My lord, we've heard that your two Galilean prisoners are preaching in the temple!" the servant panted.

> ❝ *'We must obey God rather than men.'* ❞

Thunder-faced, Caiaphas sent his guards off to arrest Peter and John again, and the next day the disciples found themselves facing the fury of the Sanhedrin.

"We expressly forbade you to mention the name of Jesus of Nazareth!" the councillors fumed.

"We must do what God wants," Peter and John insisted. "God has filled us with the Holy Spirit so we can testify that Jesus is the Savior of the world."

The members of the Sanhedrin were enraged.

"Put them to death!" the Jewish officials cried. "They have no regard for us or our laws!"

One voice rose over the uproar. "Calm down! Take the prisoners away while we discuss things properly."

It was the Pharisee Gamaliel, a teacher of the law, for whom everyone had the utmost respect.

"Friends, listen," Gamaliel continued. "In past years, several so-called holy men have risen up and tried to set up religious sects to rival the worship of God. Look what happened to them. One by one they came to a sticky end and their followers were all killed. It is bound to be the same with this Jesus of Nazareth."

The Jewish officials murmured their agreement.

"There is another reason not to overreact," Gamaliel went on. "There is a possibility—although we are all agreed that it is highly remote—that Jesus really is who His disciples say He is: the Son of God. If this were true, nothing anyone could do would stop His followers. In the end, we might even be found guilty of opposing God!"

The scowling elders could see the sense in Gamaliel's words. Grudgingly, they agreed to let Peter and John go. However, first, they had the disciples beaten and ordered them once more never to speak the name of Jesus of Nazareth again.

Reaching a verdict
The Sanhedrin was the Jews' supreme court of law. Verdicts were reached by voting. In Greek courts, jurors used voting disks like these, which come from around 300 B.C. Those with a solid hub meant the person was not guilty; those with a hole meant guilty.

Prisoner in agony
This silver and bronze figure shows a Libyan prisoner in Egypt between 1580 and 1200 B.C. Throughout history people have invented ways of hurting and torturing people they don't like, as the authorities did with Peter and John.

❧ **ABOUT THE STORY** ❧

Gamaliel's common sense saved the Sanhedrin from another miscarriage of justice. They had condemned Jesus illegally, as they had not allowed a day to pass before a guilty verdict was announced. They were about to do the same again. Luke, who wrote this story, is showing that God was in control. Jesus had to die, to fulfill God's purpose. The disciples could not die yet; they had work to do for God to fulfill His purpose.

Stephen the Martyr

As the number of people who wanted to follow Christ increased, so did the number of helpers the disciples needed. The disciples chose seven men to distribute money and food and preach Jesus's gospel. One assistant, named Stephen, stood out as being especially learned and courageous. He was full of faith and the Holy Spirit, and had the power to work miracles. He spoke with such wisdom that the teachers in the synagogues found they had met their match. Eventually, the elders bribed people to say they had heard Stephen speak out against Moses and God. Stephen was put on trial before the Sanhedrin.

"We've heard this man Stephen say Jesus of Nazareth will destroy the temple and will change the laws that Moses gave us direct from the hand of God," people lied.

Stephen listened to all the lies without blinking or saying a word. His face grew bright and shone like the face of an angel.

The high priest tried to ignore the glow of Stephen's face. "Is this so?" he questioned. "Tell us now!"

The Holy Spirit helped Stephen speak. He spoke of the Jewish people, from the

moment God had chosen Abraham to found the Jewish faith and guided him to Israel. Stephen said that God had sent Jesus of Nazareth as the fulfillment of His plan. In the past, the elders had persecuted prophets for speaking the truth, and they had done exactly the same thing to Christ.

"Jesus is the Savior of the world, sent to you by God Himself," Stephen cried. "You murdered Him!"

The Sanhedrin were outraged. They exploded with hate.

To their immense annoyance, Stephen seemed totally unaware of it all. The young man stood gazing upward, a blissful smile on his face.

"Look!" he gasped. "I can see the heavens opening!"

Stephen fell to his knees, oblivious to the riot around him.

"I can see the Son of Man sitting at the right hand of God!" Stephen gasped, with tears of joy in his eyes.

"What is this rubbish?" the Jewish officials yelled, looking up and seeing nothing but the bricks of the roof. Stephen's calmness enraged them even more.

"This man reckons he can see God!" the elders cried. "It's blasphemy—and the punishment is death!"

The officials clapped their hands over their ears so they wouldn't have to hear any more of Stephen's vision.

> " *They chose Stephen, a man full of faith and of the Holy Spirit.* "

"Take him away!" they shouted to the guards.

The soldiers dragged Stephen through the streets of Jerusalem and out of the city gates, with the furious Sanhedrin following, picking up rocks as they went. They reached the spot where stonings took place and stood Stephen up against a wall.

"Forgive them, Lord," Stephen murmured as the elders backed away. "Don't hold this sin against them."

The elders took off their cloaks and gave them to an eager young Pharisee named Saul to hold. Then they began to throw stones with glee.

"Lord Jesus, receive my spirit," Stephen cried aloud, as he sank down under the rain of rocks.

At last, Stephen lay dead. He was the first person to die in the name of Jesus Christ.

The stoning of Stephen
Stoning was the usual method of execution used by the Jews. Their law allowed it for many offenses. Jewish law said that the chief witnesses had to cast the first stone.

Stephen's gate
This street in Jerusalem is said to be where Stephen was stoned.

❧ ABOUT THE STORY ❧

Stephen was the first Christian martyr. The word comes from a Greek word which means witness. A martyr is someone who believes in his or her faith to the extent of being willing to die for it. During his trial, Stephen had spoken of the history of the Israelites, in which people had regularly disobeyed God. Now, he said, they had ignored God's message once again, by crucifying Jesus.

Saul and the Christians

THE very same day that Stephen was stoned, the Sanhedrin decided that enough was enough. They marveled that the followers of Jesus Christ were so loyal that they were even willing to die for Him. There were more followers than ever. Every day, the disciples were turning hundreds of Jews toward the new ideas of Jesus of Nazareth. The officials had to put a stop to the spread of Christ's word, and fast. They had tried ordering and threatening, and it had done no good. The Sanhedrin decided that force was the only avenue left.

Only a few hours after Stephen died, temple soldiers and the officers of the Jewish elders went marching into every house in Jerusalem, hunting high and low for followers of Jesus Christ. They upturned every house, questioned anyone who looked the slightest bit suspicious, and managed to haul off many followers. One of the keenest officers was the young Pharisee Saul, who had held the Sanhedrin's cloaks at Stephen's stoning. Saul wished with all his heart that he hadn't been lumbered with holding the garments. He would have liked to have been able to throw a few stones himself.

Saul hated the followers of Jesus Christ with a vengeance. He had been brought up a very strict Jew, and he felt that Jesus's disciples were busy undoing everything that he had always believed was important. Saul made up his mind that he would make the Sanhedrin's command his life's work. It didn't matter how long it took, he would

Early spread of Christianity
Jesus told the disciples that they were to take the Christian message to "Judea, Samaria, and the rest of the world." The early chapters of Acts show how Philip (shown in mauve) and Peter (shown in red) traveled around the whole region.

PERSECUTION IS TO MAKE A PERSON OR GROUP OF PEOPLE SUFFER FOR SOME REASON. CHRISTIANS HAVE ALWAYS FACED SUFFERING, FOLLOWING THE EXAMPLE OF JESUS, BUT THOSE WHO FLED SAUL'S MEN HELPED TO SPREAD JESUS'S WORD ABROAD. ∾

Samaria
This city was despised by traditional Jews at the time of Christ. The city had existed since King Jeroboam had made it Israel's capital after the kingdom split under King Solomon. Herod the Great built a temple there dedicated to the Roman Emperor Augustus shortly before Christ was born.

stop at nothing until every last follower of Jesus Christ was locked up, and preferably killed. Saul decided that he wouldn't stop at Jerusalem, either. After turning the holy city upside down, Saul commanded his disciple-hunters to sweep through the whole of Judea.

Never in his wildest dreams did Saul think that he was actually part of God's plan to spread the word of Jesus Christ. In forcing Jesus's followers to flee, he caused the gospel to be taken to many thousands of people who wouldn't otherwise have heard it. In every region the escaping followers passed through, they told the locals the good news of Jesus's promise of salvation. Jews everywhere begged to be baptized.

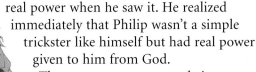

> *Now, those who were scattered went about preaching the word.*

The disciple Philip had great success in the city of Samaria. He preached passionately and worked great miracles. He healed those who were paralyzed and cured others with terrible sicknesses that racked their bodies with pain and tormented their minds. Crowds hurried to see Philip's amazing powers, and hundreds were baptized. One of the new followers was a man named Simon, who for years had conned the locals into thinking he was a magician by performing tricks and conjuring. Simon knew

real power when he saw it. He realized immediately that Philip wasn't a simple trickster like himself but had real power given to him from God.

There were so many people in Samaria who flocked to hear Philip's message that he couldn't cope with the numbers, so Philip's friends and fellow disciples of Jesus, Peter and John, journeyed down to help him. When the two disciples arrived, they laid their hands on those who had been baptized and prayed that they might receive the gifts of the Holy Spirit.

"How amazing!" cried Simon, when he saw what Peter and John were doing. "You have magic in your hands! I'd give anything to have power like that!"

The ex-magician scrabbled through his bag and pulled out the last of his money.

"Look, take this!" he cried, holding out a handful of coins. "Give me some of your magic power, too!"

Peter turned on Simon in fury. He didn't often get angry, but when he did, it was terrifying.

"May your silver be damned along with you!" Peter roared, dashing the money to the ground. "You can't buy gifts from God!"

For the first time in his life, Simon was truly humbled before Peter. He made up his mind to make the most of what he was and not strive to be anything else or to envy others their special gifts.

"I am truly sorry," he said. "Please pray for me that my sins be forgiven through Jesus Christ."

Philip
God gave Philip the gift of preaching, to spread the Christian message and to bring people to personal faith. This mosaic from the 1100s shows him casting a demon from a man.

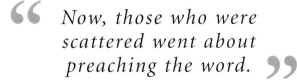

❧ ABOUT THE STORY ❧

According to Tertullian, a Christian writer in the A.D.300s, "the blood of the martyrs is the seed of the church." The church has grown most during times when Christians are being persecuted. This is partly because people decide that Christianity must be true if it is worth dying for. No one would die for a lie. It is also because early Christians amazed observers by their love for each other.

Philip and the Ethiopian

AFTER Peter and John had helped Philip in Samaria, they returned to Jerusalem. They preached the word of Jesus in many Samarian villages along the way. Philip didn't go with them. An angel of the Lord spoke to him and told him to go south instead, down the road from Jerusalem to Gaza. So Philip obediently set off down the hot, dusty, desert road. He didn't know exactly where he was going, but he remembered that Jesus had said so many times before that God would always show the way.

As Philip trudged along, he saw a chariot come slowly rumbling by with an important-looking passenger inside. The chariot bore the symbol of the queen of Ethiopia, in Africa, and Philip realized that its passenger must be one of the queen's government ministers, who was returning home after worshiping in the temple in Jerusalem.

As Philip marveled at the splendid sight, he heard a voice speaking to him, urging him gently.

"Philip, go and meet the man in the chariot," the voice said, and Philip knew it was the Holy Spirit.

Right away, Philip ran to the chariot and greeted the minister with a respectful bow.

"Good afternoon," said Philip.

The minister turned his head haughtily. He was reading a scroll of the teachings of the prophet Isaiah, and he didn't look too pleased at being interrupted. Still he was well brought up and polite, so he said "Good afternoon" back, before returning to his reading.

Philip didn't give up, though.

"I see you're reading Isaiah," he said, pleasantly. "What do you think of it? Can you understand the prophecies?"

The minister was quite taken aback by the bold question. No one in the Ethiopian royal court would ever dare approach him and talk to him like that. He was just about to scold Philip when he noticed the kindness and honesty in his eyes. There was something about Philip that made the minister bare his heart and speak quite openly.

"No, I don't really understand much of it," the minister confessed in a whisper. "How can I, when I don't have anyone to help me?"

"Well, I understand it," said Philip, with a grin.

"Do you?" said the minister excitedly. "Do you really? Then you'd better come and join me."

Philip clambered up into the regal chariot and sat

beside the Ethiopian minster. He picked up reading from the point where he had interrupted the man. As they continued the journey together he explained the Scriptures and told the Ethiopian minister all about the good news of Jesus.

> *Beginning with this scripture, he told him the good news of Jesus.*

The minister was entranced. Every word that Philip said rang true in his heart. The way of life Jesus preached was surely the only way to heaven. Jesus of Nazareth was surely the Christ foretold by the ancient scriptures!

Suddenly, the minister yelled "STOP!" at the top of his voice. The horses slowed to a halt, and the minister jumped out of the chariot.

"Look!" he said excitedly, pointing across the road. "There's a pool. I want you to baptize me as a follower of Jesus Christ right away."

He grabbed Philip's hand and hurried him across the road as fast as his legs would carry him, splashing into the water. He listened intently to Philip's prayers, joining in with them in his heart. Then came the great moment. Philip dipped him down under the water, and the minister was washed clean from all his sins. He emerged new-born, ready to begin a new life as a

follower of Christ. Philip was gone. The beaming minister looked all around, but couldn't find him anywhere. Still, nothing could dampen his spirits. He went on his way, singing God's praises and rejoicing at his new-found faith and salvation.

As for Philip, he had been mysteriously whisked away by the Holy Spirit and taken to another town where he was needed to preach the gospel. He continued to preach the word of Jesus and convert people all the way down the road to Caesarea.

A Holy King
This minister was probably a royal treasurer for the queen mother. In Ethiopia at this time it was the queen mother who ruled the country from day to day, as the king himself was thought to be too holy.

Ethiopian
In biblical times, the country of Ethiopia was in fact Nubia, which is now part of Sudan and Egypt, in northern Africa.

❧ **ABOUT THE STORY** ❧
The Ethiopian was a Gentile who had adopted the Jewish religion. He would not have been allowed to take part in Jewish ceremonies, because he was foreign. There was a Jewish community in Upper Egypt, from whom he had probably first heard about God. He is evidently very keen to find out more. This story shows how God met his spiritual need by inspiring Philip to be in the right place at the right time.

The Road to Damascus

THE YOUNG Pharisee soldier Saul had been having great success in his mission to wipe out the followers of Christ. Jerusalem's prisons were full to bursting with followers, all thanks to him. Saul was feared far and wide. Day and night, capturing followers was all he thought about.

When Saul had stormed from Jerusalem through every town and village in Judea, he went to the high priest and asked permission to extend his search to Damascus. The high priest gave Saul letters to take to all the synagogues, telling them that Saul had the authority to arrest whomever he pleased.

As the city of Damascus loomed in front of him, he rubbed his hands together eagerly. There should be plenty more followers of Jesus to hunt down there . . .

Suddenly Saul was struck by a flash of lightning which knocked him off his horse and left him cowering on the ground.

"Saul, Saul, why are you persecuting me?" a voice boomed.

"Who are you?" Saul stammered.

"I am Jesus, your sworn enemy," the voice replied.

Saul shook with fear. Deep in his heart, he knew it was the truth and he groaned aloud.

"Now rise," the voice ordered. "Continue into the city and wait there."

Saul sensed the light fading from all around him. He lowered his hands from his face and opened his eyes. Everything was pitch black.

"I'm blind!" he yelled, scrabbling around in a panic. "Help! Help! I'm blind!"

"Sir, whatever happened?" the soldiers asked, as they helped Saul up. "Why did you fall off your horse? What was that strange sound?"

"Did you not see anything?" Saul gasped. "Did you not hear the voice and what it said?"

"We heard something, Sir," the guards said. They looked at each other worriedly. Had Saul been working too hard?

Slowly and carefully, the soldiers led Saul into the city and found a room where he could stay. Saul would say nothing further to anyone. He wouldn't eat. He wouldn't drink. He hung his head, his sightless eyes gazing blankly

✦ ABOUT THE STORY ✦

This was a unique event. We do not know exactly what happened, except that Paul later said the people with him heard something, but did not see the light. Only Paul himself heard the full message and actually saw Jesus in the shining light. Paul later became an apostle— one who had seen the risen Jesus. Many visions of God include bright light, because light is a symbol of purity.

Thirteen disciples
This engraving shows thirteen disciples. Matthias has replaced Judas, and Paul (far left) has joined them. The disciples were the recognized authorities of the early church. Their teaching was regarded as coming from God.

at the ground, completely absorbed in his own thoughts.

Two whole days passed like this. The soldiers did not know what to do. On the third day, there was a knock at the door. It was a stranger named Ananias.

"The Lord told me to come and find you here," said Ananias, helping the wobbly Saul to his feet. "I know that you are the enemy of Jesus Christ, but He says that He has chosen you to spread His teachings—not just to the Jews, but to the Gentiles, too."

With that, Ananias laid his hands on Saul's trembling head. At once, scales seemed to fall away from Saul's eyes and he found he could see once more. Totally overcome with relief and joy, Saul fell on his knees and gave thanks to God. Then, to the utter astonishment of his soldiers, he begged to be baptized. He wanted to become one of the followers of Jesus Christ whom he had sought to wipe out!

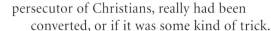

❝ *'Saul, Saul, why do you persecute me?'* ❞

Once Saul had gotten his strength back, he went to the synagogues in Damascus and proclaimed Jesus as the Son of God. People couldn't work out if the famous Saul, persecutor of Christians, really had been converted, or if it was some kind of trick.

At first, only the Jews who refused to believe in Jesus Christ decided that Saul was sincere. They felt that their greatest ally had betrayed them, and in their disappointment, they plotted to kill him. Suddenly Saul found himself being persecuted for the sake of Jesus Christ, just as he had persecuted so many others! Luckily, Saul heard of the plan and escaped.

It proved harder to convince the followers of Jesus that he really had changed. The disciple Barnabas, who believed Saul, took him to the twelve disciples. He told them what had happened on the road to Damascus, and Jesus's followers decided to accept Saul's amazing turnaround.

As an outward sign of his new inner life, Saul changed his name to Paul. He put even more energy and dedication into preaching the gospel of Jesus Christ than he had previously spent in the persecution of Jesus's followers. He was a highly educated Pharisee with extensive knowledge of the Scriptures, and he won arguments against the most learned Jewish elders in Jerusalem. The former favorite of the Sanhedrin soon became the most hated. As soon as the disciples heard that the elders wanted to kill Paul, they sent him off to Tarsus, far to the north, to teach far away from the people who had become his bitter enemies.

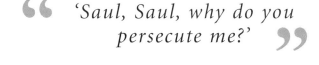

VERY FEW PEOPLE EXPERIENCE SUCH A SUDDEN CONVERSION AS THIS. OCCASIONALLY SOME DRAMATIC EVENT HELPS PEOPLE PUT THEIR FAITH IN JESUS. MOST PEOPLE GROW INTO FAITH SLOWLY. ❧

Paul's journey to Damascus
Damascus is in Syria, the country to the north of Judea. In the first century, it was part of the same Roman province as Judea. It was about 150 miles north of Jerusalem, and it would have taken Saul several days to travel there and back.

Tarsus
This was Saul's home in southeast Asia Minor (modern Turkey). Tarsus was an important city in Roman times and may have housed up to half a million people. It was sited on important trade routes. These trade routes and its port made the city rich.

Aeneas and Tabitha

THE followers who had run away from Saul's persecution spread Jesus's teachings throughout Judea and Samaria, and into Jesus's home of Galilee. At the same time, the disciples were busy traveling from synagogue to synagogue, preaching the gospel of Jesus to large congregations of Jews and winning many believers by the miracles they worked in Jesus's name.

In a town called Lydda in the northeast of Judea, Peter was told about a man named Aeneas. All the locals respected him as a good and kind man. Aeneas had been very ill for over eight years and had become paralyzed and confined to bed. His life had become a misery, with his healthy mind trapped inside a useless body.

"You must go and visit Aeneas," the people of Lydda

begged Peter. "The poor man has been terribly ill for so long. You are famous for the amazing healing miracles that you do in the name of Jesus Christ. We are sure you can cure Aeneas, too. Please help him!"

Peter went at once to Aeneas's house, and when he saw the faithful, God-fearing man lying in pain, he took pity on him straight away.

"Aeneas, Jesus Christ heals you," Peter said gently, taking his hand. "Get up now, and make your bed."

In front of all his neighbors, Aeneas swung his legs over the edge of the bed and stood up. Tears sparkled in his eyes. He flung his arms around Peter.

"I can walk!" he wept. "Praise be to God and all glory to His Son, Jesus Christ!"

A good example
Tabitha was a Christian who used her skills to help others. She was not known as a preacher, but she was known by her generosity.

Joppa
Tabitha lived in Joppa, which today is known as Jaffa and is part of the city of Tel Aviv. It is on the Mediterranean coast of Israel. It had been an important port since about 1600B.C., although tradition suggests it was built earlier by Noah's son Japheth.

The celebrations at Lydda went on well into the night, but right in the middle of it all, two followers came hurrying from the nearby town of Joppa to find Peter.

"We've been sent to ask if you'll come to Joppa right away," they begged Peter. "The people there are desperate for your help."

> " *Aeneas, Jesus Christ heals you; rise and make your bed.* "

Immediately, Peter set off for the little town. He arrived to find the sound of wailing filling the streets. A woman named Tabitha had just died, and the whole of Joppa was in mourning. Everyone had loved Tabitha. She had always put others first, never thinking about herself. Tabitha was always on the lookout for kind, generous things she could do for other people. Almost everyone in Joppa had benefited from her kindness, especially the needy.

Tabitha had been a skilled seamstress, and she had spent her own money and time in making clothes for many of the poor. Now she was gone, her dead body laid out in the upstairs room of her house, and everyone was deeply sad. The people of Joppa had heard that Peter was near, and they believed that, working through Peter, the power of Jesus Christ could help.

Peter looked around at the weeping faces of Tabitha's friends and relatives and called for silence. He knelt down beside the dead woman and prayed for a long time. Apart from Jesus Himself, only the great prophets Elijah and Elisha had ever been granted the grace to bring someone back from the dead.

Eventually, Peter opened his eyes.

"Tabitha, get up," he said firmly.

The people in the crowded room stood anxiously, scanning Tabitha's body for any signs of life. There was a gasp as her eyelids flickered a few times and then opened. Tabitha turned her head and looked straight at Peter. He stretched out his hand and beckoned, and Tabitha placed her hand in Peter's and allowed him to help her up.

The faith of the people of Joppa had been rewarded. Peter had brought Tabitha back to life, in the name of Jesus Christ.

Spinning and weaving
In biblical times, many people made their own clothes. Wool was spun into threads on a spindle (which is what the woman on the left is doing) and then woven into a garment or a piece of cloth on a wooden-framed loom. Some people specialized in this trade and sold the cloth to others.

A devout woman
This statue shows a woman worshiping God. Tabitha always worshiped God faithfully.

Peter and Cornelius

IT wasn't only Jews who were turning to follow Jesus Christ. Many non-Jews, or Gentiles, were showing a keen interest in Jesus's promise of salvation, too. For a long time, the disciples knew that Jesus wanted them to spread the gospel to Jews through the whole world, but were not sure what to do about Gentiles. In the end, the Lord showed them.

After Peter had brought Tabitha back to life, he stayed in Joppa at the house of Simon, a tanner. One day, when Peter went up on the flat roof to pray, he saw the heavens open and a sheet being let down, spread like a picnic with all kinds of animals and birds.

"Kill something and eat it," said God into his mind.

Peter was horrified. He remembered all the Jewish laws about which animals and birds were considered clean to eat, the prayer rituals that should be said before killing them and the rules about how they should be cooked.

"No, Lord!" cried Peter in horror. "I could never eat anything unclean or not prepared properly."

"You must not consider unclean anything that God has cleansed," replied the voice, sternly.

The command was repeated twice, and Peter replied the same, before the sheet finally returned to heaven.

Peter was sure that God was trying to teach him something, but what? Peter's thoughts were interrupted by a voice speaking once again into his mind.

"Three men have arrived, looking for you," said God. "Go with them, for I have sent them."

IT IS VERY EASY TO LOOK DOWN ON PEOPLE WHO ARE DIFFERENT FROM US. THIS STORY TELLS US THAT GOD REGARDS ALL PEOPLE EQUALLY, AND SO SHOULD WE. ❧

"Gentiles—keep out!"
Gentiles were allowed only into the first of three courts surrounding the temple in Jerusalem. It was here that the traders sold animals for sacrifices and where the money changers had their stalls. There were notices up all around the temple—this is one of them—telling the Gentiles not to go any farther.

The bemused Peter obediently went downstairs.

"I'm Peter," he said. "How can I help you?"

"Our master, Cornelius, has sent us to find you," the three men began. "He's a Gentile, a Roman centurion. He's always been a God-fearing man. He prays regularly and insists that his whole household do the same. He gives lots of money to charity and all the Jews in the neighborhood think very highly of him." The servants looked at each other nervously. "An angel appeared to Cornelius while he was praying and told him to send for you."

"Well, in that case, I'd better come with you," Peter said, and the three men smiled with relief.

The next day, the three servants took Peter and his companions to Cornelius's house. The centurion had gathered a welcome party of his family and friends. When Peter walked through the door, Cornelius fell on his knees before him. At that very moment, Peter understood what his vision of the picnic blanket had meant.

"Don't kneel before me," Peter said, helping Cornelius to his feet. "You're a man just as I am."

> '*God has shown me that I should not call any man common or unclean.*'

Cornelius was startled. He knew that it was unlawful for Jews to have Gentile friends and that special cleansing rituals were necessary if a Jew ever went into a Gentile house. Peter didn't seem bothered.

"I understand now that God has no favorites," Peter said. "He will welcome anyone who does what is right—no matter who they are or where they're from, whether they're Jew or Gentile, man or woman."

While Peter was speaking, everyone in Cornelius's house felt a strange glow in their hearts. They had been filled with the Holy Spirit, and they began praising God.

The Jews who had come with Peter were astonished. Yet Peter now understood.

"See?" he said. "Who can possibly say that Gentiles shouldn't be allowed to follow Christ?"

Cornelius and his household were the first Gentiles anywhere to be baptized.

❈ CLEAN AND UNCLEAN ANIMALS ❈

Jewish people live by a series of dietary laws, called *kashrut* or *kosher*. These laws set down not only which foods can be eaten, but also which foods Jews can eat with which.

LAND ANIMALS
The Jews were allowed to eat any animal that had a completely split hoof and also chewed the cud. This included cows and sheep. They were not allowed to eat camels, rabbits, or pigs.

WATER CREATURES
All fish that had fins and scales were considered clean. They could not eat any sea mammals, such as dolphins, or shellfish.

INSECTS
Only one kind of insect was clean: the hoppers (grasshoppers, locusts, etc). All other insects could not be eaten.

BIRDS
Poultry and similar birds were allowed (the Israelites ate quails in the desert after they left Egypt). Most other birds were banned as unclean, including hunting birds, such as eagles, gulls, and owls.

Tanning animal skins
This shows Egyptians tanning the skins of animals, as Simon in the story did. Tanning made the skin into soft leather.

Peter in Prison

KING Herod Agrippa hated the growth of the church of Jesus Christ almost as much as Paul had done at first. The king knew that the followers drew great strength from their faith in God and the promises Jesus had made them. He feared them because of this. He was deeply worried by the way that the disciples had stood up to the Sanhedrin, saying that they obeyed only God, not men. Herod saw this as outright defiance of all human rulers and kings.

Herod determined to wipe out the followers of Jesus Christ once and for all. He ordered his guards to arrest Jesus's followers whenever possible. The king didn't stop at imprisonment. He had James, the brother of John, put to death. When he saw how this pleased the Jewish elders, and how he gained popularity among many traditional Jews because of it, he had Peter arrested and thrown into the dungeons too.

The only thing that stopped King Herod from executing Peter right away was his concern not to be seen as a murderer. He had to be seen to give the disciple a trial first, even if it was on false charges and with bribed, corrupt witnesses. In the meantime, Herod kept Peter chained up to two soldiers—even while he slept—with a 24-hour guard outside his cell door. He knew how important Peter was to the disciples and he felt sure that the followers would try to come and rescue him. The king had also heard the strange stories of how Peter and John had disappeared from prison when the Sanhedrin had arrested them. He didn't want that to happen again.

The night before Peter was due to stand trial and face execution, he dreamed that a strange light blazed into his dingy cell and that an angel was stirring him awake.

"Quickly, get up!" the angel commanded him.

Peter dreamed that the chains and shackles fell from his feet and he was no longer bound up to the snoring soldiers on either side.

"Dress yourself," came the angel's urgent voice. "Put on your sandals."

In his hurry, Peter tripped and nearly fell over himself. The pain felt real, but Peter was sure he was dreaming.

"Wrap your cloak around you and follow me," came the final instruction.

Peter followed after the gliding angel, right through the dungeon door and past the sentries, who were all fast asleep at their posts, up the prison steps to the great iron gate. It swung open on its own, and the angel and Peter stepped out into the moonlit street. At once, the angel vanished, and Peter felt a chilly breeze brush his skin. It hadn't been a dream after all! He was really free!

"The Lord has rescued me!" Peter realized.

He hurried through the deserted city to the house belonging to Mark's mother, Mary. Peter had to get to a safe hiding place before the sun came up and Herod's guards realized that he was missing.

At last Peter arrived in front of the little door. Knock, knock, knock, he rapped softly. No answer.

"Well, it is the middle of the night," he supposed. "Everyone is probably asleep."

Thump, thump, thump. Peter knocked a little louder.

"Please wake up," Peter thought. "Hurry up and let me in before one of Herod's watchmen sees me."

No one came to answer.

 And the chains fell off his hands.

Bang, bang, bang! The desperate Peter hit the door even harder, and to his great relief he at last heard footsteps. The door swung open a little way, and an anxious pair of eyes peered nervously out at him. The eyes widened in surprise and then a mouth gasped, and the door was slammed shut in Peter's face.

Peter stood shivering on the doorstep while he heard the sound of arguing voices inside. A few moments later, the door opened a crack once more and a whole host of faces peered expectantly out.

"I told you it was!" exclaimed a voice.

"It is!" someone else cried.

Then the door was flung wide open, and Peter was ushered in. Everyone was talking at once and slapping him on the back, asking how he had gotten out of prison.

When everyone finally quietened down, Peter began to tell of his miraculous escape. By dawn, he was going over his story for the thousandth time. Peter's joyful friends wanted to hear every last detail over and over again.

Meanwhile, Herod's soldiers woke up to find Peter's cell empty. Shaking with fear, they went to tell the king—who was, of course, furious. Herod exploded with rage and ordered every guard under his command to go immediately and search high and low for Peter. It was no good. Peter was truly gone. The evil king ordered that every soldier who was on guard that night would be put to death in his place.

Roman magistrate
This carving dates from about A.D.500, but the magistrates whom Paul appeared before would have looked similar. He holds a scepter as a sign of justice, and a money bag as a sign of mercy.

Wrist chains
Prisoners in ancient times were often chained to the wall, to the floor, or to each other. It was as much to shame them as restrain them.

⬦ **ABOUT THE STORY** ⬦

This story tells of a miracle. It was not the first or last time that disciples were released from prison in some amazing way. What matters is not how it happened, but why. This was a great sign to all the Christians that God did not intend to let His message of new life in Christ be chained up by non-religious authorities. He would find a way of letting it loose. This is saying that God is greater than any human ruler.

Paul's First Missionary Journey

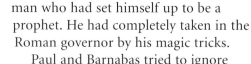

IN Jerusalem, the disciples heard that the followers who had fled Saul's persecution had spread the word of Jesus as far as Phoenicia, and the Greek states of Cyprus and Antioch. They decided to send Barnabas to guide them.

Barnabas went to Antioch first. He was met by so many eager followers that he went to Tarsus to fetch Paul to help him. For a whole year, Barnabas and Paul preached to the people of Antioch and baptized them. It was in Antioch that the disciples of Jesus were called Christians for the first time.

Paul was soon called by the Holy Spirit to sail to even more distant Gentile shores. Without questioning or hesitating, the disciple took Barnabas and John and several other followers to help him.

Paul's first port of call was the island of Cyprus. As usual, he and his companions began their preaching in the local synagogues. They worked their way across the island until they came to the town of Paphos, the home of the Roman governor, Sergius Paulus. He had heard about Jesus of Nazareth. The Roman governor summoned Paul and Barnabas to see him, so he could hear for himself.

When the disciples were ushered into the Roman governor's house, they noticed a pompous-looking local man sitting smugly next to him. Right away the Holy Spirit told Paul who he was. His name was Elymas, an evil man who had set himself up to be a prophet. He had completely taken in the Roman governor by his magic tricks.

Paul and Barnabas tried to ignore Elymas and began preaching to Sergius Paulus, but the evil magician argued with everything they said, doing his very best to keep the Roman governor from believing in Jesus. Eventually, Paul lost his temper.

"You son of the devil!" Paul cried, in a fury. "Stop trying to waylay those who want to follow the Lord!"

Paul flung out his hand in Elymas's direction, and the magician cowered away in fear.

"Feel the true power of Jesus Christ!" Paul cried at the cringing man. "You will be blind for a time, unable to see the light of the sun!"

Immediately, Elymas's eyes grew dark, and he whimpered at the governor's feet in terror. Sergius Paulus looked in astonishment at Paul and Barnabas. From that moment on, he believed wholeheartedly in all they had told him about Jesus of Nazareth.

From Paphos, Paul and Barnabas and their helpers set sail once again. After calling at Pergia, they returned to Antioch, to see how the church they had set up was doing.

Paul and Barnabas were pleased with what they found. On the first sabbath that they preached, the synagogue was packed with Jews, who had come to hear them speak of Jesus Christ and forgiveness for all. Even when they had

❧ ABOUT THE STORY ❧

From the beginning, Christianity was a religion to be spread across the world. Jesus had told the disciples to take His message to "Jerusalem, Samaria and the ends of the earth." So far, the gospel had been preached mostly as people traveled, because of persecution. Now the disciples traveled specifically in order to plant new churches. Their reason was simple. If Jesus was the Son of God, then everyone needed to know.

The first missionary journey of Paul
Paul did not make a circular journey. All the places he visited on the outward leg he visited again on the return journey, except for Cyprus. This took place about A.D. 46–48. Paul never returned to Cyprus, but Barnabas went there with Mark.

finished preaching, the congregation followed them out into the sun, urging them to continue.

All week, the Jews of Antioch spoke so excitedly about the good news preached by Paul and Barnabas that the Gentiles of the city heard of it, too. On the following sabbath, the disciples found that almost the entire population of Antioch had turned out to hear them speak.

When the Jews saw the masses of interested Gentiles, they were extremely jealous of them.

> *In Antioch the followers were, for the first time, called Christians.*

"You can't preach to them too!" they yelled, quickly working themselves up into an angry mob. "We're God's chosen people! No one can be saved unless they're Jewish!"

Paul and Barnabas stood firm.

"Don't forget that we brought God's message to you first," they reminded the Jews. "The Lord Himself has commanded us to 'be a light for the Gentiles, to bring salvation to the uttermost ends of the earth.'"

When the anxious Gentiles heard this, they were filled with gladness. They beamed with delight and gave thanks to God, and many of them were baptized right away.

Yet the Jews weren't at all satisfied. They argued and scowled and grumbled. As the days went on, they grew angrier and angrier with every Gentile whom Paul and Barnabas welcomed as a Christian. All the wealthy men and women who had been very strictly brought up in the Jewish faith were particularly outraged. Eventually they demanded that the Jewish elders drive the two followers out of the city.

Paul and Barnabas weren't downhearted. They had sown the seeds of faith among the Gentiles of Antioch, and they sailed on their way with great joy in their hearts.

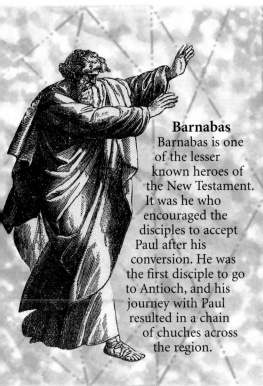

Barnabas
Barnabas is one of the lesser known heroes of the New Testament. It was he who encouraged the disciples to accept Paul after his conversion. He was the first disciple to go to Antioch, and his journey with Paul resulted in a chain of chuches across the region.

Cyprus
Barnabas came originally from Cyprus, as did several of the other disciples, so he was on familiar ground when he went back there with Paul. This Belgian tapestry, which is now in Mantua in Italy, shows Paul and Barnabas striking Elymas blind.

Faith for the Gentiles

THE chasing of Paul and Barnabas from Antioch was only the start of their troubles. In Iconium, Paul and Barnabas found that things were just as bad. They managed to win over lots people to Christ, but the traditional Jews felt outraged that Gentiles were being baptized. Paul and Barnabas were determined not to give up, but the situation grew increasingly difficult for them. People shouted them down in the synagogue and jeered at them. Eventually, the city was split into two sides who hated each other—those who supported the Jews and those who followed the disciples. When an attempt was made to stone Paul and Barnabas, they decided it was time to move on.

While many Jews were finding it difficult to accept Jesus as the fulfillment of ancient prophecies, many Gentiles

were finding it hard to give up the beliefs they had held all their lives. People had shrines to other gods in their houses, and massive stone temples to Greek gods such as Zeus dominated the towns. It was hard for them to grasp the idea of believing in just one God and His Son, Jesus Christ.

When Paul was preaching in Lystra, he saw a man who had been a cripple from birth. Paul knew that he had the faith in God to be made well, and he suddenly broke off from his preaching and shouted: "On your feet!"

The man obeyed at once. "I can walk!" he cried aloud.

The gasping crowd stared at Paul and Barnabas.

"The gods have come down to us in the form of men!" they yelled, falling on their knees before the disciples.

"All hail to Zeus, the great father of the gods!" they cried at Barnabas, bowing down.

"All hail to Hermes, his swift, silver-tongued messenger!" they worshiped Paul.

❧ ABOUT THE STORY ❧

Paul and his friends did not think about going home when they were evicted from one city. They just went on to the next. Paul picked his cities carefully. He aimed for places where there was a Jewish community. If these people became Christians, then they could share the faith with their Gentile neighbors. He also aimed for cities that had roads to travel elsewhere. The message could spread out across a wide area after he had moved on.

Paul is stoned
Stoning was the traditional way in which the Jews executed someone for blasphemy, speaking against God. This ivory from the 900s is a representation of Paul's stoning. He was very lucky to escape: the stones could fracture a victim's skull.

The birth of Athena
Athena was the patron goddess of the Greek city of Athens. She was one of many gods worshiped across the Roman Empire. She was said to have been born from the head of the great god Zeus.

The two disciples were horrified. The men and women of Iconium hadn't taken in what they had been telling them about Jesus Christ and had interpreted the miracle as the work of their own pagan gods! A priest from the temple of Zeus came with oxen to sacrifice to them.

> ❝ *'through many tribulations we must enter the kingdom of God.'* ❞

"No! No! No!" Paul and Barnabas cried. "Why are you doing this?" The disciples stopped the priests and their followers just before they had time to slaughter the oxen. "We are not gods! We are humans, just like you! We are just the bringers of the good news that there is only one, true God, who made everything."

There were other problems. The angry, nonbelieving Jews from Antioch and Iconium turned up.

"Don't listen to these strangers!" they told the people of Lystra. "They're filling your heads with an evil load of rubbish! Don't listen to them!"

The Jews stirred up the citizens into such a frenzy of hate that a mob even went after Paul and stoned him, leaving him for dead outside the city. Yet as soon as Paul recovered, he and Barnabas continued with their work undeterred. They traveled far and wide, strengthening the faith of those who did believe. They also explained that Jesus had warned that those who wanted to enter the kingdom of God would have to face a great many difficulties and dangers.

Still, it was with relief that Paul and Barnabas eventually returned to their faithful following in Antioch and rested there for a while.

Paul the letter-writer
Paul wrote many letters. The New Testament contains thirteen of them but he wrote more. The two letters to the Corinthians, the people of Corinth in Greece, refer to others which do not exist now. Some, like that to the Ephesians, were circulars, sent to several churches. Some were personal letters, like those to Timothy and Titus.

Inscription to the gods
People around Europe worshiped many gods at this time. This inscription was made by a coppersmith in Colchester, England. He put it in a temple to remind the god of his "faith."

Roman household shrine
People in the Roman Empire often had a shrine like this in their home where they would offer incense to their family god. The disciples had to explain that there was only one true God.

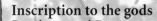

The Disciples Hold a Council

WHILE Paul and Barnabas were staying in Antioch, some followers arrived from Judea and began teaching the Gentiles that they had to adopt Jewish customs as well as be baptized if they wanted to be Christians. The two disciples argued with the followers, but the stubborn men refused to back down. In the end, Paul and Barnabas went to Jerusalem to tell the other disciples about the trouble, and to find some way to stop it.

Paul and Barnabas called the top Christians in Jerusalem together to a council in order to discuss recruiting Gentiles. When Paul told the council of the uproar they had caused by recruiting Gentiles as well as Jews into the church, the other disciples looked worried.

At once, some Pharisees who had been baptized as Christians agreed with the traditional Jewish view.

"It's true," they said. "It is the law of Moses. Only Jews can be saved. We are God's chosen people."

That was the start of a very long, heated debate. After all, it was an important issue that was in danger of dividing the church. Everyone felt strongly about his or her particular opinion. Finally, Peter stood up and called for quiet. Many people thought of him as the leader of the apostles, and he commanded a great deal of respect.

"Remember, friends," Peter began, "that God Himself told me to take the word of Jesus Christ to the Gentiles, so that they can believe in Him. I have seen with my own eyes that the Holy Spirit blesses Gentiles who are baptized, just as He does Jews. Why do you insist that only Jews can be saved?"

❧ ABOUT THE STORY ❧

The problem facing the church was whether Christianity was just a development of Judaism or something completely new. The disciples decided that it was both. Jesus had fulfilled the Jewish law through His death. So the church was something new, not a sect of Judaism. The old ceremonies could not make a person right with God. People needed only to believe in God and in Jesus.

Jewish faith today
Some practices have changed little among Jews since Bible times. One of them is ceremonial cleansing. Jews wash their hands in a special way before they eat or pray. The person who lights a candle for worship may hold out his or her hands for cleansing.

Don't get drunk
A drunken man is supported by his friends. Paul advised the people of Ephesus that they did not have to abstain from alcohol, but they did have to use it carefully.

No one dared argue with the great disciple. Everyone kept quiet as Barnabas and Paul told about all the amazing miracles God had done through them among the Gentiles. Then James stood up and reminded everyone about the words of the ancient prophets: "'I will return, and I will rebuild the dwelling of David, which has fallen . . . that the rest of people may seek the Lord, and all the Gentiles who are called by my name.'

> " 'Unless you are circumcised according to the custom of Moses, you cannot be saved.' "

"So may I suggest," continued James, "that we stop troubling Gentiles who want to join us. It is God's will that they do not have to convert to the Jewish faith before being baptized in Christ. However, I'd like to propose that we give them some guidelines, so their fellow Jewish followers will not be offended. For instance, we should instruct the Gentiles not to have anything to do with pagan religions, to be faithful to their husband or wife; and to prepare certain foods carefully."

Fortunately, this solution seemed to satisfy everyone present at the council. The disciples at once composed and copied a letter of instructions for all the Gentiles everywhere who wanted to follow the teachings of Christ. When Paul and Barnabas returned with it to the church in Antioch, the Gentiles rejoiced. They were finally officially accepted into the faith.

Marriage contract
James was anxious that the Jewish attitude to marriage be followed by the Gentiles. This is because God had shown it to be His will for all people.

Church council
This painting from Bulgaria shows the Second Ecumenical Council of the Christian church in AD381. Over the years since the meeting of the disciples there have been many important councils. As the world and people change, the church sometimes has to change to keep up.

THIS STORY SHOWS HOW CHRISTIANS WHO DISAGREE CAN SORT OUT THEIR DIFFERENCES. THE DISCIPLES MET, HEARD THE EVIDENCE AND ARGUMENTS, AND PRAYED. THEN EVERYONE STOOD BY WHAT THE LEADERS SAID. THAT IS A GOOD MODEL TO FOLLOW TODAY.

Paul's Second Missionary Journey

PAUL and Barnabas remained in Antioch for some time, strengthening the faith of the church they had established there. Then the two men decided they should split up and revisit every place in which they had they proclaimed the word of the Lord so far, to see how the new Christian communities were getting on. Barnabas picked Mark to be his assistant and sailed away to Cyprus, while Paul chose Silas as his helper, and set off through Syria and Cilicia. In every town and city the missionaries passed through, they

showed the churches the letter from the Christian council in Jerusalem regarding the baptism of Gentiles. Every day, the number of believers in Jesus Christ grew and grew.

Throughout his travels, Paul never planned his route himself. He always trusted God to show him where he should go. The Holy Spirit gave Paul signs in many different ways. One night, in Troas, he had a vision as he slept. He dreamed that a stranger stole into his room and crept silently up to his bedside. The man stood over Paul and stretched out his hands in earnest.

> ❝ *The Lord opened her heart to give heed to what was said by Paul.* ❞

"Come to Macedonia and help us," he asked.
Then the man's sad face faded away.
Next morning, Paul knew exactly where God wanted him to go. He and Silas gathered his companions and set off right away to the Roman colony in the north of Greece.

Paul directed his little company of followers to Philippi, Macedonia's leading city. They found themselves in the midst of hustling, bustling streets, noisy marketplaces, and buzzing shops and houses—but they knew no one. However, God made sure that He soon provided them with friends. The first sabbath that Paul and Silas were in Philippi, they went out of the city to a Jewish place of prayer beside a river. Many women were gathered there, and as Paul preached the good news of Jesus Christ, they listened eagerly. One woman in particular felt the joy of

Slave auction
This shows the harsh reality of the Roman slave system. The slaves had no rights of their own and could be bought and sold like cattle in a market. Many of these slaves were foreigners who had been brought to Rome as prisoners of war. A runaway slave could be executed if he or she was caught.

people to have their fortunes told. The two disciples weren't pleased at all. The slave girl followed them for days, crying out wildly after them wherever they went. Finally, Paul lost his patience. Without any warning, he turned and faced the slave girl, his face like thunder. Paul flung his hand out towards her and cried, "Spirit! I charge you in the name of Jesus Christ to come out of her!"

At once, the slave girl was quietened. She found she could no longer sense the strange unexplained things she had seen before. Her ability to see into the unknown had left her.

the Holy Spirit flood into her heart; she was a seller of fine cloth, named Lydia. Lydia begged that she and all her household be baptized right away, and she insisted that Paul and his companions come to stay with her during their stay in Philippi.

After that, Paul and Silas often returned to the river to pray and preach. One day, as they made their way there, they suddenly heard shouting behind them.

"These men are true servants of God!" came the shrill, excited voice. "They have come to tell everyone the way to salvation!"

Paul and Silas spun around to see a young slave girl hot on their heels, yelling as loud as she could and beckoning the startled passers by to come and follow them.

The slave girl had a strange gift of prophecy, and her Roman owners were delighted with it. For years, they had made lots of money out of the slave girl by charging

Paul's second missionary journey
Much of Paul's journey was overland from Antioch and through Asia Minor. Paul told the Corinthians that he faced many dangers including bandits and fast-flowing rivers. He probably walked, instead of riding animals.

Kindly slave owners
Many of the first Christians were slaves. Not all slaves were kept in chains and badly treated. Some slaves were like trusted colleagues. Slave owners could, if they chose to, free their slaves (they then became known as freedmen), and some even continued to support them as patrons. This tomb was set up by two former slaves in honor of their Roman masters.

Paul and Silas in Prison

WHEN the slave girl's Roman owners found out that her fortune-telling skills were gone, they were furious. They dragged Paul and Silas to the local courtroom to make an official complaint against them.

"These foreigners are making trouble in our city!" they yelled, stirring up an angry mob.

The Roman magistrates didn't give Paul and Silas a chance to explain.

"Arrest them for disturbing the peace!" they ordered, waving forward guards to take Paul and Silas away. "Strip them, beat them, and throw them into prison!"

Several hours later, Paul and Silas were locked by the feet into wooden stocks. Their skin bled from the Roman soldiers' whips, and their faces were black with bruises where the guards had punched them.

Paul and Silas didn't let their plight make them downhearted. Instead, they trusted in the Lord and sang hymns to God. The other prisoners were stunned. Their God must truly be wonderful to inspire such faith, they marveled. Some of them even joined in.

At midnight, the singing was suddenly drowned out by a mighty rumbling under the earth. The prison floor shook and the walls crumbled. The floor heaved, throwing the prisoners from side to side, breaking their chains, and bursting open the prison doors.

When the earthquake had stopped, the terrified jailer ran in, expecting to find his prisoners escaped. All the torches had gone out, and he could see no one. The jailer drew his sword, ready to kill himself rather than face punishment for having allowed all the prisoners to escape.

Paul and Silas were horrified when they realized what the ashamed jailer was about to do.

 Let them come themselves and take us out. ❝❞

"No! Don't! We are all here!" Paul cried.

The jailer couldn't believe his ears.

"Torches!" he cried, as guards ran in.

The jailer was amazed at the two followers of Jesus Christ. They had worked a strange miracle on a slave girl. They had been unaffected by being whipped and thrown into prison. They were unafraid of an earthquake. They made sure all the prisoners stayed in jail when they had had a chance to escape! The jailer made up his mind.

Rumbling under the earth
An earthquake happens when the pressure on two sections of the earth's crust causes the earth to split open.

Lock and key
Most doors were locked with bolts which slid across them, but the Romans also used locks and keys not unlike those we use today. This bronze lock would have been used for a small box.

Certificate of citizenship
The only way to prove you were a Roman citizen was to have an official document. This document is etched into bronze. It says that a Spanish soldier is a citizen, which meant that he had the full rights of someone who had been born into a Roman family.

Other people might say that Paul and Silas were phony, but he thought differently. He believed that the two men were truly filled with the power of God.

The jailer gave the order for the other prisoners to be chained up again immediately, but to Paul and Silas's astonishment, he led them out of the prison and back to his own house. In front of his whole household, he fell on his knees before Paul and Silas.

"Tell me what I must do to be saved," the jailer begged.

"Just believe in the Lord Jesus Christ," Paul and Silas replied, "and you will be forgiven for your sins."

The two men told the jailer and his family, and servants all about Jesus. When the jailer heard how Jesus wanted His followers to treat everyone with love and kindness, he washed Paul's and Silas's wounds and brought them food and clothes. Then he insisted that he and all his household be baptized at once, and they celebrated for hours.

The next morning Paul and Silas returned to the town's courtroom, where the magistrates smirked to themselves.

"Those strangers will have spent a horrible night in the cells," they said, gloating over their power. "They'll have learned their lesson. Let them go."

Paul and Silas weren't happy at all. They hadn't done anything wrong! They didn't want to creep away.

"We are freeborn Roman citizens," they reminded the jailer. "We want a public apology!"

The magistrates were worried when the jailer told them that they had ordered Roman citizens to be flogged without a trial. They hurried to apologize to Paul and Silas in front of the citizens, before they got in serious trouble. Then the magistrates begged them to leave Philippi. So Paul and Silas went back to Lydia's house in peace, to say goodbye to their friends before continuing on their mission.

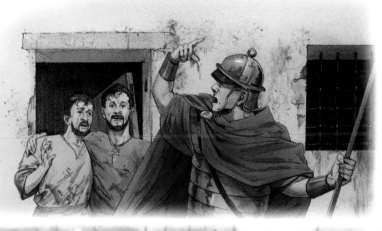

Paul arguing
This enamel plaque shows Paul arguing with both Jews and Greeks. Wherever he went, Paul got into debates. He taught that Jesus Christ was the Messiah, the person that God sent to save the people from their sins, and that He had risen from the dead. Many Greeks thought this was a crazy idea, and many Jews found it repugnant. Others believed it and became Christians.

Woman at worship
Many of the first Christians were women. Christianity liberated them, because they were considered by Jesus to be equal to men before God. Women covered their heads when they went into church. This was an important custom, because at the time only prostitutes had bare heads.

❧ **ABOUT THE STORY** ❧
This is one of many instances in the Bible when something natural—an earthquake in this case—happens at just the right time to help God's servants. It is a miracle of God's timing. God did not stop His servants from being locked up—which was unlawful, without a proper trial—but He did rescue them and at the same time so impressed others with His power that they believed in Him, too.

Paul's Travels and Miracles

PAUL and Silas pressed on to the city of Thessalonika. For three weeks Paul preached in the synagogue to argue that Jesus was the Savior. Although a large number of people believed, many Jews were outraged. They gathered together a violent mob and went to speak to the city authorities.

"Paul and his companions are trying to turn the world upside down!" they protested. "They're against the Roman emperor, because they say there is another king—Jesus!"

That night, before the Romans took any action, the followers smuggled Paul and Silas out of the city.

> **"** *And God did extraordinary miracles by the hands of Paul . . .* **"**

Paul traveled south to Athens, the main city of Greece. The city was scattered with idols of pagan gods. The streets were full of worshipers taking offerings and sacrifices to and from the pagan temples. Paul strode into the busy marketplace and preached to passersby. He also met with philosophers, men who tried to puzzle out the meaning of life and the universe for themselves.

The people of Athens loved nothing more than to hear different beliefs. While many Athenians didn't know what to make of Paul's preaching, others were keen to hear more. They took him to speak on a hill near the vast Acropolis. By the time Paul left Athens, some people had become Christians.

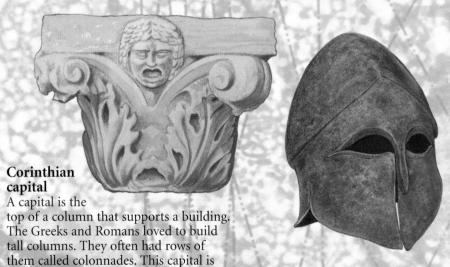

Corinthian capital
A capital is the top of a column that supports a building. The Greeks and Romans loved to build tall columns. They often had rows of them called colonnades. This capital is decorated with a face mask, like those used in the theater, and acanthus leaves under the scrolls. This design is called corinthian because it came from Corinth.

Helmet
This is a Greek helmet, which has lots of protection for the neck and a central strip to protect the soldier's nose.

Mirror
In biblical times mirrors like this were not made of glass, but of bronze which could be polished so that it gave a good, but not perfect, reflection. Paul, in his letter to the Corinthians, says that we see God's truth only dimly, or partially, as in a mirror. When we go to heaven, we shall see God "face to face."

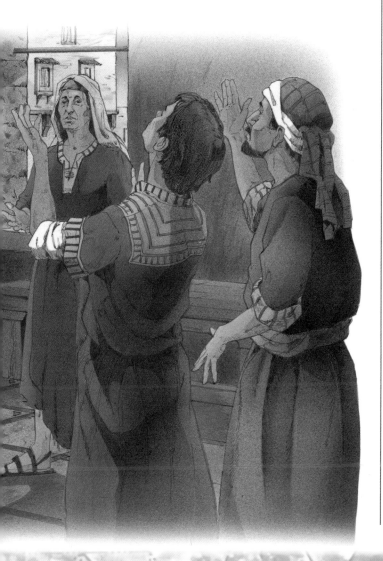

Paul's next port of call was Corinth. He stayed with a Jewish couple named Aquila and Priscilla who had fled Rome when the Emperor Claudius had ordered all Jews to leave. Paul preached in the synagogue, and Crispus, the ruler of the synagogue, asked to be baptized. Even so, most of the Jews refused to listen to Paul.

"Your blood be upon your own heads!" Paul cried in the end. "I have done my best with you, and now I will take the message of Jesus Christ to the Gentiles instead."

Paul found that the Gentiles were much more ready to believe in Jesus Christ. Many began asking to be baptized. Then one night, the Lord appeared to Paul in a vision.

"Don't be afraid to speak out in this city, for I am with you," God said. "I will make sure that no harm comes to you, for there are many people here who will turn to me."

Inspired with new faith and courage, Paul stayed for a year and six months in Corinth, and established a strong Christian community there before traveling on to Ephesus, where he stayed for two years.

Everyone who witnessed Paul's miraculous deeds was amazed. In Ephesus, seven sons of a Jewish high priest were so envious that they decided to try it for themselves. They summoned a man who they knew was possessed by an evil spirit, and they tried to cast it out, as they had seen Paul do.

The unearthly voice of the evil spirit wailed, "I know Jesus and I know Paul, but who are you?"

With a howl, the man leaped onto the seven men and they ran from the house.

After that many people who had practiced pagan rituals and black magic believed in Jesus.

The third missionary journey of Paul
Paul's third journey was very similar to his second. Once again he revisited the churches of Asia Minor. Paul was a carer as well as an evangelist. He wanted to make sure the Christians were going on with their faith.

◆ **ABOUT THE STORY** ◆

This story shows how adaptable and flexible Paul was. He did not just take one approach and organize every visit in the same way. He started in the Jewish synagogue, if there was one. When he was thrown out of one building he went and hired another. This also shows that his teaching and miracles went side by side. He always began by teaching, but the miracles often helped people believe that Jesus was for real.

Demetrius and the Riot

IN Ephesus, a silversmith named Demetrius made shrines used in the worship of the Greek goddess Artemis. He was unhappy that Paul was turning people away from Artemis to a religion in which they wouldn't need the idols he made. Demetrius called together all the other workmen.

"The numbers of people who worship Artemis are diminishing," Demetrius warned his fellow tradesmen. "It's all due to that Paul. We may lose our livelihoods, and the worship of our great goddess might die out altogether!"

The workmen were outraged at the thought. They set off through the town, shouting, "Artemis of the Ephesians is great!" Soon, people were rushing to the amphitheater for an emergency public meeting. There was utter confusion. Some people were crying, "Artemis!"; others were yelling, "Praise be to God and His Son, Jesus Christ!"; most people had no idea why they were there.

Paul's followers wouldn't let him enter the amphitheater, for his own safety, and it was several hours before the town clerk managed to quieten everyone down.

"Everyone knows that Ephesus is Artemis's special city!" he argued. "So why are you getting so worked up over the strangers who have come here? They have said nothing against our goddess. If Demetrius and the craftsmen have a complaint, let them go through the proper legal system. We would be fools to start a riot that would bring the wrath of the Romans down upon us all. Now go home!"

The situation was too fragile for Paul to remain, so he left for Macedonia.

> " 'Great is Artemis of the Ephesians!' "

❧ ABOUT THE STORY ❧

Many of the clashes between Paul and others started because the Jewish leaders regarded him as a heretic who was stirring up trouble. This story shows that there was a head-on clash between the Christian faith and other religions, too. Jesus Himself had said that He was the only way to God. The disciples taught that other religions could not bring people to know God fully and that only Jesus, God's Son, could forgive sins.

Greek gods
Artemis (also called Diana) was the patron goddess of Ephesus. There was a legend that said her image had fallen from the sky, though it was probably a meteorite. Ancient writers say that in biblical times a great stone was at the entrance to her temple. Artemis is usually portrayed with many breasts, as a goddess of fertility, but in the original Greek myths she was a moon goddess and hunter—Greek statues show her with hunting dogs. Her temple in Ephesus was one of the world's seven wonders.

Ephesus
In Paul's day Ephesus was a magnificent city. It housed at least 250,000 people and had an arena that could hold 25,000. A long road flanked with pillars led to the harbor. Paul spent two years here.

Paul in Troas

PAUL decided to return to Jerusalem. He stayed in the city of Troas for a week, encouraging the followers to remain strong and faithful when he had gone. On the night before Paul was due to leave, he spoke well into the evening. No one stirred; everyone hung on his every word. They didn't know how long it would be before the great disciple passed that way again.

On and on spoke Paul. A young man named Eutychus found himself desperately trying to stay awake and listen. Eutychus tried propping himself up in a sitting position in the deep windowsill, opening the window to let in the chill night air, sitting on his hands to make himself uncomfortable, but it was no good. His eyelids began to droop. His head nodded. Finally, he fell fast asleep, lulled by Paul's voice.

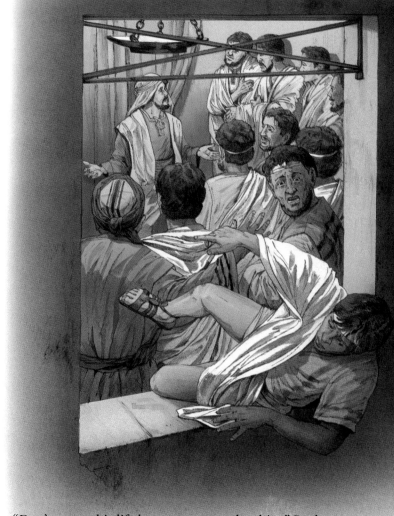

> 66 *He sank into a deep sleep as Paul talked still longer.* 99

Everyone was concentrating far too hard on what Paul was saying to notice Eutychus drifting off. In fact, the first they knew of it was when Eutychus fell out of the window and landed with a sickening thud on the ground below. There were horrified gasps as everyone dashed to the window and peered out. Eutychus was lying in a lifeless heap on the floor below.

Paul was the first to race down the stairs and reach the young man. He took Eutychus in his arms.

"Don't worry, his life has now returned to him," Paul reassured everyone.

Amazingly, through the saving grace of the great disciple, Eutychus recovered almost at once. Rejoicing, all the friends made their way back into the house, where Paul continued preaching until daybreak. They didn't stop giving thanks to God even when Paul's ship had sailed into the distance and out of sight.

THE PEOPLE OF TROAS HAD A HUNGER TO LEARN ABOUT GOD. TODAY, SOME PEOPLE TAKE FAITH LESS SERIOUSLY; IT IS A HOBBY, RATHER THAN A WAY OF LIFE. CHRISTIANS IN TROAS WOULD BE DISMAYED. ☙

Paul
Like other disciples, Paul was canonized, made a saint, so is depicted with a halo as in this mural from the 1100s from Cyprus. He was a man of great vision and energy. He cared deeply for people but could be a stern critic of those who did not live up to his own strict standards.

❖ ABOUT THE STORY ❖
Paul had a lot of friends with him by the time he reached Troas. Among them were Timothy, who was later to lead the church in Ephesus, and Tychicus, who was like a messenger who went around the churches carrying news from place to place. Luke and several others were with him, too. Paul valued the help and support of his friends, although they are not mentioned often in Acts. He did not work alone.

Paul in Jerusalem

PAUL was in a hurry to reach Jerusalem in time for the feast of Pentecost. Yet there were several sad farewells for him to make on the way.

"You won't see me again," Paul told the followers of the Ephesian church. "The Holy Spirit has warned me that suffering and imprisonment await me there. I'm not sad. The only reason I consider my life precious is because I can do the work the Lord Jesus Christ has asked me to do. Look after the church when I am gone, for many people will try to destroy your faith and lead you astray. Be alert, and God will give you His help."

At Caesarea, a prophet named Agabus took Paul's girdle and tied up his own hands and feet with it.

"The Holy Spirit has told me that the Jews of Jerusalem will bind you just like this and deliver you into the hands of the Gentiles," warned the prophet, sternly.

Paul's friends protested desperately against Paul continuing on his way. Yet the disciple stood firm.

> ❝ *'What are you doing, weeping and breaking my heart?'* ❞

"Don't weep," he begged them. "For I'm ready not only to go to prison for the Lord Jesus Christ—I'm ready to die for Him too."

The moment Paul arrived in Jerusalem, Jesus's brother, James, warned him of trouble. "There are rumors about you," James explained. "We know they're untrue, but others don't. People say that you're encouraging Jews who have converted to Christianity to give up the law of Moses and live like Gentiles!"

Paul did his best to show that the stories weren't true. He began a special week-long Jewish purification ritual, going to the temple every day to pray. Just before the seven days were completed, Paul ran headlong into a group of Jews in the temple who came from a town the disciple had visited on his travels.

"Help, everyone! Help!" they cried. "This is Paul—the man who is leading Jews everywhere astray!"

To make things worse, earlier in the day the same group of Jews had glimpsed Paul in the streets with his Ephesian friend Trophimus and wrongly assumed Paul had brought the non-Jew inside the temple.

"Paul has defiled our holy building by smuggling in a Gentile!" the Jews yelled at the tops of their voices.

"Get him!" the men and women shouted, chasing Paul through the temple courtyards and out into the road. The furious people fell on him, punching and kicking him to the ground. Just in time, a Roman tribune burst onto the scene with his soldiers.

"Who is this man?" the tribune asked the crowd, as his soldiers put Paul in chains.

"He has defiled the temple!" some people yelled.

"He has done nothing! Let him go!" cried others.

"He has broken the law of Moses!" voices roared.

"Rubbish! He's a faithful Jew!" argued still others.

The tribune ordered Paul to be taken back to his barracks. The mob followed, shouting, "Kill him!" When Paul tried to speak to them to explain, they refused to listen to him.

Paul was flung into the cells for the night, and the following morning he found himself hauled out for questioning in front of the Sanhedrin. The disciple held the burning eyes of the Jewish officials in his steady gaze.

"Brothers, I have always lived before God with a good conscience . . ." he began.

All at once, Paul realized something. Half of the council was made up of Pharisees, half of Sadducees, a Jewish sect who didn't believe in life after death. Paul suddenly saw a way to split the council's opinion and win the Pharisees over to his side.

"Of course," he said, "I myself am a Pharisee. This trial is really about the resurrection of the dead."

The annoyed Sadducees leaped up and began to argue with the Pharisees. Of course, because they were under attack, the Pharisees began to stick up for Paul.

"This man is innocent," some of them began to shout. "We can't find that he's done anything wrong."

At that, the infuriated Sadducees flung themselves on the defiant Pharisees, and the despairing Roman tribune left them to it. He ordered Paul to be taken away again, before the arguing Jews ripped him apart.

Later on, back in the dungeons, Paul heard a voice. It was the Lord calling him.

"Take courage," said God. "For just as you have testified for me here at Jerusalem, so you must also bear witness for me in Rome."

Paul's rescue
This engraving shows the chaos of the Jerusalem riot. Paul was lucky to escape alive.

Caesarea
This city was one of Herod the Great's finest achievements. He built it in honor of the Roman emperor.

❧ ABOUT THE STORY ❧

Paul was getting quite old by now. It would have been natural for him to have listened to Agabus and his friends. What was the point of walking into a trap? Paul knew that the path of obedience lay along the way of suffering. In order to achieve all he could for Jesus and to reach Rome, he had to accept more danger. He had Jesus as his model, who went willingly to the cross. Paul was practicing what he preached.

Paul Stands Trial

PAUL was in grave danger. More than forty Jews had sworn not to eat or drink until they had killed the disciple. They hurried off with their plan to the Sanhedrin.

"Ask the tribune to bring Paul down to you again, as if you want to question him further," they suggested. "We'll ambush the soldiers and kill Paul. He'll be off our hands and it won't be your responsibility, either."

The Sanhedrin were pleased with the idea, but Paul's nephew heard the plan and hurried to the barracks to tell the Roman tribune. The tribune was grateful and decided to send the disciple to safety. He wrote a letter to the provincial governor, Felix, explaining that the Jews were after Paul's blood but that he himself couldn't find the disciple guilty of anything deserving death or even imprisonment. That night, Paul was escorted out of the barracks and away by a large number of soldiers.

The Sanhedrin didn't give up. The high priest, Ananias, soon arrived with a spokesman, Tertullus, to put their case before the Roman governor. Tertullus began by trying to persuade Felix with flattery.

"It's thanks to you that we enjoy peace in our province," he said. "This man threatens our stability. He is a ringleader of the sect of Jesus of Nazareth. Now he has broken our law and desecrated our temple!"

Felix brought Paul back to give his side of the story.

"I was in Jerusalem only for twelve days," the disciple began calmly, "and these people didn't find me arguing with anyone or stirring up a riot anywhere in the city. They can't prove any of their accusations except that, yes, I worship God according to the way of Jesus Christ. I still believe everything laid down by Jewish law and I was actually purifying myself in the temple, not desecrating it!"

'I appeal to Caesar.'

Now Felix was interested in Christianity and he treated Paul kindly. He put off the Jews' demand for a judgment, saying that he wouldn't decide without further investigation, and he put Paul under house arrest, so that the disciple's friends could come and see him. Felix held Paul in this way for two years, during which time he often called the disciple to come and preach to him and his wife, Drusilla, who was a Jew. Finally, Felix was replaced by another governor, Festus, and representatives from the Sanhedrin arrived once again.

❖ ABOUT THE STORY ❖

The Roman governors were unsure what to do about Paul. They were fair, however, and gave him good protection. Paul used his citizen's right to a trial before the emperor more as a way of getting to Rome than for anything else. Paul benefited from the Roman system. God's plan had ensured the free and swift spread of Christianity across a wide area in the short space of thirty years.

Synagogue
Paul often began his ministry in synagogues, where people would know of the promised Messiah. Synagogues are Jewish centers for worship, like this one, which is the Great Jerusalem synagogue. They have separate galleries, or seating areas, for women. The service consisted of prayers, readings, and sermons.

Roman census
The Romans organized their empire very efficiently. A group of people called Censors counted all the men who owned property. This shows them at work.

"I have done nothing against the temple, the law of the Jews, or the emperor," Paul insisted. "I ask you not to hand me back to be tried among my enemies. Instead, I claim my right as a Roman citizen to be tried before the emperor himself!"

"Then to Caesar you shall go," replied Festus.

Before he could send Paul off, King Agrippa and his wife, Bernice, arrived. Festus organized a royal audience, so Agrippa could question Paul too.

Paul was grateful for the chance to explain. He told how he had been a strict Pharisee who had persecuted Christians; how Jesus Christ had spoken to him on the road to Damascus and totally changed his life; and how he had preached to both Gentiles and Jews, which was the real reason why so many Jews were seeking his death. Finally, Paul reminded the king of the prophets who foretold that Christ would suffer and rise from the dead and that He would bring salvation to all the world.

"Paul, all your research into the Scriptures has driven you crazy!" scoffed Festus in a loud voice.

"I am not crazy," replied Paul, calmly. "The king knows about these things, and I'm sure that he believes in the words of the prophets. Don't you, King Agrippa?"

"Hmm," said Agrippa, thoughtfully. "I think that you're trying to turn me into a Christian in a very short time!"

"Whether now or later, I wish that everyone would become what I am," Paul said with a sad smile, "except for these chains, of course."

Later on, in private, Festus, Agrippa, and Bernice went over everything again and again. They all agreed that Paul had done nothing wrong. They sighed. If the disciple hadn't appealed to be tried in Rome, he could have been freed right away.

Christians fighting the lions
There is a story in the Old Testament of Daniel surviving a night in a lion's cage. Sadly, many Christians in the first two centuries A.D. did not survive their ordeals with lions. They were thrown to the hungry beasts as "entertainment" for the crowds.

The Colosseum
This amphitheater in Rome still stands. In Paul's time it held 50,000 people. It was used for gladiatorial displays.

The Voyage to Rome

PAUL and several other prisoners sailed for Rome, under the protection of a centurion named Julius. Julius treated Paul with great kindness, and when the ship called at Sidon, he let the disciple visit his old friends. Then it was back to the boat for several days' hard sailing to Cyprus, for the wind was against them. Paul wasn't surprised that it was slow-going. He was an experienced sailor and knew that the stormy season was near. On the way to Crete, the ship was beginning to struggle against the gusts and the waves, and they barely made it to a harbor. Paul advised Julius that they should winter there, but the captain and shipowner just scoffed. They assured the centurion that it would be better to winter in a harbor on the other side of the island. As soon as a gentle south wind blew up, they set sail once again, cautiously keeping close to the shore.

The warm breeze didn't last long. A wild northeasterly gale came from behind the mountains, sweeping down over the sea and whipping up the waters, so that the ship was tossed and turned and driven far offshore. As the howling storm went on into the night, the terrified crew slid around the slippery decks trying to lash together the heaving, straining boards of the ship with ropes. Next day, as the waves crashed over the boat, they threw furniture and cargo overboard in an effort to keep afloat. On the third day, as the waves grew yet higher, the desperate crew hurled even spare sails and rigging into the deeps to lighten the load. Day after day, the storm continued to rage around them, showing no sign of ever blowing over. The sailors couldn't remember when they had last glimpsed the sun or the stars. They couldn't tell where the blackness of the sky ended and the blackness of the water began. It felt like the end of the world.

Everyone huddled together in deep despair, certain that they would meet a watery death.

"Take heart," Paul reassured them. "Last night, an angel of God told me that we will eventually run aground and that the ship will go down, but none of us will die."

Finally, during the fourteenth night of the storm, the crew realized that the ship was running into shallower water. There was a sudden scramble as they raced to let down anchors before the boat was tossed onto the rocks that lurked in the darkness. At last, there was a glimmer of hope! Everyone wept with relief when the rays of dawn began to light up

the horizon. They had been sure they would never feel the warmth of the sun again. To their joy, they could see land only a little way off. They cast off the anchors and hoisted the foresail and began to make for a bay. As they tried to run ashore, the bow stuck fast in a sandbank. To everyone's horror, the stern of the ship began to break up fast in the crashing surf. There was no other choice but to abandon themselves to the mercy of the sea and jump overboard before the ship went down.

Incredibly, just as Paul had said, all 276 people made it safely to shore. Some swam. Others floated on broken bits of the ship. The soaked, shivering survivors were welcomed to the island of Malta by the local people, who made a bonfire to warm them up.

> ❝ *'I now bid you take heart; for there will be no loss of life among you, but only of the ship.'* ❞

The locals soon realized that there was something unusual about Paul. An angry viper came slithering out of the fire, trying to escape from the heat, and sank its fangs into his hand. The Maltese people knew that a viper bite was fatal, and they fully expected Paul to die swiftly from the poison. They waited anxiously but nothing happened.

"He must be a god!" they whispered to each other.

The Roman governor of Malta, Publius, was just as generous as his people, and he gave the survivors lodgings in his own quarters. When Paul found out that Publius's father was terribly ill, he healed him to repay the governor's kindness. The news soon got out that the strange man who hadn't died from the snakebite had miraculous healing powers. Maltese from all over the island brought their sick to be cured by Paul. After three months it was time to set sail once again. Paul had won the greatest respect from the people of Malta, and they loaded down the ship with all kinds of provisions and gifts.

Finally, they reached Rome. The other prisoners were handed over to the captain of the guard and imprisoned. Paul, though, was given special treatment. He was allowed to live under house arrest. He awaited trial for two years, and during that time many people came to hear him preach about Jesus Christ and the kingdom of God. Paul also regularly wrote letters to all the friends he had made on his travels, urging them to keep the faith. He continued to do this right up to the very last days of his life, when he knew that he was going to be put to death for the sake of his belief in his master and teacher, Jesus Christ.

Paul's journey to Rome
This took place in the winter of A.D.59–60. It was not Paul's first experience of shipwreck. Before this journey he had told the Corinthians he had been shipwrecked three times, but did not say where.

❧ ABOUT THE STORY ❧
Sea travel in Paul's day was hazardous. The ships were relatively small, powered only by oars and sails. Navigation was by the stars. Most ships hugged the coast so that they would know where they were. No one sailed in winter, which was where the captain's gamble about the weather failed. Luke, the writer of the story, wants us to see that God would not let His servant die before his work was complete.

The Revelation to John

THE disciple John was in prison on the Greek island of Patmos, praying one sabbath, when he heard a voice filling his mind.

"Write down what I am about to show you and send it to the churches," it instructed.

John spun around to see Jesus Christ behind him, blazing with light brighter than the sun.

"Don't be afraid," Jesus said. "I am the first and the last. I died but I shall live for ever. I hold the keys of death."

John saw a door opening into heaven.

"Come here and I will show you the future of the world," thundered the voice. Suddenly John found himself standing before the very throne of God, surrounded by countless angels singing, "Blessings and honor and glory and might for ever and ever, amen!"

The Lord showed John the mighty battle between good and evil that was being played out on the earth. John saw the happiness of men and women who believe in the salvation of Christ, and the misery and fear of those who do not repent. He saw angels of destruction sweep over the earth to kill wicked men and women with plagues, as warnings to all those left to repent before it was too late. John heard the souls of those who had been killed for their Christian beliefs cry out to God, "O Lord, avenge us and wipe out the world and all its wickedness." God comforted them and told them it was not time.

There were others to come who would win their place in heaven by being martyred in Jesus's name.

John saw a woman representing the people of God giving birth to the Messiah. She stood with the moon under her feet and crowned with twelve stars. Then war broke out in heaven itself. The archangel Michael led God's angels against Satan and his wicked angels, and flung them down from heaven to earth. John watched as the furious Satan and his army went off to tempt all those who follow Jesus's teachings. Great evils rose up, and many people abandoned God to follow Satan. God sent angels over the earth, reminding people that they should fear His judgment and turn again to the Lord while there was still time.

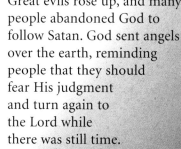

Then John witnessed the end of the world. Jesus, the Lamb of God, was triumphant. There was rejoicing in heaven as Satan was flung into a lake of fire. God then passed judgment on everyone who had ever lived. If their name was not in His book of life, they were destroyed, along with Satan.

Finally, John saw a new heaven and a new earth, which looked like the holy city of Jerusalem. The city shone and sparkled as though it were made from diamonds and gold and decorated with precious jewels in every color of the rainbow. Through the middle of the city flowed the river of life, as clear as crystal. On either side of the river grew groves of the healing tree of life. The gates of the city stood open, welcoming everything that was good. The city was lit with the glory of God, and there was no temple—because God Himself was there.

"Behold, God is living with all His people in His

> " *'I am the Alpha and the Omega, the beginning and the end.'* "

kingdom on earth," John heard a voice proclaim. "Pain and sorrow and death are no more."

John heard Jesus Christ speaking to him one last time. "Let all who are thirsty come and drink from the waters of life. I will be coming soon to judge the living and the dead, and the good will be blessed for ever. I am the first and the last, the beginning and the end."

"Amen," whispered John. "Amen!"

A glimpse of heaven
Artists have tried to portray John's vision of heaven with God surrounded by a sea of glass. However, it is really beyond words and imagining.

❧ ABOUT THE STORY ❧

The Book of Revelation is something of a mystery to people today, but in the 1st century A.D. it was a source of great encouragement. It is written largely in picture language which the Christians of the time would have understood clearly. It is really a series of sketches of the battle between good and evil, which takes place all through human history. It shows that God and His church always triumph in the end.

The Church Since the Apostles

CHRISTIANITY continues to grow around the world. In places, Christianity is growing at an amazing rate. In Russia and China, for example, Christianity is growing very fast. But the church today is very different. This is how it developed.

Expansion and argument: A.D.100–700

After the death of the apostles, Paul's prophecy that false teachers would attack the church came true. There were cults such as the gnostics, the forerunners of today's "new age" movements. These people who did not believe in Jesus were called heretics. They denied important teachings; for example Marcion (d.160) rejected the Jewish elements in the New Testament.

These attacks were countered by writings built on the apostles' teaching. Justin Martyr (c.100–165) defended Christianity against Roman philosophers. The African Tertullian (c.160–225) showed how Jesus could be God and man. In 325 the Council of Nicea defined the basic truths of Christianity (although controversy continued for some time). Despite the arguments and continued persecution, the church grew. In 395 the Roman Emperor Constantine saw a vision of Christ and declared Christianity to be the official religion of the Empire. By 404 the Bible had been translated into Latin, and Augustine of Hippo (354–430) had produced the basis of Christian belief as it is today. Christianity spread across Europe. Columba went to Iona (northeast England) and Saint David converted Wales.

Aurelius Augustinus
Also called Augustine of Hippo, he was baptized by St Ambrose in A.D.386. He was a great writer, and wrote *Confessions* in A.D.400, about his own life.

Division and darkness (700–1400)

Then came a period that many Christians today are ashamed of. There were the Crusades, in which western kings tried to force Christianity on countries of the east. There were corrupt popes and clergy who were more interested in worldly wealth than spiritual truth. And in 1054 there was a major split which still exists to this day. The churches of the east (now called the Orthodox churches) divided from the churches of the west over an important but obscure teaching about the relationship of the Holy Spirit to Jesus Christ.

Crusades
These are the kinds of soldiers and knights that fought in the Crusades.

St Thomas Aquinas
He became a monk in 1244, and quickly became a great teacher. His teachings and writings largely represent the teachings of the Catholic Church.

However, there were good points. Thomas Aquinas (1225–74) was an important religious writer whose work is still influential, especially in the Roman Catholic Church. The great cathedrals of Europe were built, including Rheims, Cologne, Salisbury, and York. Groups of traveling preachers called for reform and spread the gospel as the first Christians had. Among them was John Wycliffe (1330–84), who was influential in leading the church back to belief in the detail of the Bible.

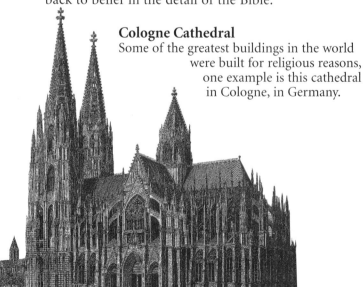

Cologne Cathedral
Some of the greatest buildings in the world were built for religious reasons, one example is this cathedral in Cologne, in Germany.

Reformation and renewal (1400–1800)

The most famous controversy came when a German monk, Martin Luther (1483–1546) nailed his 95 theses (statements for discussion) on the door of Wittenburg Church in 1517. He criticised many practices and beliefs which, he said, departed from the teaching of the Bible. From then on, other "Protestants" (protesters) added their voices to his—among them Huldreich Zwingli, in Zurich, and John Calvin, in Geneva. This period, when the beliefs, or doctrines, of the Church changed, was called the "Reformation."

Martin Luther
Luther's reforms began after a trip to Rome. He disagreed with the sale of indulgences, that is, people buying forgiveness.

The Roman Catholic Church continued under the Pope, but other churches began: Lutherans on the Continent, Presbyterians in Scotland, and Anglicans (Church of England) in England. The Reformation in England was a mixture of political and spiritual forces. Henry VIII was glad of an excuse to rid himself of the authority of the Pope so that he could get divorced.

Roman Catholicism continued much the same, but Protestantism divided further as groups rediscovered old truths which they emphasized. These divisions were signs of life and vitality. The Baptist churches stressed the need for personal commitment in the rite of baptism. John Wesley (1703–91) founded Methodism when the Church of England disagreed with his open-air preaching and emphasis on spreading the word of Christ.

John Calvin
In 1559 Calvin founded a religious academy in the city of Geneva, Switzerland, which later became a university.

Henry VIII
When the Pope refused to declare that Henry's marriage to his first wife, Catherine of Aragon, was illegal, Henry made himself head of the church, and allowed his own second marriage.

Change and decay (1800 to present)

Over the last 200 years there have been enormous social and cultural changes. "Enlightenment" thinking (which emphasized the importance of human reason) and the growth of science challenged many Christian beliefs. Only late in the 1900s did western society begin to recognize a "spiritual" dimension to life.

The Roman Catholic Church made major changes at the Second Vatican Council (1962–5), including allowing mass to be celebrated in local languages and not Latin. The Protestant churches began to talk and work together (and in some cases reunite), and the World Council of Churches was formed in 1948.

The charismatic (or Pentecostal) movement and the work of evangelists such as Billy Graham have brought thousands of (often young) people into the churches. But it is overseas where stories of growth that parallel those of the Acts of the Apostles are to be heard today. The missionary movement of the 1800s saw people from the west spread the gospel in Africa, India, China, and South America. In the year 2000 there were more Christians (580 million) in Latin America than in Europe (420 million). In Africa, the growth was from 230 million in 1985 to 400 million in 2000. The Holy Spirit is still at work.

Television evangelist
Billy Graham claims to have converted millions of people to Christianity.

Modern cathedrals
This modern cathedral in Brazil, South America, shows that the church has a modern and developing outlook. It is an energetic and exciting force in many parts of the world.

Faith, Love, and Charity

THE Acts of the Apostles tells of people who risked everything for Jesus Christ. Their example has inspired thousands of Christians in every century since. Others have preached the message of Jesus in new places, believing that it is the most important message anyone could ever hear. And still others, inspired by the love of Jesus, have sacrificed all to care for the sick and poor. Some, like the apostles, have even been killed by jealous opponents. Here are a few of their stories.

St Francis of Assisi (c.1181–1226)

The son of a wealthy Italian cloth merchant, Francis lived a worldly life until he had a vision of Jesus. Then he gave up everything to teach the gospel. Others joined him in his mission, and the Franciscan order of monks was born. He wrote a simple rule of life for their communities, which still exists today. He had a simple faith and a great love of nature.

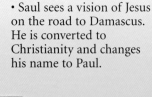

Mother Julian of Norwich (c.1342–1420)

We do not know anything about Mother Julian's background. She became a hermit devoted to prayer at St. Julian's Church in Norwich, in eastern England. She received fifteen visions from God, which she wrote in a famous book, *Revelations of Divine Love*. She showed how sinful people could become united with a caring God in a mystical experience of spiritual love.

Elizabeth Fry (1780–1845)

The daughter of a banker in Norwich, she married a merchant. They were Quakers (the Christian group also known as The Society of Friends). She came from a wealthy background, and she was upset by the conditions of women in prison. She began to teach them the Bible, provide them with clothes, and help them to improve themselves. She also campaigned for many prison reforms.

William Booth (1829–1912)

A Methodist from Nottingham, England, he moved to London but left the church because people did not like his fiery preaching. He was even sent to prison for it. His own mission in the east end of London helped the poor, and preached the gospel. In 1878 he formed the Salvation Army, which fought social evils like child labor. The Salvation Army is famous for its social work across the world.

TIMELINE

• Jesus is crucified in Jerusalem by the Roman authorities.

• Matthias is chosen to replace Judas Iscariot as the twelfth apostle.

A.D.33

DISCIPLES VISITED BY THE HOLY SPIRIT AT PENTECOST

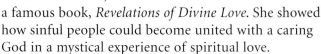

EARLY CHRISTIAN BAPTISM STONE

PENTECOSTAL ALTAR

• Peter heals the beggar by the Beautiful Gate.

• Philip baptizes the Ethiopian government minister.

• Saul sees a vision of Jesus on the road to Damascus. He is converted to Christianity and changes his name to Paul.

PETER HEALS AENEAS

Gladys Aylward (1902–1970)

This famous British missionary spent all her money on a one-way ticket to China in 1930. In 1938 she helped many children to safety from the China-Japan war. She later ran an orphanage in Taiwan.

Helda Camara (born 1909)

A Roman Catholic priest in Brazil, he became a bishop in 1952 and an archbishop in 1964. He spoke against the bad conditions of the poor, criticizing the government and rich landowners, whose policies caused the poverty and oppression. He was opposed by some even in his own church.

Mother Teresa of Calcutta (1910–1998)

Born in Macedonia in eastern Europe, she was a Roman Catholic nun who worked among the poor children of India. She founded the Sisters of Charity and became a world-renowned figure, always seen dressed in her blue robe. She was awarded the Nobel Peace Prize in 1979.

This is a nun of the Sisters of Charity helping deprived children.

Trevor Huddleston (1913–1998)

He went to South Africa, where he worked in Soweto. He became Bishop of Stepney, in east London, and was later made Archbishop of the Anglican Province of the Indian Ocean. He campaigned actively against apartheid, a system in South Africa of keeping different races apart.

Martin Luther King, Junior (1929–1968)

He followed in his father's footsteps to become a Baptist pastor in Montgomery, Alabama. He soon became involved in the struggle for civil rights among his fellow black people. He resigned from his church in 1959 to give all his time to black rights. He spoke for nonviolent action and reconciliation between black and white people. This means that he wanted black and white people to get along peacefully. He was murdered by a white man in Memphis, Tennessee, in 1968. The third Monday in January is celebrated as Martin Luther King Day.

Desmond Tutu (born 1931)

Tutu was made Anglican Archbishop of Cape Town, South Africa, in 1986. He was a passionate campaigner against apartheid, and successfully called on the west to impose economic sanctions (refusing to buy goods) on South Africa. He took a nonviolent approach to his protest, and after apartheid was abolished he became Chair of the Truth and Reconciliation Commission, set up to try to overcome the hate and distrust that resulted from apartheid.

PAUL AND BARNABAS
WORSHIPED IN LYSTRA

• The disciples hold a council and decide to allow Gentiles into the Christian Church.

• Paul leaves on his second missionary journey.

• Paul is arrested in Philippi.

JERUSALEM

• Riots in Ephesus.

• Paul leaves the city of Troas to return to Jerusalem.

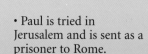

PAUL WRITING HIS LETTERS

EGYPTIAN
STATUE
OF A
PRISONER

• Paul is tried in Jerusalem and is sent as a prisoner to Rome.

• Paul is martyred in Rome for his belief in Jesus Christ.

A.D.60

241

People and Places

Glossary

Index

People and Places

Aeneas Worthy man of Lydda in Galilee who was paralyzed and restored to health by Peter.

Ananias Wealthy early follower of the apostles, husband of Sapphira. Claimed to have sold all his goods to give the money to the poor but kept some and was struck dead for lying.

Ananias Jewish follower of Christ in Damascus who laid hands on the blinded Paul and so restored his sight.

Andrew First apostle to be called by Jesus, brother of Simon Peter.

Annas Former High Priest, father-in-law of Caiaphas, who interrogated Jesus.

Antioch, Syria Capital of Roman province of Syria where Christians were first so-called. Paul escaped from it once in a basket.

Archelaus Son of Herod the Great, ruler of Judea, avoided by Joseph and Mary on return from Egypt; soon replaced by Roman governors.

Augustus Roman Emperor at the time of Jesus's birth who ordered a census of all tax-payers. This forced Mary and Joseph to travel to Bethlehem when Mary was about to give birth.

Barabbas Robber whose release the Jerusalem mob demanded instead of Jesus's when Pilate offered them the choice.

Barnabas Companion of Paul on his first missionary journey. He brought Paul to Jerusalem after his conversion in Damascus.

Bartholomew One of the apostles.

Bartimaeus Blind beggar of Jericho whose sight Christ restored.

Bethany Village 3 miles east of Jerusalem where Mary, Martha and Lazarus lived and where Christ raised Lazarus from the dead.

Bethlehem City in Judea where Jesus was born in a stable, fulfilling an ancient prophecy, and where the Three Wise Men came.

Caesarea Important city on the coast built by Herod the Great and named after Augustus Caesar.

Caiaphas Head Priest, leader of the Sanhedrin, who plotted against Jesus and interrogated him.

Cana Town in Galilee where Jesus performed His first miracle, turning water into wine when a wedding feast had run out of wine.

Capernaum Town on the west shore of the Sea of Galilee, home of Peter and other disciples, where Jesus began His mission, preaching in the synagogue after being baptized by John.

Cleopas One of the disciples whom the risen Christ encountered on the road to Emmaus and who did not recognize Him.

Cornelius Roman centurion who was told by an angel to send for Peter. Peter baptized him as the first non-Jewish Christian.

Damascus City in east Syria where Paul was going to persecute Jewish Christians when he was blinded on the road.

David Greatest king of Israel, ancestor of Joseph.

Demetrius Silversmith of Ephesus who stirred up a riot against Paul because he feared that Christianity would damage his statue-making.

Elijah Old Testament prophet who appeared along with Moses at the Transfiguration to the amazed disciples.

Elizabeth Wife of Zechariah and mother of John the Baptist, whom she bore in old age.

Elymas Scoundrel who deceived Roman governor Sergius Paulus until Paul blinded him.

Emmaus Village where Jesus appeared after the Crucifixion to the apostles and had supper with them before they realized who He was.

Ephesus City in western Asia Minor (Turkey) where there was a riot against Paul and in favor of the pagan goddess Artemis.

Eutychus Young man of Troas who was overcome by sleep during a long sermon by Paul and fell from a window.

Gabriel Archangel sent to announce coming births of John to Elizabeth and of Jesus to Mary.

Galilee Region of northern Israel/Palestine where Jesus grew up and began His ministry.

Galilee, Sea of, also called Lake Tiberias Lake in northern Israel/ Palestine where Jesus walked on the water.

Gallo Roman governor of Corinth who was not interested in Jewish complaints against Paul preaching to Gentiles (non-Jews).

Gethsemane Garden on the Mount of Olives outside Jerusalem where Jesus went to pray on the night before the Crucifixion and where he was arrested by the soldiers of the Sanhedrin, led by Judas.

Golgotha Place of execution (literally, hill of the skull) outside Jerusalem where Jesus was crucified.

Herod, The Great King, Ruler of Judea and bloodthirsty tyrant, who learned of the birth of the Messiah from the Three Wise Men. Ordered the massacre of all male children under two in Bethlehem. Father of Antipas and Archelaus.

Herod Antipas Son of Herod the Great, tetrarch (ruler) of Galilee. Married his niece and sister-in-law Herodias, for which he was condemned by John the Baptist. Imprisoned John the Baptist and, when Salome, Herodias's daughter, demanded John's head in return for dancing, Herod Antipas gave it to her.

Herodias Cousin and wife of Antipas, mother of Salome and enemy of John the Baptist who had attacked her.

Iconium City in Asia Minor (Turkey) where Paul and Barnabas were hailed as Greek gods for healing a crippled man.

Jairus Synagogue elder who begged Jesus to save his daughter, who was dying. When Jesus came to the house, servants said that Jairus's daughter was dead but Jesus said she was only sleeping and cured her.

James Son of Alphaeus, an apostle.

James Son of Zebedee and a fisherman by trade. Called James the Great Apostle who, with his brother John and Peter, formed the inner ring of apostles. Proposed a compromise over the admittance of Gentiles.

James the Less Traditionally recognized as the brother of Jesus, of whom little is known.

Jericho Ancient city east of Jerusalem.

Jerusalem Capital of Judea. Its great temple, rebuilt by King Herod, was the focus of Jewish religious life. Jesus's mission ended there in His trial and crucifixion, but the apostles regarded it as their base for many years. Destroyed by the Romans after a Jewish revolt in 70 AD.

Jesus Christ, son of God Born of Mary, a virgin, in a stable in Bethlehem to which she and her husband Joseph had gone for the census. Worshipped by the shepherds and the Three Wise Men. Grew up in Nazareth, Galilee. At the age of 12 he argued in a Temple of Jerusalem with the elders. Baptized by his cousin John the Baptist, His first miracle was at Cana, where He turned water into wine. Chose 12 local followers, mostly simple men such as Peter the fisherman, when He began his ministry. More miracles followed, including raising Lazarus from the

dead. His teachings were delivered mostly in the form of parables, such as the Prodigal Son or the Good Samaritan, which increasingly angered the Pharisees and Sadducees. Entered Jerusalem on a donkey in triumph on Palm Sunday. He was seized on the Mount of Olives, tried before the Sanhedrin and Pontius Pilate, and crucified. On the third day He rose from the dead and, after appearing several times to His followers, ascended into heaven.

John, St. Son of Zebedee, apostle, fisherman and brother of James.

John the Baptist, St. Cousin of Jesus, six months older, son of Elizabeth and Zechariah. Became a preacher, introduced baptism as the first step on the road to salvation, baptized Jesus, whom he recognized as the Messiah. Imprisoned by Herod Antipas for attacking Herod's marriage. Was beheaded to please Salome.

John the Evangelist, St. Writer of the fourth, most philosophical Gospel.

Jordan River in which John the Baptist baptized people, including Jesus.

Joseph, St. Descendant of King David, who discovered that Mary, his future wife, was pregnant though still a virgin and was told by the Angel Gabriel that God was the father. Took his wife to Bethlehem and then, warned by an angel, fled from Herod's massacre to Egypt. Died before Jesus began preaching.

Joseph of Arimathea Wealthy follower of Jesus who asked Pilate for permission to take Jesus's corpse and bury it. Helped by Nicodemus.

Judaeus One of the apostles, also called Thaddeus.

Judas Iscariot Apostle who betrayed Jesus for 30 pieces of silver. At the Last Supper, Jesus gave him a piece of bread, telling him to do what he had to do. Judas then led soldiers to the Mount of Olives, where he identified Jesus by embracing Him. Later, he hanged himself in remorse.

Judea Area around Jerusalem where the purest Jews lived.

Lazarus A beggar who sat outside the gates of Dives and begged a rich man for scraps. When they both died, Lazarus went to heaven, the rich man to hell, from which he looked up and begged Abraham for mercy — in vain.

Lazarus of Bethany Brother of Mary and Martha who died and was raised from the dead by Jesus after four days in the tomb.

Levites Priestly tribe, noted for their concern with ritual purity.

Luke, St. Evangelist, writer of the third Gospel.

Lystra City in Asia Minor (Turkey) where Paul was stoned for preaching.

Mark, St. Evangelist, the writer of the second Gospel, which was actually the first to have been compiled. May have been an apostle.

Martha of Bethany Sister of Mary and Lazarus, who worked hard to get food for Jesus and the disciples when they came, and was upset that her sister Mary merely sat at Jesus's feet.

Mary Mother of Jesus. She conceived Him while a virgin and married Joseph, an older man. After giving birth to Jesus in Bethlehem in a stable, she fled to Egypt and returned later to Galilee. Was present at the Crucifixion. According to Catholic dogma, she ascended bodily into heaven.

Mary Magdalene Despite Mary's sinful past, Jesus cast out her demons, and she became devoted to Him, being at the cross when He died and being the first person to see Him resurrected.

Mary of Bethany Sister of Martha and Lazarus who, when Christ visited them, spent her time listening to Him rather than serving food. Later, one of the women who went to Jesus's tomb and found it empty.

Matthew, St. Apostle, writer of the first Gospel and originally a tax collector, also called Levi. Son of Alphaeus.

Matthew, St. Evangelist, probably a Greek-speaking Jew from Syria.

Matthias Apostle chosen to replace Judas.

Moses Old Testament prophet who had led the Israelites out of Egypt and received the Ten Commandments, which formed the basis of the old Mosaic Law of the Jews, on Mount Sinai.

Nazareth Town in Galilee, home of Joseph and Mary and where Jesus grew up.

Nicodemus Wealthy Pharisee who came to Jesus for secret teaching and who provided the spices for His burial.

Paphos Capital of Cyprus where Paul converted the governor Sergius Paulus.

Paul, St. Native of Tarsus. Originally called Saul and an avid persecutor of Christians as a devout Jew. He was blinded on the road to Damascus by God. Sight restored by Ananias, he returned to Jerusalem to become the greatest missionary of all, traveling across Asia and Europe and writing many epistles. Believed in letting uncircumcised Gentiles become Christians. Martyred in Rome.

Peter, Simon Chief of the apostles, called the Rock (Petros) by Jesus and chosen by Him as the founder of the church in Rome. The first apostle to recognize Jesus as the Messiah, he still fell asleep on the Mount of Olives and then three times denied knowing Christ when questioned. Later, as the leading apostle, he was martyred in Rome.

Pharisees Intellectual elite of Judea (their name means separated ones) famous for being learned and pious. Rivals of the Sadducees and much criticized by Jesus.

Philip One of the apostles who preached very successfully in Samaria.

Philippi City in Macedonia (northern Greece) where Paul and Silas preached but were imprisoned for expelling a slave girl's evil spirits.

Pontius Pilate Roman Procurator (governor) of the Roman province of Judea at the time of Jesus's trial. Interrogated Jesus and tried to have Him released but bowed to popular pressure and released Barabbas instead, then tried to wash his hands of the affair. Considered a saint by some eastern churches.

Sadducees Social elite of Judea, devoted to the letter of the Mosaic Law, who did not believe in immortality. Rivals of the Pharisees and equally attacked by Jesus, whom they plotted to kill.

Salome Daughter of Herodias, who bewitched her stepfather Herod Antipas by her dancing and, as reward, demanded and was given the head of John the Baptist.

Salome Mother of the apostles James and John, one of the women at the foot of the cross who took spices to the tomb.

Samaria City and region of north Palestine whose Jewish inhabitants were considered impure by Judean Jews because they intermarried with non-Jews and did not observe all the Laws of Moses.

Sanhedrin Supreme Council of the Jews in Jerusalem before whom Jesus was brought for trial, as were some apostles, later.

Sapphira Wife of Ananias and like him struck dead for lying about giving away all her money when she had really kept some.

Sergius Paulus Roman governor of Cyprus converted by Paul.

Silas One of Paul's chief companions on his missionary journeys.

Simon of Cyrene The strong man in the crowd made to carry Jesus's cross when He was too tired to hold it.

Simon the Magus Sorcerer from Samaria who tried to buy Peter's magic with money.

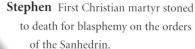

Simon the Zealot An apostle.

Stephen First Christian martyr stoned to death for blasphemy on the orders of the Sanhedrin.

Tabitha Woman of Joppa who was raised from the dead by Peter.

Tarsus City in Cilicia (southern Turkey), with the privilege of Roman citizenships for all its inhabitants, including Paul, who was born there.

Thomas, St. One of the apostles. Called Doubting Thomas because he doubted Jesus's resurrection until he actually touched His wounds.

Tiberias Town and Lake (also called Sea of Galilee) in northern Israel.

Zacchaeus Tax collector of Jericho who climbed a tree to see Jesus and jumped down, offering to give half of what he had to the poor.

Zebedee Father of the apostles James and John.

Zechariah Husband of Elizabeth. An elderly priest, he saw the archangel Gabriel in the temple who told him Elizabeth would have a child. When Zechariah refused to believe Gabriel, he was struck dumb until John's birth.

Glossary

altar
A holy table or platform where people made offerings or sacrifices to God.

angel
A messenger from God.

anoint
The ritual of marking with oil or ointment a person who has been chosen for holy use, such as a priest. In the New Testament Jesus is referred to as "the anointed one" because he was chosen by God to spread His word on Earth.

apostle
One of the original group of 12 men picked by Jesus from His disciples (followers). They were closer to Him than anyone else, and learned from Him how to carry on His teachings after His death. The apostles were Peter, James and John, Andrew, Thomas, Bartholomew, Philip, Matthew, James the Less, Thaddeus, Simon the Zealot and Judas Iscariot (who, after his betrayal, was replaced by Matthias). Saul, who converted to Christianity after Jesus's death, and became Paul, was also considered an apostle.

archangel
An angel of the highest level. Gabriel and Michael were archangels.

banquet
A large feast, often in celebration of a person or event.

baptism
The ritual of becoming a Christian, marked by sprinkling water on the head, or by immersing a person in water, also known as Christening. Jesus commanded that His followers be baptized to show they had made the decision to be Christians. The water represents cleansing.

blessed
A holy person may bless someone after that person has died to make them holy.

census
An official way of counting how many people live in a region, country or town.

centurion
A soldier in the Roman army who was in charge of 100 men (*cent* means 100).

chariot
A two- or four-wheeled vehicle that is pulled by horses. In ancient times, chariots were used in wars and races.

Christian
The name given to people who follow the teachings of Jesus Christ.

citizen
A person who lives in a particular town or country.

cleansed
In a religious context, the action or state of being free of evil, sins and guilt. When people are baptized, their souls are said to be cleansed, so that they can start their new life afresh.

conscience
Having a sense of what is right and wrong.

constellations
Groups of stars that form patterns in the sky. Through their studies of star constellations and their meanings, the Three Wise Men found their way to the baby Jesus.

contract
An agreement between two or more people that is written or spoken.

crucifixion
A means of execution by tying or nailing a person to a wooden cross. It was used by the Romans as a punishment for major crimes such as robbery or murder. However, Jesus was crucified for high treason which Caiaphas, the high priest, charged him with.

debt
Money or goods owed by one person to another.

demon
An evil spirit or the devil. In Bible times, people who were insane were often described as being possessed by demons.

denarii
The currency (money) that was used in Jerusalem at the time of Jesus Christ.

disciples
People who believed in and followed the teachings of Jesus Christ. The first disciples were those who heard Jesus preaching as he traveled around Galilee. The 12 apostles were chosen from the many disciples.

divine
Belonging to or to do with God.

empire
A group of countries or states that is ruled by one person who is called the emperor, king or queen.

eternal
Describes something that is forever, with no beginning or end. God is said to be eternal. Eternal life, or eternity, is the life promised by God that continues after death.

frankincense
Resin of trees found in east Africa and Arabia, which is burned to produce a sweet scent. It was used during religious ceremonies. One of the wise men who visited the baby Jesus was said to have brought a gift of frankincense as a symbol of God.

Gentile
A word that originally meant belonging to the same people. In the Bible, it refers to peoples who were not of the Jewish race. Jesus, although of the Jewish race, was determined that His message was for Gentiles as well as Jews.

gladiator
A swordsman trained to fight with other men or animals in a large arena. Unarmed early Christians were pitted against armed Roman soldiers with the taunt that if their God was so great He would protect them.

Gospel
A written record of Jesus's life and teachings. These are known as the Gospels, which means "good news." The Gospels now form part of the New Testament.

govern
To control the affairs of a country or state.

halo
A ring of light that is sometimes pictured around the heads of saints or angels in paintings to show that they are holy.

healer
A person who has the ability to heal others, without the aid of medicine, but through faith in God, for example. God gave Jesus the gift of healing and He gave it to His apostles.

holy
Describes a person, a place, or an object that is sacred, or has a special relationship to God. Jesus, His apostles, and saints are said to be holy and Jerusalem is described as a holy city.

Holy Spirit
An invisible, life-giving, divine force which is one of the ways God chose to make His presence known to people on earth. The most vivid example is when He visited the apostles in the form of the Holy Spirit, following Jesus's death.

hypocrite
A person who pretends to have feelings or beliefs about something or someone but who really feels or believes the opposite.

kingdom of God
A spiritual place that Jesus described as within reach of everyone who follows His teachings, and tries to live their life in a Christian way.

leper
A person with an illness called leprosy that caused paralysis and deformity. Because of this, and because people in Bible times believed the disease to be catching, lepers were avoided, and made to live together in isolated places called leper colonies.

martyr
A person who chooses to suffer greatly or be put to death rather than give up their religious beliefs.

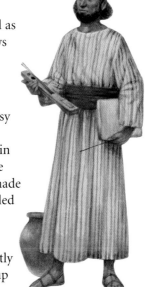

Messiah
One chosen by God, savior, or anointed one, usually referring to Christ. The word Christ is the equivalent word in Greek.

ministry
The work of teaching about God and how Christians should live their lives, as done by Jesus in his three years of traveling and preaching around Judea, and by priests today.

miracle
An amazing or supernatural act or event, or mighty work, which is performed through the power of God. Jesus's many miracles during his ministry in Galilee included healing the sick, raising the dead to life, and making five loaves and two fishes stretch to feed a crowd of 5,000 people.

mission
A special purpose or reason for acting. Jesus's mission, given to Him by God, was to spread His word.

myrrh
Oil from African and Asian plants used in medicine and perfumes. It was one of the symbolic gifts given to the baby Jesus by the Three Wise Men, representing mortal man.

oasis
A place in the desert where water is found and plants can grow.

parable
A story that draws from real life to make a teaching point. Jesus used people and situations His audience would be familiar with to teach them about the kingdom of God. This made the point of His stories easy for people to remember and to understand.

Pharisee
Member of a strict religious sect. The word actually means "separated ones." The Pharisees were generally ordinary people, not priests, who closely followed Jewish law to the letter. Sometimes they extended the ways that these laws were applied to make them even harder for others to follow.

pilgrimage
A journey taken by believers to visit a religious shrine. It can also mean the journey through life toward the hope of eternal life.

prefect
A Roman official who ruled over a region, as in Judea during the time of Jesus.

priest
A person whose job is to perform religious duties, and to advise on the teachings of God.

prophesy
To be able to tell what will happen in the future. The coming of the Messiah was prophesied in the Old Testament, and Christians believe that Jesus fulfilled that prophecy.

purify
To make pure and clean. In the religious sense, this means freeing a person of sin, by praying or by being blessed by God or a priest.

religion
Worshipping or believing in God or other gods.

repentance
The feeling of being truly sorry for wrong thoughts or deeds, coupled with the determination to try to do better in the future.

resurrection
Being restored to life after death. Jesus's resurrection, three days after He died on the cross, is the central point of the New Testament, and of Christian faith.

ritual
Set words and actions that make up a religious ceremony.

sacrifices
The offering of animals or people for the worship of a god.

Sadducees

A small group of traditional Jews, mostly connected with the families of priests, who were influential in the temples at the time of Jesus. Unlike the Pharisees, they did not believe in life after death.

Samaritans

People from various places, who, in Old Testament times, were sent by the invading Assyrians to live in the city of Samaria in the northern kingdom of Israel. The Jews were banished from Israel by the Assyrians, and felt the Samaritans had not only taken over their cities but also mimicked the Hebrew faith. The Samaritans were subsequently despised by Jews for generations, but Jesus makes a point of featuring them in His stories to drive home the point that the kingdom of God is open to everyone.

Savior

A person that saves somebody from danger. Jesus is described as a savior because He saved us from sin by showing us the Christian way of life.

scribes

Writers and learned people who, because of their skills, became important in matters of government and administration. Jewish scribes were closely associated with the Pharisees and high priests, and were responsible for passing on their knowledge of Jewish law and scriptures.

scriptures

The writings contained in the Bible that are accepted by the various faiths as the word of God, or people directly inspired by God. For the Jewish people, the Scriptures are the 39 books of the Old Testament. For Christians, the Scriptures also include the New Testament.

sermon

A speech designed to teach listeners about particular aspects of faith or religion, and how they should behave.

soul

Your soul is who you are – it is your life force. It is the part of you that Christians believe will live forever. Heaven is described as the kingdom of souls.

spiritual

Belonging or relating to the soul.

tribute

Something that is done or said to give thanks to something, sometimes a god.

unmerciful

Showing no kindness when punishing somebody.

vision

A supernatural image seen by someone. The Bible tells of many visions that were sent by God, which enabled people to foretell or forewarn of coming events.

symbol

An easily recognizable visual aid that helps people understand something that is hard to describe or show, such as an emotion or feeling. The dove is used as a symbol of innocence in the Bible, although it has also become a symbol of peace.

synagogue

The building where Jewish people worship God. In Jesus's time, the synagogue had separate seating for men and women and also served as the school for Jewish children.

Index

H

I

J

K

L

This edition is published by Southwater

Distributed in the UK by
The Manning Partnership
251–253 London Road East
Batheaston
Bath BA1 7RL
tel. 01225 852 727
fax 01225 852 852

Published in the USA by
Anness Publishing Inc.
27 West 20th Street
Suite 504
New York
NY 10011
fax 212 807 6813

Distributed in Canada by
General Publishing
895 Don Mills Road
400–402 Park Centre
Toronto, Ontario M3C 1W3
tel. 416 445 3333
fax 416 445 5991

Distributed in Australia by
Sandstone Publishing
Unit 1, 360 Norton Street
Leichhardt
New South Wales 2040
tel. 02 9560 7888
fax 02 9560 7488

Southwater is an imprint of Anness Publishing Limited
Hermes House, 88–89 Blackfriars Road, London SE1 8HA
tel. 020 7401 2077; fax 020 7633 9499

© Anness Publishing Limited 2000, 2001

Previously published in four separate volumes: Birth of Jesus, Jesus in
Galilee, The Resurrection of Jesus and Road to Damascus.

Publisher: Joanna Lorenz
Managing Editor, Children's Books: Gilly Cameron Cooper
Project Editor: Jennifer Williams
Designer: Roger McWilliam

10 9 8 7 6 5 4 3 2 1

PHOTOGRAPHIC ACKNOWLEDGEMENTS
Page 12 (BL) Sonia Halliday Photographs; 18 (BL) Guy Mansfield, Panos
Pictures; 32 (BR) Penny Tweedie, Panos Pictures; 52 (BL) The Stock Market; 70
(BL) Sonia Halliday Photographs; 84 (BC) The Stock Market; 98 (BR) Frank
Spooner Pictures; 105 (BR) The Stock Market; 128 (BL) J. C. Tordai/The
Hutchison Library; 135 (BL) Gianni Dagli Orti/CORBIS; 147 (BR) Richard T.
Nowitz/CORBIS; 153 (BR) AFP/CORBIS; 161 (BL) Richard T.
Nowitz/CORBIS; 165 (BC) Dave Bartruff/CORBIS; 170 (BL) Richard T.
Nowitz/CORBIS; 172 (BR) Richard Hamilton Smith/CORBIS; 173 (BL) Richard
T. Nowitz/CORBIS; 179 (BC) Arte & Immagini/CORBIS; 180 (BL) John
Hatt/The Hutchison Library; (BR) J. C. Tordai/The Hutchison Library; 181 (TL)
The Hutchison Library; (BL) The Hutchison Library; (BR) Dorig/The Hutchison
Library; 186 (BL) John Hatt/The Hutchison Library; 190 (BR) Sonia Halliday
Photographs; 194 (BL) Michael Nicholson/CORBIS; 200 (BL) Sonia Halliday
Photographs; 203 (BC) Sonia Halliday Photographs; 204 (BR) Hanan
Isachar/CORBIS; 206 (BC) Jayne Taylor/Sonia Halliday Photographs; 209 (BR)
F. H. C. Birch/Sonia Halliday Photographs; 210 (BR) Neil Beer/CORBIS; 217
(BR) Arte & Immagini/CORBIS; 221 (BC) Sonia Halliday Photographs; 231
(BC) Sonia Halliday Photographs; 237 (BL) Historical Picture Archive/CORBIS;
238 (BL) Bettmann/CORBIS; (CR) Arte & Immagini/CORBIS; 239 (C) Archivo
Iconografico, S.A./CORBIS; (C) The Salvation Army International Heritage
Centre; 241(BR) Paul Velasco/CORBIS. All other images are from the Miles
Kelly Archive.

Every effort has been made to trace the copyright holders of all images that
appear within this book. Anness Publishing Ltd apologizes for any unintentional
omissions and, if notified, would be happy to add an acknowledgement in
future editions.